New Highlight

4

Cornelsen

2

two

* Fakultativ (wahlfreie Bestandteile des Lehrwerks)

4

four

Unit **6*** ist nur Pflichtstoff für den E-Kurs in Nordrhein-Westfalen.

 Als Hörtext oder Song auf der Audio-CD vorhanden; die Track-Angaben beziehen sich auf die Vollfassung (Bestellnummer 344630): 1⦿2 = CD 1, Track 2.

W ⦿ Zusätzliche Aufgaben auf der CD-ROM im Workbook

 Kann dem Portfolio-Ordner hinzugefügt werden

Aufgaben:

○ leicht   ◐ mittel   ● schwierig

Interkulturell

Wiederholung

Begleitend zum Schülerbuch finden sich unter www.new-highlight.de interaktive Online-Übungen, die am Ende jeder Unit bearbeitet werden können.

* Fakultativ (wahlfreie Bestandteile des Lehrwerks)

Next stop: USA

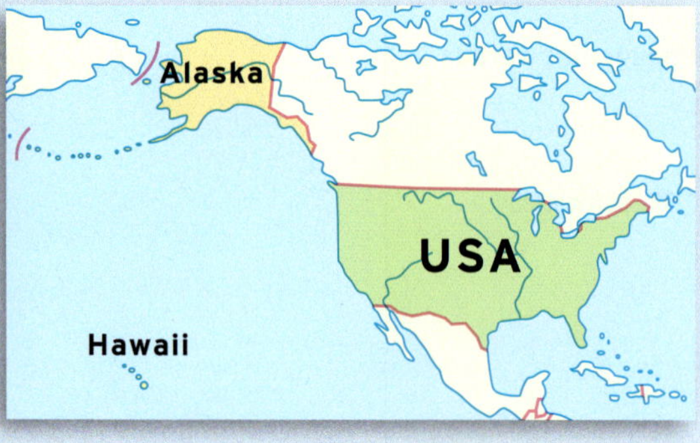

Neah Bay
Anacortes
Olympic National Park ★
Seattle
Washington

Montana

North Dakota

South Dakota

Bend
Oregon

Idaho

Wyoming

Nebraska

Pacific Ocean

Nevada

Utah

Colorado

Kansas

San Francisco
San Jose

California

Las Vegas

Hollywood
Santa Monica
Los Angeles

Arizona

Phoenix

New Mexico

San Diego

Texas

500 km

Alaska

USA

Hawaii

1 **Songs about the USA**

1⊙2 Listen to the songs and look at the map.
What places can you hear?
Put up your hand when you hear a name.
Then write the names on the board.

2 **Places in this book**

Work with a partner. Look quickly at the units
in this book.
What places can you find? Can you find them
on this map?

NORTH
WEST • EAST
SOUTH

500 km

Maine

VT
NH • Boston
New York
MA
RI
CT
New York
New Jersey
Detroit
Pennsylvania
Philadelphia
Delaware
MD
Washington, D.C.
West Virginia
Virginia

Michigan
Wisconsin
Chicago
Indiana
Indianapolis
Ohio
Illinois
Iowa
-ta
-ca

Missouri
Kentucky
Tennessee
North Carolina
Greenville
South Carolina

Atlantic
Ocean

Arkansas
Georgia
Missis-sippi
Alabama
Dallas
Louisiana
Houston
New Orleans
Florida
Epcot + Sea World
Kennedy Space Center
Miami
Gulf of Mexico
-nio

VT = Vermont
NH = New Hampshire
MA = Massachusetts
CT = Connecticut
RI = Rhode Island
MD = Maryland

Tip:
Use the Internet. Go to:
www.new-highlight.de
Find the window for the
webcode and put in:
NHL-4-7
Or look at a map.

PROJECT The USA from east to west

a) Work with a partner. Find out:

- How many states are there in the USA?
- What's the capital of the USA?
- What's the biggest city in the USA?
- What's the population of the USA?
- What countries are the USA's neighbours?
- Which two states aren't near the others?
- How far is Los Angeles from New York City?

b) Work in groups. Make a map of the USA for your classroom.

- Put in the most important rivers, lakes and mountains.
- Put in the states, cities and towns that are in this book.
- Put some interesting facts on your map: capital, population, …

▶W 2, 1–2

AMERICAN ENGLISH

1 **American pronunciation**

a) British English (BE) and American English (AE) sound different.
Listen to the five kids. Who's British? Who's American?

I think ... is British/American.

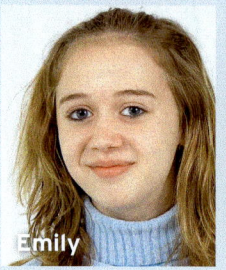 **Emily**
 **Kenichi**
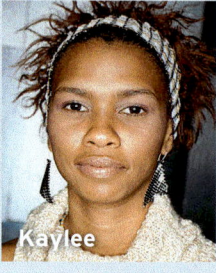 **Kaylee**
 **Luke**
 **Shanna**

b) How do British people say these words?
Read them out.

c) Listen to the words in British and American
English. Can you hear what's different?

1 later – better
2 park – world
3 fast – dancing
4 got – shopping
5 Tuesday – new

2 **Special American words and phrases**

Listen to the conversations. Then listen again and match the phrases (1–5)
with the pictures (a–e).

1 Hi, you guys.
2 Gimme five!
3 How ya doin', Ally?
4 Have a nice day!
5 Awesome!

3 **British and American words**

1⊙6 **a)** Some American English words are different. Start a list in your exercise book. Look at the photos here. In your list, write the British English words for the things. Then listen and check.

🇬🇧	🇺🇸
1 flat	apartment
2 ...	store
3 ...	sidewalk
4 ...	subway
5 ...	cellphone

b) **GAME**
Make ten cards. Write the British English and the American English words from 3a). Mix the cards up. Can you put the right words together?

flat

apartment

● **4** **American English spelling**
American spelling is sometimes different. Work with a partner. Look at the underlined words in American English spelling. Write the words in British spelling. Then check in the *Dictionary* (pages 160–179).

Tips for travelers to the USA

OAKBROOK CENTER
More than 160 stores and restaurants

1 mile = 1.609 **kilometers**

Read about our favorite places.

New York T-shirts in all colors

▶ W 2, 3

Unit 1

The Big Apple

Lower East Side

Chinatown

Little Italy

The Financial District

The Statue of Liberty and Ellis Island

1 **Before you listen: Where is New York City?**

It's in the east/west of the USA.

Tip:
Check on the map
on pages 6–7.

2 **Where's what in New York?**

1○7 **You're in Manhattan at the top of the Empire State Building. Look at the photos and map on pages 10 and 11. Listen and pick the right answers.**

The places on this page are north/south of the Empire State Building.
The places on page 11 are north/south of the Empire State Building.

▶W 3, 1

The Empire State Building

Times Square

Central Park

Harlem

3 At the top of the Empire State Building

Listen to the tour. Are these sentences true or false?

1⊙8

1 Manhattan is one of the five areas of New York.
2 Lower East Side, Little Italy and Chinatown are immigrant neighbourhoods.
3 New York is the financial capital of the world.
4 About 17 million immigrants came to the USA through Ellis Island from 1890 to 1920.
5 In Central Park you can only find poor people.
6 In Times Square you can find famous theatres.
7 Harlem was famous for rap music.

4 AND YOU? Talk to a partner about the photos.

I think ... looks ...
I'd like to see ... because ...

→ beautiful • boring • busy • cheap • cool • dirty •
dangerous • exciting • expensive • great • modern •
good for shopping/food/sightseeing/sports/ ...

▶ W 3, 2–3

SIGHTSEEING IN NEW YORK

1 Listen to the dialogue. Pick the right answers.

1◉9

1 Tyrell and Jazmin are at Central Park / the Empire State Building.
2 They're going to Ground Zero / Chinatown.
3 Then they're going to Tyrell's apartment in Harlem / Little Italy.

2 Listen again. Who ...

1◉9

1 ... has to be more careful with the traffic?
2 ... lives in Greenville and thinks New York is more exciting?
3 ... always makes dinner at 18.30?
4 ... doesn't get much pocket money?

3 At a deli: Look at the menu.

a) **How much is a ham sandwich?** It's ... dollars.
   How much are potato chips? They're ... cents.
   Which is more expensive – white bread or brown bread?

 b) **Listen. What does**
1◉10 **the tourist ask for?**

Make your own sandwich!

Grilled chicken	$5.00	**BREAD:** white, brown, roll, pita, bagel: free
Beef	$5.25	
Black Forest ham	$5.00	
Smoked salmon	$6.25	Lettuce, tomato: free
Cheese	$4.25	Cheese 50 cents
Egg salad	$3.75	Potato chips 50 cents

ALL DRINKS ONLY $2!!

---

c) Listen and read the dialogue.

1◉11

ASSISTANT Hi guys, what would you like?
JAZMIN I'll have a beef sandwich on a roll with lettuce, tomato and cheese, and potato chips. And an orange juice, please.
ASSISTANT That's $8.25.
JAZMIN My cousin is paying!
TYRELL Here you are.
ASSISTANT Thank you. Have a nice day!

d) Look at the menu. Make a new dialogue.

PROJECT Your school deli

Organize an American deli in your school for one day:

- **Write a menu.**
- **Make a list: Who's bringing what? Who's doing what?**
- **Make sandwiches and sell them at lunchtime.**
- **Everybody has to speak English!**
- **What will you do with the money?**

Look at www.new-highlight.de **for help.**
Put in the webcode NHL-4-12.

▶W 4, 4

ON THE SUBWAY

1 Find Chambers Street on the subway map. Listen and look at the map. Find where Tyrell lives.

2 Work with a partner. Read the sentences. Your partner finds the place on the map.

Partner A

1 From Times Square, take line 1 south to the end of the line.

2 From Central Park North, take line 2 or 3 south. Change at 42nd Street to line 7. Travel two stops.

Partner B

1 From Washington Square at W 4th Street, take line F east. Travel four stops.

2 From Grand Central, take line 4, 5 or 6 north to 86th Street. Then walk three blocks west.

3 You're at Times Square.
Partner A: Pick a station or a place. Tell your partner how to get there.
Partner B: Find the place on the map.

– Take line ... south/north/east/west to ...
– Change at ... to line ...
– Travel ... stops.
– Walk ... blocks north/south/east/west.

W 4, 5

MTA **New York City Transit**
Manhattan Subway Map
©2006 Metropolitan Transportation Authority Unauthorized duplication prohibited 022806

1 **Who was Malcolm X?**

a) **Look at the photos and the quotes by Malcolm X in the boxes. Pick the right answer.**

b) **Read Malcom X's story. Check your answer to exercise 1a).**

Malcolm X ...

a) sang rap songs   **b)** helped to change history   **c)** made films

The story of Malcolm X

1⊙13

> **"If you're born in America with a black skin, you're born in prison."**

Malcolm Little was born in Omaha, Nebraska in 1925. He had seven brothers and sisters. In 1931, when Malcolm was six years old, his father died. The police said it was an accident. But Malcolm thought a group of white people killed him because his father often had problems with white people. Later his mother became ill, so the children had to leave their home and live in different families and children's homes. These were the most terrible years of Malcolm's life.

5

Malcolm was one of the best pupils at his school. He
10 wanted to be a lawyer. But a teacher told him that that wasn't a job for black people. At that time, black people couldn't sit next to white people on buses or trains, or in restaurants and cafes. And black children often had to go to different schools from white children. So Malcolm left
15 school when he was fifteen and he moved to Harlem in New York. He started to steal. In 1946 he went to prison for seven years.

> **"Without education, you're not going anywhere in this world."**

In prison Malcolm read lots of books and learned about a group of black Muslims. They wanted a better life for black Americans –
20 a life without white people. Malcolm Little changed his name to
25 "Malcolm X" because for him "Little" was a slave name. And he started to fight for the rights of black people. He talked on the radio and on TV about freedom for black people and he wrote angry newspaper
30 articles. For some people he was dangerous because it was OK for him to use violence to change things. But he became one of the most popular speakers in America.

> **"Usually when people are sad, they don't do anything. But when they're angry, they bring about a change."**

In 1964 Malcolm's life changed: He travelled to Mecca and came back with a new name (El-Hajj Malik El Shabazz). Now he thought that violence was wrong. And he fought for a better life for everybody everywhere: black and white. But on February 21st, 1965, three men killed Malcolm X in Harlem. On that day America lost one of the most important men in its history – a man who helped black people to fight for their dreams. 35

2 When and where: Match the sentence parts.

1 Malcolm was born
2 Malcolm's father died
3 Malcolm left school
4 He started thinking about black rights
5 Malcolm's life changed
6 Three people killed Malcolm

a) when he was fifteen.
b) in 1931.
c) in Harlem.
d) after his trip to Mecca.
e) in 1925.
f) in prison.

3 Pick the right answers.

1 Malcolm had
   a) two different names.
   b) three different names.
   c) four different names.

2 When Malcolm was a child
   a) his parents died.
   b) things were hard for him.
   c) he had a happy life.

3 When Malcolm was young, black people
   a) had different rights from white people.
   b) couldn't use buses.
   c) had rights like white people.

4 After 1964 Malcolm X thought that violence was
   a) sometimes OK.
   b) always OK.
   c) never OK.

5 In his last years Malcolm wanted rights for
   a) American people.
   b) black people.
   c) everybody.

4 Malcolm X's life

**a) Finish the sentences.
Tell the class.**

I think Malcolm was a/an ... man.
He had a/an ... life.

→ boring • brave • dangerous •
exciting • hard • important •
interesting • stupid • tough •
wild

b) Write a summary of Malcolm X's life (about 50 words). Put your ideas together with these words:

→ and • but • because • then

Tip:
Write only the most important things. You can use some sentences in exercises 2, 3 and 4.

▶W 5, 6–8

1 Food

a) Make lists with the class. What are the words in the pictures?

These words are on page 12.

Fruit and vegetables   **Meat and fish**   **Other food**

b) Write the lists in your exercise book and put in more words.

● **c) What did you have for breakfast and lunch yesterday? Tell the class.**

▶ Wordbank 1, p. 126

2 Money

a) What's the right word?

→ pocket money • cents • dollars

1 $ (American money).
2 You get it from your parents.
3 There are one hundred in $1.

b) WORD LINK Which verb can't you use?

find get kill borrow lose
save spend steal win | MONEY

● **c) AND YOU? Talk to a partner.**

1 How often do you get pocket money?
2 What do you do with your pocket money?

3 The story of Lil' Kim

Finish the story with the words and phrases from the box.

The words and phrases are all in the story pages 14–15.

→ fought • killed • lost • violence • was born • went to prison

Lil' Kim ... in 1975 in New York. She lived in a poor neighbour-hood where there was lots of ... and other problems. She ... hard and became a rapper. Her boyfriend Notorious B.I.G. helped her, but in 1997 somebody ... B.I.G. Lil' Kim was devastated when she ... him but she worked hard and became a big star. Then in 2005 she had problems with the police: She ... for 10 months. When she came out, she said sorry to her fans.

4 WORD SEARCH The time and date

a) Write these times and dates in numbers.

They're all on pages 11–16.

1 eighteen ninety (p. 11)
2 half past six (p. 12)
3 February the twenty-first (p. 15)
4 nineteen sixty-five (p. 15)
5 two thousand and five (p. 16)

● **b) Write five dates or times. Say them to your partner – but don't show them! Your partner writes them. Are they right?**

Tip:
1950: You say "nineteen fifty"
1998: You say "nineteen ninety-eight"
2007: You say "two thousand **and** seven"

16

sixteen

▶ W 6, 9–11 ▶ W ⊙

1 What are they like?

a) Write the opposites.

New York

Greenville,
South Carolina

	New York	Greenville
1	big	small
2	...	boring
3	expensive	...
4	...	clean
5	busy	...
6	...	safe

b) Look at the photos. Talk about the girls.

Britney   Kimberley

I think Britney/Kimberley is .../looks ... .

→ beautiful • friendly • healthy •
ill • nervous • quiet • sad •
shy • sporty • tired

c) AND YOU?
What's your area like? Use words in a).
What are you like? Use words in b).

2 Travel

a) Put the words from the green box in the network. Then find more words.

→ a park • presents • with friends •
an amusement arcade • food •
a museum • with family • car •
in a holiday flat • bus • in a hotel •
postcards • clothes • a church •
underground/subway • plane

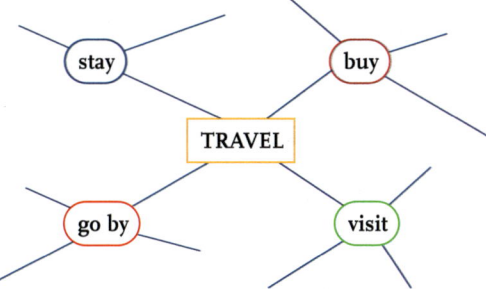

stay   buy

TRAVEL

go by   visit

● **b) Write about a trip. Use words from 2a). It doesn't have to be true!**

I/We travelled to ... . I went by ... .
I stayed ... . I visited ... . I bought ... .

3 SAY IT IN GERMAN

Tell your partner about
the advert in German.

Tip: Pick the most important things: What? Where? When?

Welcome to New York City

"SEE IT ALL"

Downtown Manhattan Heliport, Pier 6 East River
Hours : Monday – Saturday   9:00 a.m. - 6:30 p.m.
reservations suggested
212-355-0801
Hours : Sundays Only   11:00 a.m. - 6:00 p.m.
VIP/West 30th Street Heliport.

W W W . H E L I N Y . C O M
ID required

Free Gift with this Ad

DELUXE	ULTIMATE	NEW YORKER
$275	$179	$129

Helicopter Flight Services, Inc.
New York City Sightseeing Tours   No.45

NYC

H E L I N Y

17

seventeen

► W 7, 12–14 ► W ⊙

LISTENING Dates, times and places

1 Three dialogues

a) Look at the adverts, notes and cards. What are they?

1 Adverts for …
2 Notes about …
3 Appointment cards for the …

b) What's the American English word for *shopping centre*? Put it in your list.

c) Now listen to the three dialogues. Pick A, B or C.

1◉14

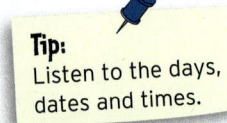 **Tip:** Listen to the days, dates and times.

1

A
Get it all
at the Manhattan Mall!
The most exciting shops in NYC!
Open every day
9 a.m.–9 p.m.

B
Get it all
at the Manhattan Mall!
The most exciting shops in NYC!
Open Mon.–Sat. 9 a.m.–9 p.m.
Sunday 10 a.m.–7 p.m.

C
Get it all
at the Manhattan Mall!
The most exciting shops in NYC!
Open Mon.–Sat. 9 a.m.–9 p.m.
Sunday 10 a.m.–6 p.m.

2

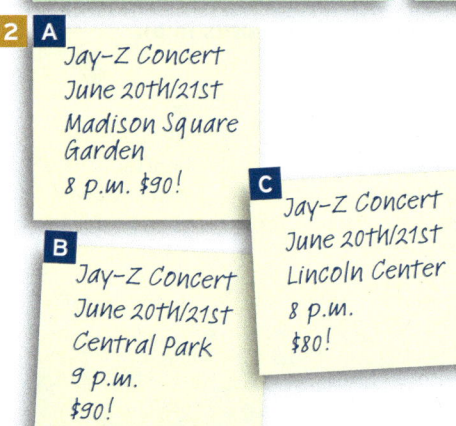

A
Jay-Z Concert
June 20th/21st
Madison Square
Garden
8 p.m. $90!

B
Jay-Z Concert
June 20th/21st
Central Park
9 p.m.
$90!

C
Jay-Z Concert
June 20th/21st
Lincoln Center
8 p.m.
$80!

3

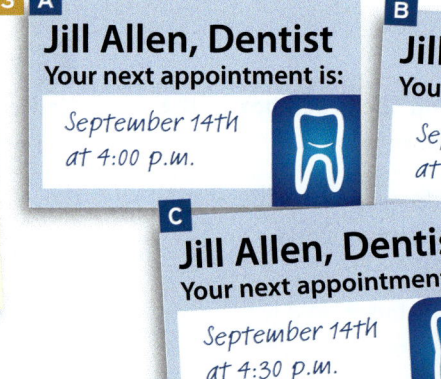

A
Jill Allen, Dentist
Your next appointment is:
September 14th
at 4:00 p.m.

B
Jill Allen, Dentist
Your next appointment is:
September 14th
at 3:30 p.m.

C
Jill Allen, Dentist
Your next appointment is:
September 14th
at 4:30 p.m.

d) Compare your answers with a partner. Then listen again and check.

1◉14

2 Put in *to/at/in/on*. You can listen to the dialogues again and check.

1◉14

1 On Sunday we open … 10 a.m.
2 They're … June.
3 They're … June 20th/21st.
4 … Madison Square Garden.
5 You have to go … the dentist.
6 Your appointment is … Tuesday.

● 3 AND YOU? Do you have any plans, appointments or invitations?

I have tickets for … / I have an invitation to …
I'm going to go to … / I'm going to meet …

on Saturday / at 3 o'clock /
at the sports club / at my house

▶W 8, 15 ▶W ◉

SPEAKING Invitations

 1 **Brianna's invitation**

1⊙15
- **What is Brianna doing on Saturday evening?**
- **When should Tyrell be there?**
- **What can Tyrell bring?**

BRIANNA   Do you have any plans for Saturday night?
TYRELL   No, not really.
BRIANNA   I'm having a party. Do you want to come?
TYRELL   That sounds great, thanks. When should
          I be there?
BRIANNA   About 7 o'clock. There'll be some pizza
          and salad.
TYRELL   That sounds good. Can I bring anything?
BRIANNA   Yeah, can you bring some CDs?
          Your music is better than my music.
TYRELL   OK. Thanks for the invitation. See you then.

 2 **Tyrell's invitation**

1⊙16   **a) Finish the dialogue.**

TYRELL   Do you have ... for Friday evening?
JUSTIN   No, ...
TYRELL   I'm having a movie night. Do you ...?
JUSTIN   That ..., ... When ...?
TYRELL   About 6 o'clock . There'll be lots of movies
         and music concerts on DVDs.
JUSTIN   That ... . Can I bring anything?
TYRELL   Yeah, can ... some popcorn?
JUSTIN   ... . See you then.

**b) Read the dialogue
in a) with a partner.**

3 **ROLE PLAY**
**Partner A: Invite partner B to
a party. Look at your card on
page 94.**
**Partner B: Look at your card
on page 94.**

4 **INTERPRETING** **You and your brother are at a cafe.
You meet an American girl. Your brother wants to invite her
to a party, but he's too shy to speak English. Help him.**

BROTHER   Frag sie doch, ob sie zu unserer Party am
          Samstagabend kommen will.
YOU   (to American girl) Do you want to ...?
GIRL   That sounds great, thanks. Can I bring a friend?
YOU   (to your brother) Sie kommt gern. Darf sie ...?
BROTHER   Ja, klar. Sag ihr, dass die Party um 18 Uhr
          anfängt. Hier ist unsere Adresse.
YOU   (to American girl) That's fine. The party starts ...

Remember:
on Monday, **on** Tuesday ...
at 9 o' clock, **at** night, ...

▶ W 8, 16–17 ▶ W ⊙

READING Party invitations

1 **Read the invitations, Tyrell's letter and his e-mail.**
- Why are these two birthdays special? (Tip: How old are Destiny and Diego?)
- What does "RSVP" mean, do you think? Pick the right answer.

    a) Please come.   **b)** Please tell me/us if you can come.

Destiny Moore is **16!**

Please join us for a
Sweet Sixteen party
for Destiny Moore –
the sweetest teen in New York!
Dinner and dancing
Tuesday, November 3rd, at 7 p.m.
Place:
Daleesha's Restaurant
West 125th Street
Harlem, NY 10027

RSVP to Mr and Mrs Moore by October 15th

| To | everybody |
| From | Diego Garcia <diegoG@hotwire.com> |

PARTY!!

I'm having a party
'cause I'm going to be sixteen
So come on over –
my house is the scene!

October 7th is the date
The party starts at six – don't be late
There'll be lots of music, food and fun …
The most awesome time for everyone!

RSVP by October 1st please!

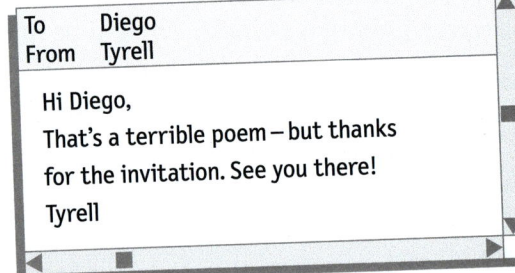

Dear Mr and Mrs Moore,

Thank you for the invitation.
I'm afraid I can't come because
it's my grandma's 60th birthday
on the 3rd.

Best wishes,
Tyrell Stone

| To | Diego |
| From | Tyrell |

Hi Diego,
That's a terrible poem – but thanks
for the invitation. See you there!
Tyrell

2 **True, false or not in the text?**
Read the texts again. Write *true* or *false*. If you can't find the information,
write *not in the text*.

1 Destiny's party is on November 3rd, at 19.00.
2 Diego's party is on a Saturday.
3 The two parties are at home.
4 There's food at the two parties.

5 There's dancing at Destiny's party.
6 Destiny's party finishes at 11 p.m.
7 Diego's parents are sending the invitations to his party.
8 Tyrell can go to the two parties.

3 Parties in the USA and Germany
Ask and answer the questions with a partner.

	YOU	YOUR PARTNER
Do your friends send invitations like Destiny's?		Yes, they do. / No, they don't.
Are 16th birthdays special in Germany?		Yes, they are. / No, they aren't.
Why is 16 a special age in the USA? Look at Destiny's card.		It's special because you can ...
What other special parties do people have?		For their ...th birthday. / For a wedding. / ...

WRITING Party invitations

1 AND YOU? Imagine you can have a big party and money isn't important. Make notes about these things:

- When will it be?
- Where will it be?
- Who will you invite?
- What music will you play?
- What will you eat?
- How will it be special?

> IDEAS
> - at home / at a football club / at a hotel / at a club / at a shopping centre / on a beach / at a swimming pool / ...
> - all my friends and family / all the class / my best friends / ...
> - rap / house / techno / ...
> - hamburgers / sandwiches / pizza / salad / fruit salad / cake / ...

2 Copy and write this invitation.
OR make your own special invitation.
Use your notes from exercise 1.

Tip:
If you have computers in class, find a party invitation on the Internet. Write it. Then send it to your partner.

INVITATION

Your name: _____
Place: _____
Date: _____
Time: from _____ to _____
RSVP to _____ by _____
Write your message here: _____
_____
_____

3 Your answer

a) Give your invitation to a partner. Read your partner's invitation.

b) Answer your partner's invitation. Give your answer to your partner.

Tyrell's letter and e-mail on page 20 can help you.

THE AMERICAN DREAM?

1 Read the article and answer the questions. **What problems did Lanh and Maria have? Are they happy in the USA? Why or why not?**

Did you know that about 3 million people in New York City were born in other countries? Lanh and Maria tell us about life in the USA.

My name is Lanh Nguyen and I was born in Vietnam. When I came to the USA I was only seven years old.
The hardest thing was the language. But that became easier very quickly. The second problem was the different way of life. One example is the food – so much meat! In my family we eat healthier food with lots of vegetables. But I think New York is great – it's much more international than the cities in Vietnam. I love living here. Teenagers in the USA have more freedom than in Vietnam. My dream is to be a cook and have the coolest restaurant in New York.

My name is Maria Cortez. I moved here from Costa Rica when I was 14. My dad's biggest dream was to live in the USA. He wanted a better life for us. And one day he won a lottery so we could live in America. When you're young, it's OK to move to a new country. But it's harder when you're older. I don't like New York. It's too busy and there's too much traffic. But the worst thing is when people think you're stupid because your English isn't good. Mom and dad were happier in Costa Rica too. Now they miss our country.

2 **AND YOU?**
Would you like to live in the USA or another country? I'd like to live in …
What would you like there? What would you miss? I'd like … / I'd miss …

3 **WORD SEARCH**
a) Find these words on this page.

1 That became … very quickly. (Lanh)
2 In my family we eat … food. (Lanh)
3 It's … when you're older. (Maria)

b) Now find these.

1 The … thing was the language. (Lanh)
2 My dream is to be a cook and have the … restaurant in New York. (Lanh)
3 My dad's … dream was to live in the USA. (Maria)

4 WORD SEARCH

a) Find these words on page 12.

1 Who has to be ... ... with the traffic? (ex. 2)
2 Who lives in Greenville and thinks New York is ... ...? (ex. 2)
3 Which is ... ... – white bread or brown bread? (ex. 3)

b) Now find these words on pages 14 and 15.

1 These were the ... ... years of Malcolm's life. (lines 7–8)
2 But he became one of the ... ... speakers in America. (line 31)
3 On that day America lost one of the ... ... men in its history. (lines 37–38)

5 OVER TO YOU! Finish the checkpoint.

CHECKPOINT

Vergleiche mit *-er/est* und *more/most*

- Bei einsilbigen Adjektiven (z. B. *hard*) und zweisilbigen Adjektiven auf *-y* (z. B. *happy*) hängst du ... bzw. ... an das Adjektiv.
- Bei dreisilbigen Adjektiven (z. B. *expensive*) und manchen zweisilbigen Adjektiven (z. B. *famous*) setzt du ... bzw. ... vor das Adjektiv.
- *good* und *bad* haben unregelmäßige Formen:
  good, ..., ...
  bad, ..., ...

Tip:
Write the checkpoint in your exercise book.

Tip:
Learn these three forms together.

▸ Eine Übersicht über diese Regeln findest du auf der *Summary*-Seite 136.
▸ Extra Practice, pp. 97 ff.
▸ W 10–11

NACH DIESER UNIT KANN ICH ...

über die Sehenswürdigkeiten von New York sprechen.	▸ *In Times Square there are lots of theatres. I'd like to go to Central Park.*
Vergleiche anstellen.	▸ *New York is more exciting than Greenville. It's my biggest dream.*
über Daten und Uhrzeiten sprechen.	▸ *Malcolm X died on February 21st 1965. The party starts at 7 p.m.*
ein Sandwich in einem „Deli" bestellen.	▸ *I'll have a roll with beef and tomato, please.*
jemanden den Weg mit der U-Bahn oder zu Fuß beschreiben.	▸ *Take line 2 or 3 to 125th Street. Walk three blocks to 128th Street.*
jemanden einladen.	▸ *Do you have any plans for Saturday evening? I'm having a party on Saturday. Do you want to come?*
eine Einladung annehmen oder ablehnen.	▸ *That sounds great, thanks. / I'm afraid I can't come.*

Unit 2

Life in LA

A

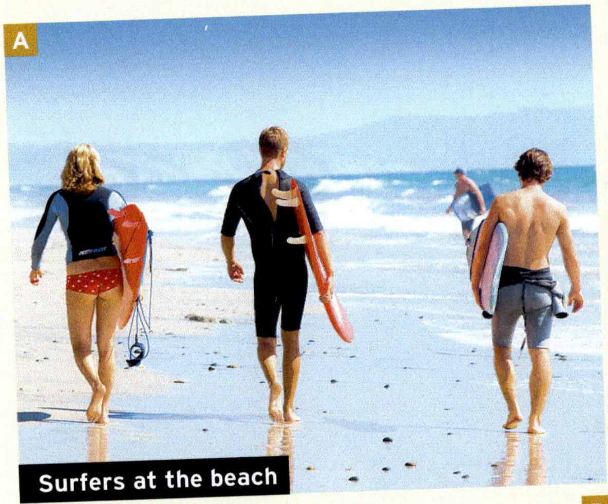

Surfers at the beach

B

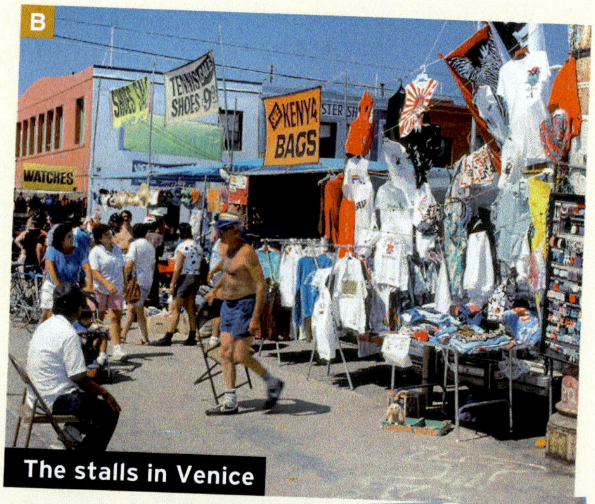

The stalls in Venice

C

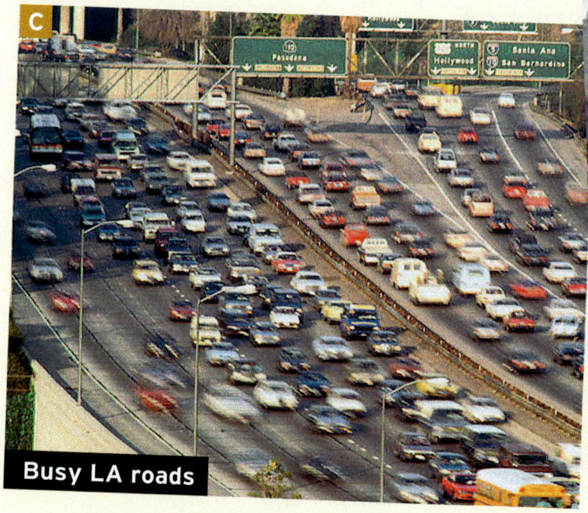

Busy LA roads

D

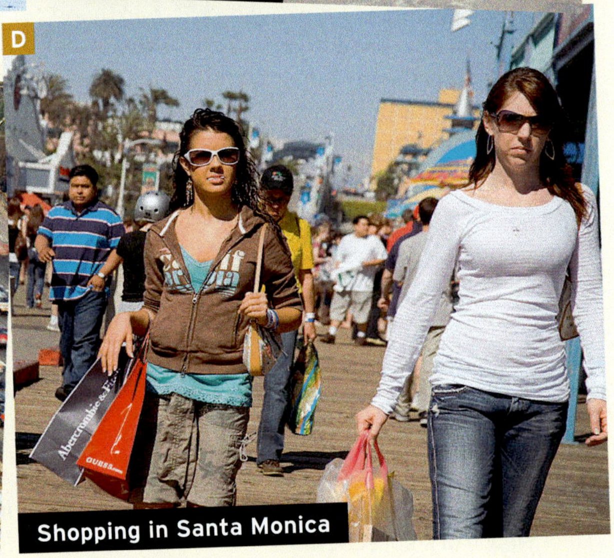

Shopping in Santa Monica

1 My Los Angeles video diary

1 ⊙ 17 Listen to the video diary about LA. Which five pictures on pages 24 and 25 is the teenager talking about?

2 About the pictures

1 ⊙ 18 Listen. Look at the pictures. What's right: a), b) or c)?

3 AND YOU? Tell the class.

I think LA is cool because ... But some things aren't so good, like ...

The boardwalk

A homeless man

Smog

Disneyland

4 Talk about a photo

Partner A: Partner B has picked a photo. Find out which photo.
Ask some questions like these:
What can you see?
How many people are there?
What are the people doing?
What's happening?
How do the people look?
What's the weather like?

Partner B: Pick a photo. But don't tell Partner A which photo.
Answer Partner A's questions:
– I can see ...
– There are ...
– They're ...
– A man is/Some people are ...
– The man looks ...
– It's nice/terrible/ ...

▶ W 13, 1–3
▶ Wordbank 2, p. 127

FREE TIME IN LA

1 **Look at A, B and C. What are they about?**

→ TV • outdoor activities • dancing

A is about ...   B is about ...   C ...

A

TODAY'S HIGHLIGHTS

NEWS
Good Morning America   7 a.m. KABC

SPORTS
Baseball   5 p.m. NBC
Action from New York.

MOVIES
Best Man, Worst Friend   8 p.m. ABC FAMILY
A great family movie.

SERIES
Back Home   10:30 p.m. CBS
12 stars from Big Brother meet again!

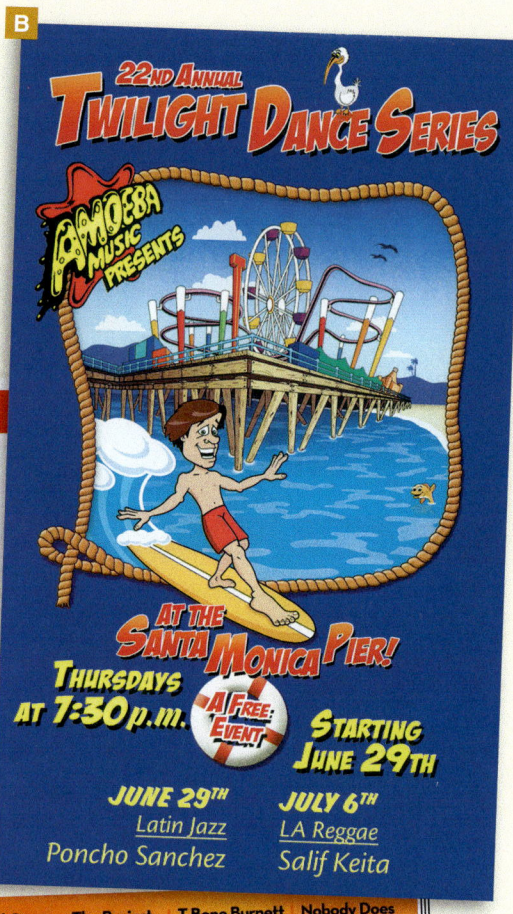

B

2 **What do we learn in the texts?**
Pick the right answers.

1 There's sports on TV ...
a) early in the morning.
b) in the afternoon.
c) late at night.

2 If you want to go to *Twilight Dance* ...
a) you have to pay.
b) you don't have to pay.
c) you only pay on Thursdays.

3 The magazine has information about ...
a) films and TV.
b) music in Santa Monica.
c) things to do in LA.

C

3 **What is it in German?**

highlights	**a)** Schlagzeilen	**b)** Höhepunkte	**c)** Lampen
twilight	**a)** Abenddämmerung	**b)** Tageslicht	**c)** Sonnenaufgang
Get out!	**a)** Steh auf!	**b)** Hau ab!	**c)** Geh raus!

Tip:
First find the words
in the text. Check
with a partner. Then
check in a dictionary.

PROJECT A media survey

TV, films and computers are very important today. Which are most important for young people? Do boys and girls like the same things? Do this survey and find out.

a) Ask your partner these questions. Write the answers in your exercise book.

Are you – a boy/a girl?

TV	Films	Computers
1 How much TV do you watch every day? a Less than an hour b One or two hours c More than two hours	**4 How many films do you watch every week?** a No films b One or two films c More than two films	**7 Do you have your own computer?** a Yes b No
2 Do you have a TV in your room? a Yes b No	**5 How often do you go to the cinema?** a Every week b Sometimes c Never	**8 How often do you use a computer?** a Every day b Sometimes c Never
3 What kind of TV programmes do you prefer? a Sport b Chat shows c Series d ... ▶ Wordbank 3, p. 127	**6 What kind of films do you prefer?** a Action b Comedy c Romance d ... ▶ Wordbank 3, p. 127	**9 How often do you use the Internet?** a Every day b Sometimes c Never

b) Collect the results on the board.

c) Present the results in class.

Media Survey Class 8 B

		BOYS	GIRLS
1 TV time	< 1 hour	2	5
	1–2 hours	4	7
	> 2 hours	6	3
2 TV in room		6	4
3 Favourite TV programmes		Series	Series
4 Films every week	0	1	2
	1–2	5	8
	2+	6	5

In the survey, we found out that two boys and five girls watch less than one hour of TV every day. But four boys and seven girls watch one to ...
Ten pupils in our class have a TV in their room – six boys and ...

Most pupils prefer ...
Lots of pupils watch more than two films every week – six boys and ... But most pupils only watch between one and two ...

d) Look at the questions in the survey and write about you and the media.

I watch about 1 hour of TV every day. I don't have a TV in my room. I prefer series and ...

e) Write a report about the survey in your class (50–70 words). How many pupils did you ask? Are boys and girls different? You can use the ideas in c).

▶ W 14, 4–6

1 **Look at the pictures. Try to answer the questions.**

a) Where do you think the story is happening?

b) Do you think that all the teenagers in the photos are friends?

c) Who would you like to be, the girl in the first picture or one of the teenagers in the second picture?

Lucky thing!

1⊙19

Saturday 9.15 a.m., 3rd Street, Santa Monica

Richard Bailey was waiting for his daughter.

"Hurry up, Caitlin! We'll be late," he shouted.

Ten minutes later they were driving along the freeway

5 towards Hollywood.

"Now remember Caitlin," Richard said. "You're the best.
You can get this role. This is a day that you'll always
remember. It could be the start of a great career in TV."
Caitlin was looking at the invitation to the audition that

10 the studio had sent.
She was feeling
nervous. But she
didn't say anything.

> **KABC STUDIOS LA**
> **invites:** Caitlin Bailey
> **to an audition for:** TEEN TALK
> **on:** Saturday, October 3rd at 10 a.m.

10.15 a.m., Santa Monica Boardwalk

Two friends, Lee and Nina, were on the 15
boardwalk. They had their surfboards. It
was a nice morning. Lots of people were
jogging, walking and cycling. After ten
minutes the two friends arrived at Venice.
This was always a busy place, with lots of 20
stalls, food places and music. And there
were homeless people who were sleeping
on the grass. Lee and Nina sat on the
grass too, watched the people and had
their sandwiches. 25

12.30 p.m., KABC Studios, LA

Caitlin left KABC Studios. Her dad was sitting in the car. "How was it?" he asked.

"Terrible," she answered. "First, I was standing in line for a long time. Then, the man who

asked the questions wasn't very nice. He was the director, so I won't get the role," she said.

"Well, we have to hurry up," her father answered. "Or we'll be late for your photo shoot." 30

"Appointments, auditions, photo shoots! I need a break, Dad!" Caitlin answered.

"Think of your future, Caitlin," Richard said and they went towards Santa Monica.

1.30 p.m., Santa Monica Beach
Lee and Nina were in the sea on their surfboards. The waves were great. The water was
35 cold. But they were fine because they were wearing wetsuits.

1.40 p.m.
Caitlin was on Santa Monica Beach too.
She was wearing nice, expensive surfing
gear, but she wasn't surfing. A photographer
40 and a make-up artist were with her. The
photographer was taking photos. "Turn to the
left … no, not too much … now turn to the
right … look at me … smile … look happy …",
the photographer was shouting. Caitlin looked
45 at the sea. She saw something that made her
jealous – surfers. "Lucky things!" she thought.

1.50 p.m.
Lee and Nina walked along the beach. Nina saw a girl who was
standing on the beach in nice clothes.
50 "Look at that girl," she said to Lee. "She's a model."
"Yeah, it must be a photo shoot for a magazine," he answered.
"How do you get a job like that? Lucky thing!" Nina thought.

2 **Who is it?**

1 He does lots of things for his daughter.
  But is he really helping her?
2 She loves surfing. But she'd really like
  to be a photo model.
3 He loves Venice, the sea, free time …
4 She has a busy life and no free time.

3 **Finish these sentences.**

1 In the morning Caitlin went …
2 At the same time Lee and Nina were …
3 After the audition Caitlin wasn't …
4 Then she and her dad went to …
5 At 1.30, Lee and Nina …
6 Caitlin was doing a …

4 **On Saturday**
evening:
Write the dialogue.

CAITLIN	today – terrible day
DAD	this – could – the start – great career
CAITLIN	tired – need – break
DAD	think of – future
CAITLIN	want – some – free time
DAD	OK – go to the beach – next weekend

5 **Caitlin's e-mail**
You're Caitlin. Write to your friend
Alice. Tell her about Saturday.
Use words and phrases from the story.

To Alice	From Caitlin
Hi Alice, Saturday was a terrible day. First I went to KABC Studios for an audition. I was waiting …	

▶ W 15, 7–9

1 A Santa Monica scene

a) What can you see?

Work in teams of three or four pupils. Who can find the most things, activities, people?

The words are in the story on pages 28–29.

b) Finish these sentences with words from a).

1 The waves are great. Let's go ...
2 The water is cold. You need a ...
3 We can ride our bikes on the ...
4 Look. There's a cool T-shirt ...
5 That man has no home. He's ...

2 Networks: Finish these networks in your exercise book.

MEDIA — TV

TV PROGRAMMES — Sport

FILMS — Comedy

▶ Wordbank 3, p. 127

3 Definitions: What do you call ...

1 ... somebody who takes photos?
2 ... somebody who knows all about make-up?
3 ... somebody who surfs?
4 ... big roads that you find in the USA?
5 ... small shops that you find in Venice?
6 ... the track that goes along the beach?

4 Pick some of these words and ask your partner:

→ director • model • teenager • surfboard • wetsuit

What do you call somebody who
is/makes/wears ...
What do you call something that
you need when/you wear when ...

5 WORD SEARCH *Who* or *that*?

a) Find the right words on pages 28 and 29.

1 This is a day ... you'll remember. (ll. 7–8)
2 Caitlin was looking at the invitation to the audition ... the studio had sent. (ll. 9–10)
3 There were homeless people ... were sleeping on the grass. (ll. 21–23)
4 The man ... asked the questions wasn't very nice. (ll. 28–29)
5 She saw something ... made her jealous – surfers. (ll. 45–46)
6 Nina saw a girl ... was standing on the beach in nice clothes. (ll. 48–49)

b) When do you use *who* and *that*?
Look at the answers to a). Make a rule.

You use ... for people.
You use ... for things.

▶ W 16, 10–12   ▶ W ⊙

DICTIONARY WORK

1 **What's the text about?**
Read the advert and find
out what a SEGWAY is.

a) It's only a toy for kids.
b) You can travel to places on it.
c) You use it for sport.

Tip:
There are lots of new words
in the text, but you don't have
to understand everything.

2 **Do you know the words?**
**a) What German words do
these words sound like?**

1 batteries   **2** forwards
3 maximum

SEGWAY

The SEGWAY can take you to places that cars and bikes can't go – like stores, offices, airports and streets. With a SEGWAY you can go shopping, go to work or just have fun. The SEGWAY is clean, quiet and good for the environment. You don't need gas – the SEGWAY uses batteries. You can charge the batteries anywhere – in the home or in the office. Using the SEGWAY is easy. To go forwards, you lean forwards. To go backwards, you lean backwards, to go left or right, you lean left or right. Maximum speed: 12.5 miles per hour (mph)
Price: $4000-$5500

b) Now find the three words in the advert.
Do you think that you were right? Then check the words in a dictionary.

3 **Find the words in the advert, look at the context and pick the right meaning.**

gas   **a)** *Nomen* Gas, (AE) Benzin   **b)** *Verb* (mit Gas) vergiften
charge   **a)** *Nomen* Gebühr   **b)** *Verb* berechnen   **c)** *Verb* aufladen
speed   **a)** *Verb* rasen   **b)** *Nomen* Geschwindigkeit

4 **Three dictionary entries**
Read the three entries. Then find the words
in the SEGWAY advert and look at the context.
What's the right meaning in German?

environment /ɪnˈvaɪrənmənt/ *Nomen* **1** Umgebung, Umwelt **a bad environment** ein schlechtes
häusliches Milieu
2 the environment die Umwelt **laws to protect the
environment** Gesetze zum Umweltschutz

lean¹ /liːn/ *Adj (Fleisch)* mager; *(Person)* schlank
lean² /liːn/ *Verb* (**leaned, leaned** /liːnd/, *BE auch* **leant,
leant** /lent/) **1** *ohne Obj* sich lehnen **lean backwards**
sich zurücklehnen **lean over to one side** sich zur Seite
lehnen **He leaned across the table to pick up the phone.**
Er beugte sich über den Tisch, um den Telefonhörer
abzunehmen. **lean forwards** sich vorbeugen
2 *ohne Obj* **lean against/on sth** sich an etw lehnen, sich
auf etw stützen
3 *+ Obj* lehnen **Please don't lean bicycles against the
shop window.** Bitte keine Fahrräder an das Schau-
fenster lehnen.

office /ˈɒfɪs; *AE auch* ˈɔːfɪs/ *Nomen* **1** Büro **the firm's
head office** der Hauptsitz der Firma **an office block** ein
Bürohaus
2 *(AE) (Arzt-, Zahnarzt-)* Praxis
3 *(oft in Zusammensetzungen)* Amt **the Foreign Office**
das Auswärtige Amt **the tax office** das Finanzamt
4 *kein Plural* Amt, Amtszeit **the chairman holds office
for one year.** Der Vorsitzende ist ein Jahr lang im Amt.
the party that is in office die Regierungspartei

From: *Das Oxford Schulwörterbuch, Oxford University Press, 2007*

▶ W 17, 13   ▶ W ⊚

LISTENING Phone messages

1 An important message

1⊙20 **a)** Caitlin's mum wrote three phone messages. Listen to the phone call. Which message do you hear?

b) Listen again and check.

A
PHONE MESSAGE
For: Caitlin
From: KABC Studios
Message: Call Jack between
          8 p.m. and 10 p.m.

Tel.:   310-555-0719

B
PHONE MESSAGE
For: Richard
From: Brown's Books
Message: New movie book has come.
          Please pick it up
          tomorrow after 10 a.m.
Tel.:   310-555-4570

C
PHONE MESSAGE
For: Caitlin
From: Bob Brown
Message: Call Bob after 8 p.m.

Tel.:   310-555-0901

2 Can I take a message?

1⊙21 **a)** Listen. What's right − a), b) or c)?

1 Caitlin is talking to ...
a) Bob Brown.
b) her dad.
c) a woman at KABC Studios.

2 Bob Brown ...
a) is at home.
b) can't come to the phone.
c) isn't at the studio.

3 Bob can call Caitlin ...
a) on her mobile.
b) at home.
c) at school.

b) Write this message in your exercise book.

PHONE MESSAGE
For: Bob ...
From: ...
Message: Call Caitlin on her ... after ...
Tel.:   310-555-2279

c) Finish the message. Then listen again and check.

> **Tip:**
> mobile (BE)
> = cellphone (AE)

3 Caitlin's news

1⊙22 **a)** Listen and make notes.

1 Who's calling?
2 Who's answering the phone?
3 What can Caitlin have?
4 How does Caitlin feel?
5 When can Caitlin come to the studio?
6 Who must come too?

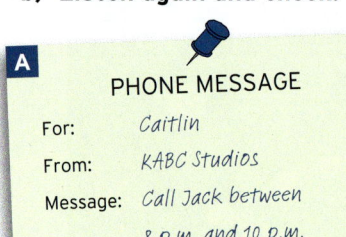
> **Tip:**
> Before you listen, read the questions and write the question words in your exercise book.

b) SAY IT IN GERMAN
Tell a partner about the phone call − in German. Use your notes for a).

▶ W 18, 14   ▶ W ⊙

SPEAKING Phone calls

 1 Two phone calls

1◉23 **a) Listen to or read the two dialogues.**

CAITLIN	Hi. Can I speak to Josh, please?
MAN	Josh? (*Er*), I think you have the wrong number.
CAITLIN	Oh, sorry.
MAN	No problem. Bye.

CAITLIN	Hi. Can I speak to Josh, please?
MRS STONE	I'm afraid he isn't here. Can I take a message?
CAITLIN	Yes, please. Can you tell him that Caitlin called? Can he call me back? My new number is 310-555-2279.
MRS STONE	OK, Caitlin. No problem. Bye.
CAITLIN	Thanks, Mrs Stone. Bye.

b) Answer these questions.

1   Who has a wrong number?
2   Who wants to speak to Josh?
3   Who isn't at home?
4   Who can take a message?
5   Who has a new number?

c) Practise the phone calls with a partner.

2 SAY IT IN ENGLISH

a) Make a phone call with a partner. Write the dialogue on the left or on the right.

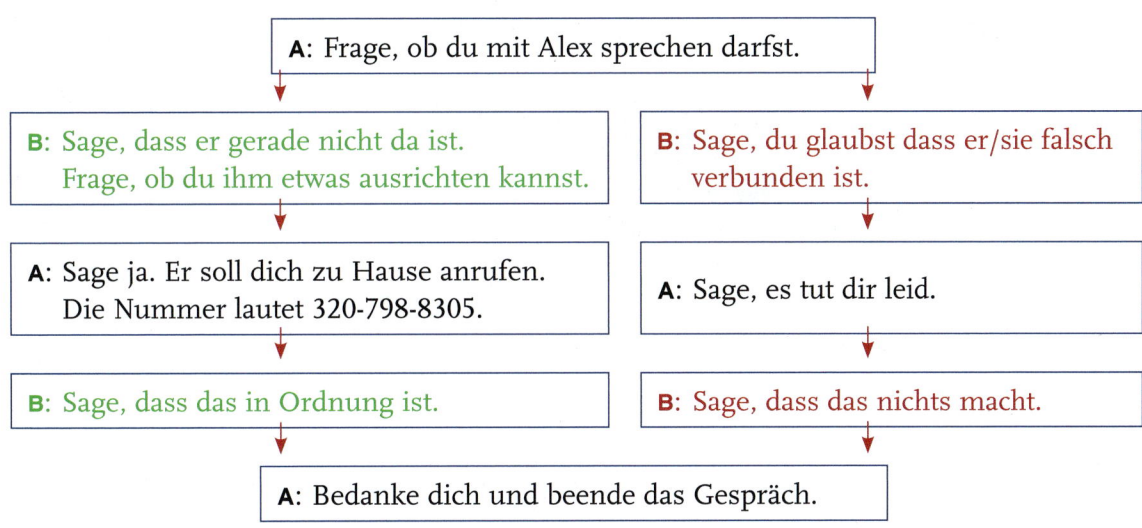

A: Frage, ob du mit Alex sprechen darfst.

B: Sage, dass er gerade nicht da ist. Frage, ob du ihm etwas ausrichten kannst.

B: Sage, du glaubst dass er/sie falsch verbunden ist.

A: Sage ja. Er soll dich zu Hause anrufen. Die Nummer lautet 320-798-8305.

A: Sage, es tut dir leid.

B: Sage, dass das in Ordnung ist.

B: Sage, dass das nichts macht.

A: Bedanke dich und beende das Gespräch.

b) Act the dialogues with a partner.

3 ROLE PLAY

Partner A: Look at your card on page 94. Then phone Partner B.

Partner B: Look at your card on page 94. Answer Partner A and write the message.

▶ W 18, 15 – 16   ▶ W ◉

READING A teen newspaper online

1 Look at the six articles in LA YOUTH.
Which article do you think looks the most interesting?

Tip:
You can read LA YOUTH online:
www.LAYOUTH.com

LA YOUTH – the newspaper by and about teens

I won a ticket to see my favorite band!

Nattalie, 16, won a ticket to see *My Chemical Romance*. And she met her hero, Gerard Way, the lead singer.

A day that made a difference

Mel Shin and her class went to Mexico for a day. They took food and clothes to orphans there.

Is Disneyland uncool for teens?

Is it only for young kids?
Some people say yes.
Some people say no.
Write to us and tell us what you think.

Halloween tricks

Three teen writers tell funny stories about this "scary" day: Fred (16), Katherine (17) and Stephanie (16).

CD reviews

Our teens recommend *The Pixies*, *Within Temptation* and the movie soundtrack for *The Chorus*.

TV or not TV?

Could you give up TV for two weeks? No TV at home! No TV at friends' houses!
Sue Li (16), Connie (16) and Nicole (15) try.

2 Correct these sentences.

1 Nattalie met a famous film star.
2 Mel Shin bought clothes in Mexico.
3 All teenagers love Disneyland.
4 Three teenagers tell Christmas stories.
5 The teenagers hate the *Pixies* CD.
6 Three teens watched TV for two weeks.

3 Find words in the text that mean:

1 somebody who you find great
2 kids who have no parents
3 not fun or interesting
4 something makes you frightened
5 tell somebody that something is good
6 film music

▶ W 19, 17

WRITING An article for a teen newspaper

1 TV or not TV?

Look at these sentences. Are they FOR TV or AGAINST TV? Write two lists.

1 You can learn lots of things on TV.
2 People watch too much TV – they don't read books or newspapers.
3 TV is like a drug. When you start, you can't stop.
4 You can relax when you watch TV. That's great.
5 If you watch too much TV, you won't do outdoor activities.
6 If you don't watch TV, you can't talk to your friends about your favourite shows.
7 It's nice to sit with your friends or family and watch TV together.
8 In our family everybody wants to watch something different. So we often fight.
9 TV helps you to forget your problems.
10 TV programmes can help teens with their problems.

2 For and against TV

Read this article and pick the right words. Write the article in your exercise book.

Tip:
This article has four paragraphs. Every paragraph has a different main point.

Useful phrases:
• This is what I think.
• On the one hand, ...
• On the other hand, ...
• All in all I think ...

Is TV good (**1**) bad? Could I live (**2**) TV? This is what I think.

On the one hand, I think that TV is great. When I'm tired (**3**) school, I watch some TV. When I'm sad, it makes me (**4**). When I'm bored, TV is (**5**).

On the other (**6**), you shouldn't watch too much TV. Some teens watch TV for 3 or 4 (**7**) every day. They don't (**8**) their homework or sport. That (**9**) good!

All in all, I think TV is OK. But you mustn't (**10**) TV too much.

1 and / or / if
2 without / with / for

3 at / between / after

4 happy / bored / hungry
5 boring / stupid / fun

6 foot / hand / head

7 minutes / days / hours
8 do / like / find
9 is / isn't / wasn't

10 play / see / watch

3 For and against computer games

Write an article for a teen newspaper.

You can use ideas from exercise 1.

You can write a text like exercise 2.

Look at the tip and useful phrases in exercise 2.

4 TV and you

Write 50–70 words. Do you watch TV? When? How much? Could you live without TV? Is TV good? What's good? What isn't so good? Why?

▶ W 19, 18   ▶ W ⊚

LOOK AT LANGUAGE

A LETTER TO *LA YOUTH*

1 **Is Disneyland uncool? Is it only for young kids? What do you think?**

2 **What is the letter about?**
Pick a main point for every paragraph.

→ Disneyland is for everybody • Long lines • The rides

Dear LA Youth,

Last summer I went to Disneyland with my younger brother. It was a Saturday. When we arrived, lots of people were waiting at the gates. They were standing in long lines, so we had to wait too. Kids were running everywhere. After an hour

5   we went in. (Tip number 1 – don't go to Disneyland on the weekend!)

First we went on *The Pirates of the Caribbean* ride. We were in a boat and pirates were shouting, singing and fighting! It was OK. One pirate looked like Johnny Depp. But I didn't have my

10 camera! (Tip number 2 – bring your camera!) Then we went on the *Splash Mountain* ride. That was a roller coaster ride in a mountain. It was fun. But there was lots of water and we were very wet. (Tip number 3 – bring a jacket!) Then we went on another ride – *Space Mountain*. It was great. Our train was going very fast. Everybody was screaming. But my brother was crying. (Tip number 4 – don't bring young kids on the *Space Mountain* ride!)

15 In the night I was feeling tired, so we watched the fireworks.

Is Disneyland only for young kids? No, Disneyland is cool for teenagers too. But you should remember my tips.

Sophie (16)

3 **WORD SEARCH**   *was/were*
a) **First guess the missing words in these sentences.**

1   When we arrived, lots of people ... waiting at the gates. (ll. 2 – 3)
2   They ... standing in long lines. (l. 3)
3   Kids ... running everywhere. (l. 4)
4   Pirates ... shouting. (l. 8)

5   Our train ... going very fast. (l. 13)
6   Everybody ... screaming. (l. 13)
7   My brother ... crying. (ll. 13 – 14)
8   In the night I ... feeling tired. (l. 15)

b) **Now check your answers in the letter on this page.**

4 WORD SEARCH

Look at the pictures. Guess the missing words. Check on pages 28–29.

1 Richard Bailey ... ... for his daughter. (l. 2)

2 Caitlin ... ... at the invitation. (l. 9)

3 I ... ... in line for a long time. (l. 26)

4 Lots of people ... . (l. 15–16)

5 Homeless people ... ... on the grass. (ll. 20–21)

6 They ... ... wetsuits. (l. 33)

5 OVER TO YOU!

Finish the sentences in the checkpoint and make the rule.

Tip:
Write the checkpoint in your exercise book.

CHECKPOINT

Past progressive: was/were + -ing

Wenn du sagen willst, was in der Vergangenheit gerade im Gange war:
Nach *I, he, she, it* benutzt du ...
Nach *we, you, they* benutzt du ...
Das Verb endet auf ...

► Eine Übersicht über diese Regeln findest du auf der *Summary*-Seite 133.

► Extra Practice, pp. 100 ff.

► W 20–21

NACH DIESER UNIT KANN ICH ...

über eine Umfrage berichten.	► *In the survey we found out that boys watch more TV than girls.*
Telefonnachrichten notieren.	► *Message for Anna: Call your dad after 8 p.m.*
Anrufe machen/beantworten.	► *Can I speak to Josh, please? / I'm afraid he isn't there. / Can I take a message?*
meine Meinung über Fernsehen sagen.	► *On the one hand, I think TV is great. On the other hand, too much TV isn't good.*
erzählen, was in der Vergangenheit gerade im Gange war.	► *Caitlin was looking at the invitation.*
genauere Informationen über Personen oder Sachen geben.	► *The man who asked the questions wasn't nice. She saw something that made her jealous.*

Unit 3
At Sullivan High

1 Read the school brochure.
- Where is Sullivan High?
- Find AE words for *pupils*
and *years*.

2 Listen to the tour of the school.
Put the photos A-E in the right order.

Photo ..., photo ..., photo ...

3 Match the photos with the
phrases from the box.
Then listen again and check.

 medical classroom • flag • locker •
cheerleaders • security check

4 Write sentences for the photos.
Use the words in exercise 3. Example:
Students put their books in lockers.

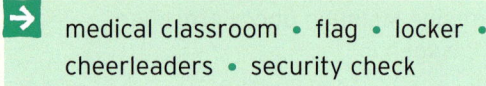

► W 25, 1

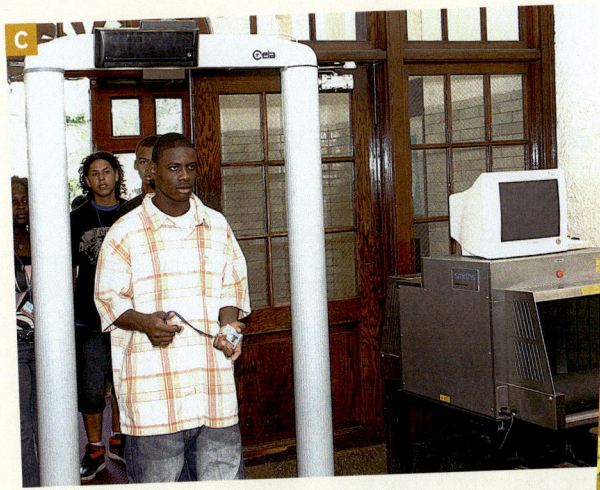

Tip: You can find more pictures of Sullivan High School on their website.

5 **Compare your school with Sullivan High School. What's the same? What's different? Make lists with a partner.**

→ a swimming pool • flags • cheerleaders • extra classes after school • lockers • a homework club • summer classes

At Sullivan High School and at our school there is/there are	At our school we don't have	But at our school we have
– lots of pupils	– a medical classroom	– first aid lessons
– ...	– ...	– ...

►W 25, 2–3

BASKETBALL DREAMS

1 Is basketball popular at your school? Do you watch it on TV?

2 Work with a partner. Look at the pictures and finish the file.

BASKETBALL FILE

Teams:	There must be ... teams of ... players.
Place and equipment:	You need a basketball ... and two ...
Gear:	You should have a T-shirt, shorts and basketball shoes.
What you must do:	Players must get the ball in the ... to get points.
Points:	Free throw = 1 point, shot = 2 points, long shot = 3 points.
Rules:	Players mustn't touch other players and they mustn't kick the ... (these things are fouls).

3 SONG *YMCA*

1◉25 **a)** Listen to the song. Do you know it?
Do you like it? Tell the class.

I think it's great / cool / OK / bad / terrible.

b) Listen again and read the words.
Does the song have a happy ending?
Find the lines in the song that tell you.

● **c)** Finish the summary of the song.

The singer had a problem. He wanted to ...,
but he didn't have ... . Then ... helped him.
The singer played at ... . One day there was
a ... . The singer made ... . Now he's a ...

I spent many long days with nothing to do
Which way should I go? I have no clue
A basketball in my hand, but I got no hoop
Gotta find me a place so I can shoot
I got dreams of being like Michael J.
But a ball's no good with no place to play
Till this old man came, showed me the way
Now I play at the YMCA

Five years later, the old man came
So happened to be the day of the big game
The score was tied, 3 on the clock
It's up to me to make the last shot
So I got the ball, jumped sky-high
Released the ball, then closed my eyes
Now I'm a star and it's OK
Thank you for the YMCA

It's fun to stay at the YMCA
It's fun to stay at the YMCA
They have everything for young men to enjoy
You can hang out with all the boys
It's fun to stay at the YMCA
It's fun to stay at the YMCA
You can get yourself clean
You can have a good meal
You can do whatever you feel

▶ W 26, 4

4 **Candice from Sullivan High**

1 ⊙ 26 **Listen. What's Candice's problem?**

Her basketball shoes are ... . But good shoes are really ... and cheap shoes are ...

What should I do?

You shouldn't worry, Candice.

5 **Read the website advert.**

1 How much are the shoes?

2 What's special about the shoes?

3 Where can you buy the shoes?

4 What's the AE word for *trainers*?

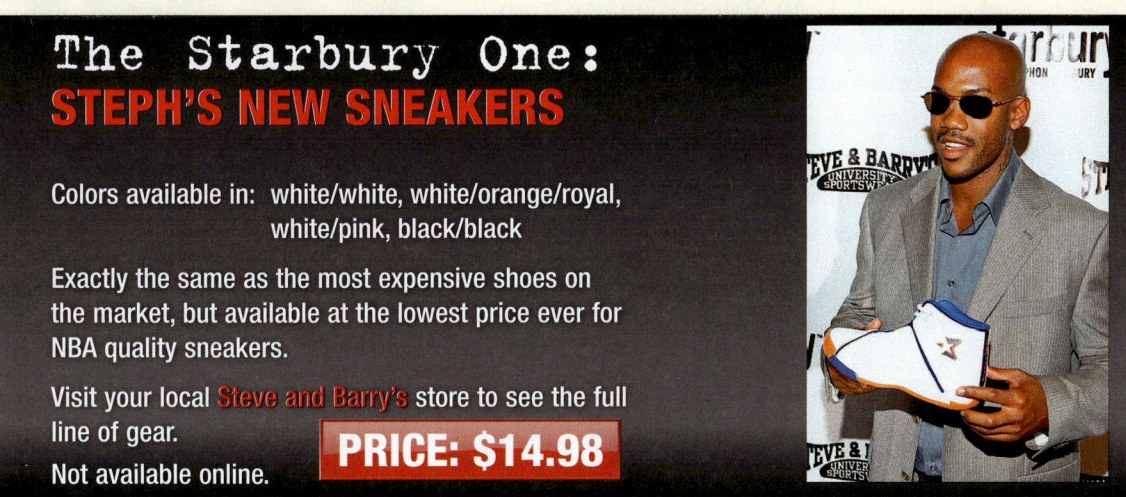

The Starbury One:
STEPH'S NEW SNEAKERS

Colors available in: white/white, white/orange/royal, white/pink, black/black

Exactly the same as the most expensive shoes on the market, but available at the lowest price ever for NBA quality sneakers.

Visit your local Steve and Barry's store to see the full line of gear.

Not available online.

PRICE: $14.98

6 **AND YOU?** **Tell the class: How important are brands for you?**

Brands are important. They show that you're cool.

I agree. People laugh if you have cheap gear.

I think the ... brand is cool.

Brands like ... are too expensive.

I don't agree. You shouldn't pay lots of money for a name.

...

Clothes should look good. You shouldn't wear them because they have a special label.

PROJECT Team sports

- **Work in five groups. Each group picks one of these team sports: baseball, American football, soccer, softball, volleyball.**
- **Go to www.new-highlight.de. Find the window for the webcode and put in NHL-4-41.**

- **Make notes about your sport. Print out photos or find other pictures.**
- **Make a file like the basketball file in ex. 2.**
- **Make new groups. Now you're the expert for your sport. Present your file: For ... there must be ... / you need ...**

Tip:
The *Presentation Phrases* at the start of the book can help you.

▶W 26, 5–6

1 **Can you remember these words?**
If you can't remember, check them
in the *Dictionary* **(pages 160–179).**

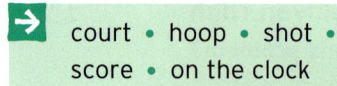

→ court • hoop • shot •
score • on the clock

2 **Read the story. Who won the game?**

1 ◎ 27

Fair play

It was the day of the basketball game between Sullivan
High School and North High School. Candice from
Sullivan High loved basketball. She wasn't very good at
other school subjects, but she was great at sport. Her
5 dream was to become a famous basketball player when
she finished school. Her family lived in a small
apartment in a neighbourhood with lots of drugs and
violence. Candice wanted a better life for her family –
she needed a good job.

10 The cheerleaders left the court and the two teams came on. Candice felt confident. "It'll be
a good game," she said to her friend April from the Sullivan team. Lana Hill from the
North team said, "New shoes, Candice? They look good, but they won't make you faster,
you know. North is going to win today." "Not with you on the team!" Candice said.

The game started and soon Candice got the
ball. She moved down the court and threw the   15
ball at the hoop – two points. The Sullivan
students cheered.

The game was fast. At half-time Candice had
scored 12 points but it was 24–18 to North.
"Too bad!" said Lana to Candice and smiled.   20
"We're going to win!"
"Don't be so sure," said Candice.
"Well done, girls! You played well – but you
must move faster!" said Ms Harris, Sullivan's
coach. She looked at Candice. "Do your best,   25
Candice! ... OK, let's go. Good luck!"

The game started again. The Sullivan team played faster. Now there was a minute on the
clock: 44–42 to North! Candice ran. She got the ball and she was ready to shoot. But
suddenly somebody's arm hit her in the face and she felt a terrible pain in her right eye.
"Foul!" April shouted.   30
"Lana," Candice thought. Candice was really angry, she wanted to hit Lana. She started to
walk across the court. Then she stopped. "Wait a minute," she thought. "Don't do anything
stupid."

Candice looked at the referee. He was talking to Lana. Then he gave Candice a sign – she had two free throws. "I mustn't miss," Candice thought. First throw: Candice's eye hurt and she couldn't see the hoop. The shot missed. Second throw: The shot missed again. The game was over. 44–42 to North.

35

Candice walked off the court. She felt bad. And she felt stupid. "Basketball star," she thought. "Forget it!"
Then Ms Harris stopped her.
"Hey, Candice," she said. "Don't be sad. You're the best player that I've trained. You play by the rules and you have self-control, that's very important. You have a good future – you shouldn't give up your dream."

40

45

3 Who's who? Match the names with the people in the story.

1 Candice
2 Lana
3 April
4 Ms Harris

a) Sullivan's coach
b) a Sullivan team player
c) a North team player
d) Candice's friend and Sullivan team player

Tip:
Find the first place in the text where you can read the names.

4 A report about the game
a) Finish the sentences.

1 Sullivan High School played against ... High School. (ll. 1–2)
2 The game was ... . (l. 18)
3 At half-time the score was ... . (l. 19)
4 When the game started again, the Sullivan team played ... . (l. 27)
5 Lana's arm hit Candice ... . (l. 29)
6 Candice had two free throws. Her shots ... . (l. 36)
7 In the end, the score was ... to ... . (l. 37)
8 The coach said Candice shouldn't ... her dream. (l. 46)

● **b) Write a report about the game for the Sullivan School website.**
Yesterday Sullivan High School played ... The game ... . It was a ... game.

Tip:
Pick sentences from exercise 4a). Put in words like *suddenly, then, so.* Then say what the game was like.

5 What is fair play?
Put the sentences together.

1 You play
2 You help
3 You don't fight

other players.
with the referee.
by the rules.

6 AND YOU? What do you think?

– Fair play is the most important thing in sport.
– Fair play is important, but you don't always have to play by the rules.
– The most important thing is to win.

▶ W 27, 7–9

1 Match the phrases with the pictures.

These phrases are in the story on pages 42–43.

→ Too bad! • Good luck! • Well done!

2 Sport words

a) Match the words with the pictures.

These words are on pages 40–43.

→ kick • score • miss • cheer • hit • throw

3 A sport network

Work with a partner. Put in words from pages 38–43, then find more words.

shorts   cheerleader

Sports gear   People in sport

SPORT   gym

Other sports words   Places and equipment

free throw   clock

▶ Wordbank 4, p.128

● **b) Write sentences for the pictures.**

1 The football player has scored!   2 The people are …

4 WORD SEARCH Imperative

a) Find these sentences on pages 42 and 43.

1   … your best, Candice! (ll. 25–26)
2   … a minute. (l. 32)
3   … it! (l. 40)
4   … … so sure! (l. 22)
5   … … anything stupid. (ll. 32–33)
6   … … sad. (l. 42)

b) Write what the coach says.

1   😊 drink – lots of water
2   😊 wear – good shoes
3   😊 use – the right equipment
4   😠 hurt – other players
5   😠 do – dangerous things
6   😠 lose – your self-control

▶ W 28, 10–13   ▶ W ◉

1 **School subjects and activities**

a) Work with a partner. Make a list of school subjects and activities.

English, maths, homework club, ...

▸ Wordbank 5, p.129

2 **At school**

a) Look at Sullivan's timetable and finish the sentences.

1 School starts at ...
2 School finishes at ...
3 Lessons are ... minutes long.
4 There are ... minutes between lessons.
5 Lunch is at ... or at ...

b) Write about your school.

b) Talk to your partner about your school subjects and activities. Use the phrases in the box.

→ I (really) like ... • I love ... •
I'm not keen on ... • I can't stand ... (because) ...

Lesson	Time
Class meeting	7:45 – 8:00
1	8:04 – 8:50
2	8:54 – 9:40
3	9:44 – 10:30
4	10:34 – 11:20 (lunch)
5	11:24 – 12:10 (lunch)
6	12:14 – 1:00
7	1:04 – 1:50
8	1:54 – 2:40
9	2:44 – 3:30

3 **About school and me**

a) Put in the words in the box.

→ about • at • by • in • near • on

I'm Mack. Let me tell you ... me. I live ... my school. I usually walk there, but sometimes I go ... bus. My favorite sport at school is baseball. I'm not ... the school team. At school I'm good ... art and computers. ... the future, I'd like to be a detective.

b) Make notes about you. Then tell a partner. Talk about:

live near school? walk to school? favourite sport? school team? good at? future?

4 **In the classroom**

a) WORD LINK Work with a partner. Find words or phrases that come after each of these verbs.

→ look at • play • sit • talk to • wear

Look at the board / the teacher / ...

b) Look at the photo for one minute. What are the people in the photo doing? What are they wearing? Then close your book and write sentences about the photo.

Some students are ... . One boy / girl is ...

c) Compare your sentences with a partner.

LISTENING Giving orders

Tip:
First read the questions. Then listen. You don't have to understand every word. Only the answers to the questions are important.

 1 American school scenes

1⊙28 **Listen to six conversations. Pick the right answer. Then listen again and check.**

1 Who's speaking?
a) a student
b) a parent
c) a teacher
d) a coach

2 What are the girls talking about?
a) shopping
b) the cinema
c) a basketball game
d) a party

3 What's the boy wearing?
a) sneakers
b) a jacket
c) walking shoes
d) a cap

4 What are the students going to do?
a) write a report
b) watch a DVD
c) listen to a CD
d) do a test

5 Where are they?
a) in the classroom
b) in the school car park
c) at the bus stop
d) in the playground

6 What are they going to do?
a) go to school
b) go to the hospital
c) leave school early
d) phone Nick's dad

2 Match the phrases from the listening texts in exercise 1 with the right pictures.

1 Put your tray back.
2 Don't leave anything in the car.
3 Put your shoes over there.
4 Don't forget the popcorn!

 3 INTERPRETING An American exchange student at a German school has a problem.

1⊙29 **Listen. Then practise the conversation.** The phrases in exercise 2 can help you.

WOMAN	Stell dein Tablett zurück. Lass deine Sachen nicht auf dem Tisch liegen!
GIRL	Why is she shouting? What's she saying?
YOU	She says put … . And don't …
GIRL	Oh, er sorry. Tell her I didn't know.
YOU	Sie … . Sie …
WOMAN	In Ordnung, aber sage ihr, sie soll ihr Glas da drüben hinstellen. Und sie soll ihre Tüte nicht vergessen.
YOU	She says OK, but …

▸ W 30, 17–18   ▸ W ⊙

SPEAKING What you must do and mustn't do

1 An exchange student

1 ⊙ 30 **Read the dialogue or listen to it. Which of these things (1–5)
can you wear or bring to Sullivan High?**

CANDICE	What do you want to know about school?
ADRIENNE	What about clothes? What must you wear?
CANDICE	Well, you don't have to wear anything special. But you mustn't wear T-shirts with bad messages or bad pictures on them.
ADRIENNE	OK. Can I bring my cellphone to school?
CANDICE	Yes, but you must turn it off and leave it in your locker.
ADRIENNE	What about my MP3 player?
CANDICE	That's OK. You can use it in class. But you must turn it off if the teacher asks you.

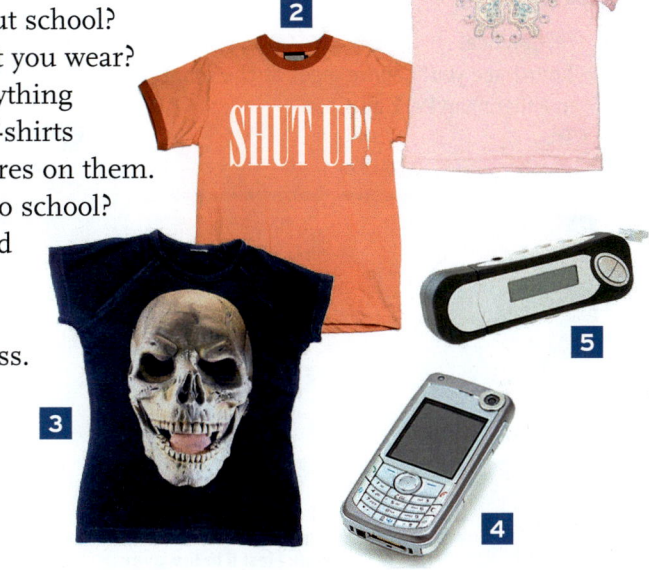

2 A new student
Finish the dialogue.
Then read it with a partner.

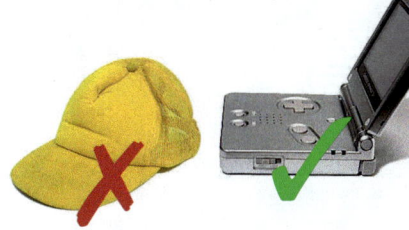

MIGUEL	What do you want …?
DAN	What about …? What …?
MIGUEL	Well, you … anything special. But you … baseball caps.
DAN	OK. … my video game player to school?
MIGUEL	Yes, but you … and leave it in your locker.

3 ROLE PLAY

You're going to talk about what you must do and
mustn't do at your school.
First make two lists with your partner.

You mustn't wear … (dirty clothes, short T-shirts, …)
You mustn't bring … (alcohol, drugs, skateboards, …)

Partner A: You're a pupil. Look at
your card on page 95.

Partner B: You're an English
exchange student. Look at your
card on page 95.

4 SAY IT IN GERMAN What do these signs at Sullivan High mean?

In the classroom   In the computer room   On a door

BE RESPECTFUL.
Don't be late.

NO E-MAIL
INTERNET ONLY FOR SCHOOL PROJECTS

DRUG-FREE ZONE
HATE-FREE ZONE

▶ W 30, 19   ▶ W ⊙

READING Messages

1 Match the messages (1–4) with the photos (A–D).

A

> **1** | To: Candice   From: Troy
>
> Hi, Candice!
> I must see you! Can we meet at the fountain in Millennium Park at 4 p.m.?
> Troy

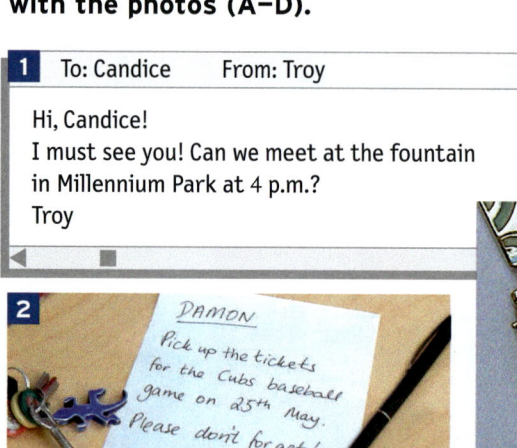

2

DAMON
Pick up the tickets for the Cubs baseball game on 25th May.
Please don't forget!

Dad

B

C

D

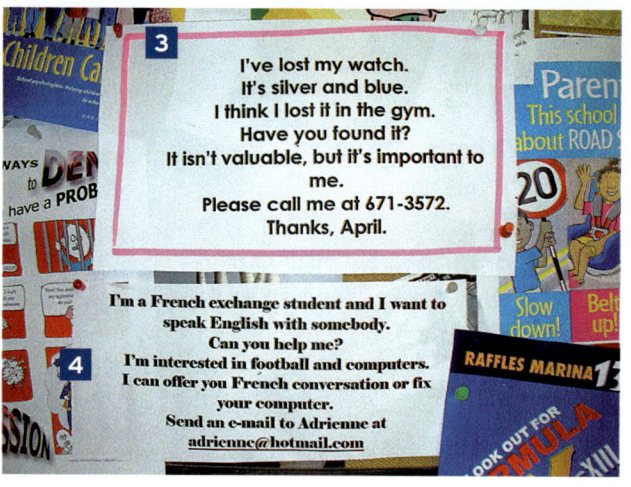

3
I've lost my watch.
It's silver and blue.
I think I lost it in the gym.
Have you found it?
It isn't valuable, but it's important to me.
Please call me at 671-3572.
Thanks, April.

4
I'm a French exchange student and I want to speak English with somebody.
Can you help me?
I'm interested in football and computers.
I can offer you French conversation or fix your computer.
Send an e-mail to Adrienne at
adrienne@hotmail.com

2 Pick the right answer a) or b).

1 Troy wants to meet Candice
a) in the morning.
b) in the afternoon.

2 Damon
a) has tickets for a baseball game.
b) has to get tickets for a baseball game.

3 April wants to
a) buy a new watch.
b) find her watch.

4 April's watch
a) is expensive.
b) is special.

5 Adrienne is
a) a student from another country.
b) an American student.

6 Adrienne would like to
a) learn French.
b) practise her English.

►W 31, 20

3 **What is it in German?**
Find these words on page 48.
Pick the right German word.
Then check in the *Dictionary*
(pages 160–179).

Remember:
Read the sentences.
The context can
help you.

4 **SAY IT IN ENGLISH**
Find these phrases in English
in messages 1–4 on p. 48.

1 **fountain**	**a)** Quelle	**b)** Rathaus	**c)** Brunnen
2 **silver**	**a)** silbern	**b)** albern	**c)** sinnvoll
3 **valuable**	**a)** nützlich	**b)** hygienisch	**c)** wertvoll
4 **fix**	**a)** stehlen	**b)** reparieren	**c)** benutzen

1 Können wir uns treffen?
2 Bitte nicht vergessen.
3 Hast du sie gefunden?
4 Kannst du mir helfen?

WRITING Messages

1 **You're an exchange student at Sullivan High. Pick a) or b).**

a) **You want to find somebody who can
speak English with you. Write a message
for the school noticeboard.**
Message 4 on p. 48 can help you.

- **Say who you are and ask for help.**
  I'm ... and I ...
- **Say what you're interested in.**
  I'm interested in sport/music/
  computer games/...
- **Say what you can offer.**
  I can offer German/... conversation.
  I can fix your .../...

b) **You've lost your bag.
Write a message
for the noticeboard.**
Message 3 on p. 48 can help you.

- **Say what your bag is like.**
  It's big/blue/new/...
- **Say what's in it.**
  My books/pencil case/
  lunch ... is/are in it.
- **Ask if somebody has found it.**
  Have you ...?
- **Write your e-mail address.**
  Send an e-mail to ...

2 **Put your message on the board in
your classroom. Read the other messages.**

 3 **Pick one message from
exercise 2 and write an e-mail.**

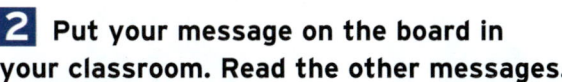

Hi ...,
My name's .... I saw your message
on the noticeboard.
I would like to .... I'm interested in ... /
I've found .... It was in ...
You can ...
(your name)

1 **Read the information about paramedics.
Say if the sentences are true or false.**

1 Paramedics help people in accidents.
2 Paramedics have easy jobs.
3 Paramedics only work Monday to Friday.
4 It's important to be healthy when you're a paramedic.
5 The training is very short.
6 You get lots of money as a paramedic.

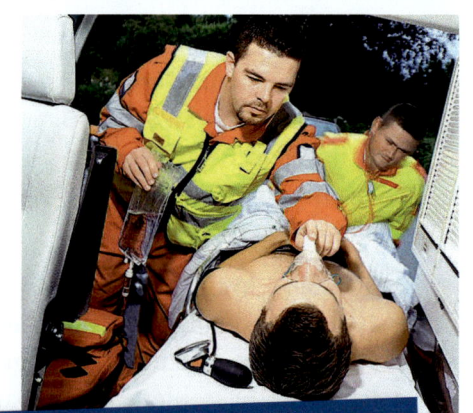

Sullivan High School Medical Career Academy
Career information: Paramedic

Do you know the people who bring people in the hospital on TV shows like *ER*? They're paramedics. They give people first aid when they have an accident or become sick. Then they take them to hospital.

Paramedics have hard jobs. As a paramedic, you must work in the evening and on the weekend and the work can be dangerous. You must be very fit and you mustn't be nervous. You mustn't panic when things are difficult and you mustn't be too emotional when somebody dies. The training is hard too – you must do 1000–2000 hours of training.

You shouldn't become a paramedic if you want to earn lots of money. But you should become a paramedic if you want an exciting job where you can really help people.

If you would like more information, then you should talk to the teachers in the Medical Career Academy.

2 **WORD SEARCH** *Must* or *mustn't*? Put in the words. Then check on this page.

1 You ... work in the evening.

2 You ... be very fit.

3 You ... be nervous.

4 You ... panic when things are difficult.

5 You ... be too emotional when somebody dies.

6 You ... do 1000–2000 hours of training.

3 **WORD SEARCH**

Should or shouldn't? **Guess, then check on pages 40–41.**

1 You ... have a T-shirt, shorts and basketball shoes. (p. 40, ex. 2)
2 What ... I do? (p. 41, ex. 4)
3 You ... worry, Candice. (p. 41, ex. 4)
4 You ... pay lots of money for a name. (p. 41, ex. 6)
5 Clothes ... look good. (p. 41, ex. 6)
6 You ... wear them because they have a special label. (p. 41, ex. 6)

4 **OVER TO YOU!**

Finish the checkpoint.

Tip:
Write the checkpoint in your exercise book.

► Eine Übersicht über diese Regeln findest du auf der *Summary*-Seite 135.
► Extra Practice, pp. 104 ff.
► W 32–33

CHECKPOINT

Die Hilfsverben *should/shouldn't* und *must/mustn't*

• Mit ... rätst du jemandem, etwas zu tun.
• Mit ... rätst du jemandem, etwas nicht zu tun.
• Mit ... sagst du, was jemand tun muss.
• Mit ... verbietest du jemandem, etwas zu tun.

NACH DIESER UNIT KANN ICH ...

Schulen in den USA und Deutschland vergleichen.	► *At Sullivan High there are extra classes in summer, but at our school there aren't any lessons in summer.*
über Sport und Sportregeln sprechen.	► *There must be two teams of five players. A free throw is one point.*
jemandem raten, etwas zu tun oder nicht zu tun.	► *You should play to win. You shouldn't worry.*
jemandem sagen, was er/sie tun muss.	► *You must turn off your MP3 player.*
jemandem verbieten, etwas zu tun.	► *You mustn't bring skateboards.*
jemanden anweisen, etwas zu tun oder nicht zu tun.	► *Put your tray back! Don't forget, please!*
eine kurze Nachricht schreiben.	► *Have you found my schoolbag? It's black and green. I think I left it in the gym.*

Unit 4

The Evergreen State
Welcome to Washington State, in the north-west of the USA.

Visit Olympic National Park – with its mountains and forests.

a bear a deer a cougar

Washington is famous for wild animals.

Visit the Makah Reservation in Neah Bay. There's a big festival every August.

---

 1 A holiday trip

2⊙1 **a) Read the two questions. Then listen and look at the brochure.**

1 Which places in Washington did Emma visit?
2 What animals did she see?

b) Listen again. Are these sentences true or false?

1 The trip started in Seattle.
2 There are lots of trees in the national park.
3 They didn't go to the sea.
4 They visited a reservation.
5 Emma liked Anacortes.
6 She took a photo of a whale.
7 She didn't buy presents for her friends.

▶ W 35, 1

Anacortes – you can go whale watching here.

Washington's islands – great for fishing and boat trips.

Seattle is Washington's biggest city.

Cape Flattery – popular for hiking.

Park Rangers – always ready to help.

2 **Brochure game**

a) First write all the things that you can see in the brochure.

mountains, trees, animals, ...

b) Then play this game with your partner.

A I see something that starts with b.

B Is it a bear?

A Yes, it is. / No, it isn't. Try again!

3 **Your Washington holiday**

a) Work with a partner. Plan your holiday. Pick three places. Think about what you want to see and do there.

b) Tell the class.

– First we want to go to ...

– We want to see / meet / ...

– Then we want to ...

Tip:
Make notes about your plans. Use your notes when you're talking to the class.

▶ W 35, 2–3

IN A NATIONAL PARK

1 Pick the right sign or brochure:

a) You want to go camping in a national park.
b) You want to find out about trees and animals.
c) You're worried about fires in national parks.
d) You want to go hiking in a national park.

1

Are you concerned about wildfires?

- Smoking in the forest is dangerous.
- Driving a car on grass can start a fire.
- Making campfires is OK, but only on campgrounds.

2

BE A JUNIOR RANGER

OREGON STATE PARKS

Are you interested in finding out about forests? Do you like learning about the environment? Do you like watching wild animals? JOIN THE JUNIOR RANGERS.

3

Bear country

- Hike in groups.
- Make lots of noise when you hike.
- Keep young children near you.

4

Welcome to Heart O' the Hills Campground

1. Feeding wild animals is prohibited.
2. Thank you for keeping the campground clean.

National Park Rangers

2 National park words

a) Find words in the texts that mean:

1 A fire in a forest
2 A place where you can go camping
3 A club for young people
4 A wild animal in Olympic National Park
5 People who work in national parks

b) Find nouns for these verbs:

1 drive a ...
2 find out about ...
3 feed ...
4 learn about the ...
5 make lots of ...

3 Look at the texts and finish these sentences. Find as many examples as you can.

1 In a national park you shouldn't smoke, ...
2 In a national park you can ...
3 In a national park you should ...

▶ W 36, 4

PROJECT A wall newspaper about national parks

a) Look at this wall newspaper about Olympic National Park.

1 Which activity would you pick?

2 What animals would you like to see?

OLYMPIC NATIONAL PARK

WHERE?
In Washington State, in the north-west of the USA

NEAR?
Port Angeles

ENVIRONMENT?
Mountains, forests, rivers and lakes

ANIMALS?
Bears, cougars, deer and beavers

deer beaver

ACTIVITIES?
Hiking, boat trips and camping

ENTRANCE FEE?
$5 for a person or $15 for a car

INFORMATION?
At visitor centers or on the Internet: www.nps.gov/olym

b) Make groups of three or four.

1 Pick another national park on the map of the USA.

2 Find out about the national park. Go to www.new-highlight.de and put in the webcode NHL-4-55.

Tip:
Use the questions in the Olympic National Park wall newspaper.

3 Make a wall newspaper about your national park.

4 Ask and answer questions about the parks.

Tip:
An "expert" from each group should stand near the wall newspaper and answer questions.

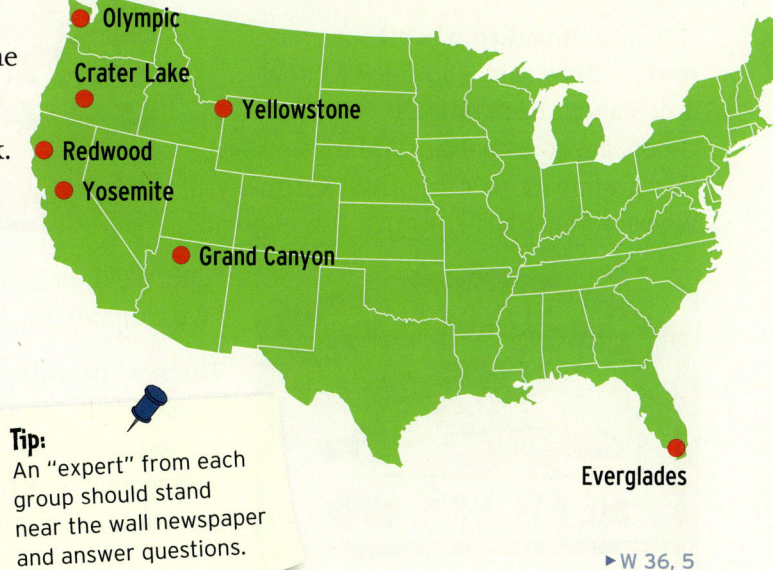

▶ W 36, 5

1 **Look at the pictures. What do you think happens in the story?**
This story is about two … . They live in … . First they go camping in …
Then they drive to … . They hear stories about whale …

Roots

2⊙2

Toby Brown sat in his big, old car. Mark, his
friend, sat next to him. The two boys had their
camping gear – tents, food and clothes. It was
early when they left Anacortes and the town
5 was quiet. The teenagers were looking
forward to getting out of town for the
weekend.

Toby and Mark from Anacortes

After leaving Port Townsend, the boys drove to Port Angeles. Then they turned left and
drove into Olympic National Park, to the Heart O' the Hills Campground. They put up their
10 tent and ate some food.

Toby loved outdoor activities like camping and hiking. So that afternoon the two boys hiked
to Hurricane Ridge. It was great up there. The boys could see the beautiful, blue sea in the
north and the Olympic mountains in the south. In the evening they sat at the campfire and
planned the next days.
15 "What about going to Neah Bay?" Mark said.
"Neah Bay?" Toby answered. "My grandma came from that town. But I've never been there!"
"Really? It's on a reservation," Mark said.
"Was your grandma Native American?"
"Yeah, sure!" Toby answered.
20 "But that means that you're Native
American too! That's interesting!"
Mark said.
"My grandma died when I was very
young," Toby said. "So I don't know
25 much about her family."
"Roots are so important," Mark said.
"My grandparents came from Germany.
We went there last summer. It was great."

A campground in Olympic National Park

"OK. We'll go to Neah Bay tomorrow," Toby said.
"We can look for my grandma's family, the Parkers." 30

The next morning the boys drove along a narrow,
lonely road near the sea. In the afternoon they
arrived at a small, quiet town – Neah Bay. The
teenagers stopped at the visitor center. The man
there told Toby where the Parker family lived. 35

The Parker family was very happy to meet Toby and his friend. Their house was small, so the two boys put up their tent in the garden. That evening there was a big party. All the family came – and neighbours too. There was lots of great Makah singing and dancing.

A nice, old woman was there – Halma Parker. She
40 remembered Toby's grandma. She was her cousin.

Later, everybody sat at the fire and Halma told stories. She talked about the days before white people came to Neah Bay.

"The Makah people didn't live in tepees, but in long-
45 houses. All the family lived together – grandparents, parents, children, uncles, aunts and cousins. Fishing was very important. But whale hunting was the most important thing. The men used small canoes. It was very dangerous, but they were good at whale hunting.
50 Life wasn't always easy, but our people were happy. Then the white people came. They brought illnesses and lots of Makah people died. They prohibited our language. They fished in our ocean. And they prohibited whale hunting. So in the end lots of our young people had to leave Neah Bay and go to work in the white people's
55 towns and cities. Your grandma too, Toby! Some people never came back. They forgot their roots. Roots are important, Toby!"

Whale hunting in the past

Tip:
You can find out more about the Makah people at www.makah.com

57

fifty-seven

---

2 **True, false or not in the text?**

1 The two boys went to Olympic National Park in Toby's car.
2 They saw animals on Hurricane Ridge.
3 They made a campfire.
4 Going to Neah Bay was Toby's idea.
5 Mark's family visited Germany last year.
6 The boys stayed in the Parkers' house.
7 Fishing was important in Neah Bay.
8 Toby's grandma left Neah Bay in 1900.

3 **Neah Bay today**

 a) Listen to the end of the story.
2⊚3 – Do people live in longhouses now?
– Is there lots of work in Neah Bay today?
– Do people fish with canoes?
– Do they hunt whales?
– Who comes to Neah Bay every summer?
– Will Toby go back to Neah Bay?

b) Listen to Little Steven's song about
2⊚4 **Native Americans. Is it happy or sad?**

● **4** **Back in Anacortes: Finish the dialogue between Toby and his mom.**

MOM Hi, Toby. How was your trip?
TOBY Hi, Mom. It was …
MOM What places did you visit?
TOBY First we … . Then we …
MOM Did you meet the Parkers?
TOBY …

MOM Where did you stay in Neah Bay?
TOBY …
MOM What's Neah Bay like?
TOBY …
MOM Do you think that you'll go back?
TOBY …

▶ W 37, 6–9

1 **Hobbies: What are they saying?** These words are in the story on pages 56–57.

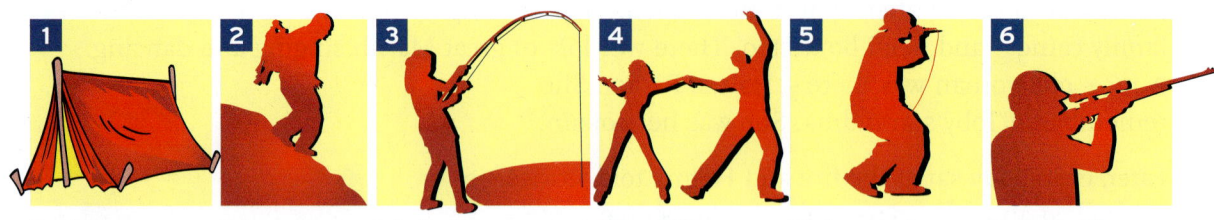

Let's go ...   I love ...   My hobby is ...   They like ...   He's good at ...   I don't like ...

2 **Signs**

a) What do these signs mean in German? Tell a partner.

CAMPING IS

COUGAR COUNTRY

Campfires only on the campground

Welcome to Anacortes in beautiful Washington.

Join the Junior Rangers now!

NO HUNTING!

b) What do these signs mean in English? Tell a partner.

BOOTFAHREN
nicht gestattet

ZELTLAGER
GESCHLOSSEN

EINTRITT €10

ANGELN
VERBOTEN

3 **WORD SEARCH** Find the missing adjectives.

1 Do you like watching ... animals? (p. 54)
2 Keep ... children near you. (p. 54)
3 Toby sat in his ..., ... car. (p. 56, l. 1).
4 The boys could see the ..., ... sea. (p. 56, l. 12).
5 The boys drove along a ..., ... road. (p. 56, ll. 31–32)

6 They arrived at a ..., ... town. (p. 56, l. 33)
7 A ..., ... woman was there. (p. 57, l. 39)
8 The men used ... canoes. (p. 57, l. 48)

> **Tip:**
> Adjectives tell you about people, places and things. Adjectives make a text more interesting.

4 **Make it interesting.**

a) Put the adjectives in the right place.

It was a night in March (**cold**). Toby and Mark were at a campground (**lonely**). They were in their tent (**small**). Toby was reading a book (**good**). Mark was listening to his MP3 player (**new**). Then Toby heard a noise (**terrible**). The boys looked out and saw a bear (**big/black**).

b) Put in: *old, tired, nervous, black, lonely, funny, quiet.*

Toby and Mark shouted and the ... bear ran into the forest. The ... boys didn't sleep that night. There was no noise in the forest. It was very ... . They talked and told ... stories all night. In the morning the ... boys put their things in the ... car and they left the ... campground – quickly!

▶ W 38, 10–13   ▶ W ⦾

USING MIND MAPS

1 **A good job?**
Would you like to be a park ranger?
Read the text and find out.

2 **Main points**
a) What's this text saying?
Pick two main points.

– A ranger's life is terrible.
– A ranger's job is easy.
– A ranger does many jobs.
– A ranger has a boring job.
– A ranger has to be fit and sporty.
– A ranger's work is dangerous.
– A ranger has a great job.

b) Does your partner agree?

NATIONAL PARK RANGERS

Park Ranger

Rangers have to do lots of different jobs. They look after the national parks (the animals, forests, rivers and lakes). They give information to visitors. Rangers work on the park campgrounds too and they often lead tours in the parks. When hikers get lost in the parks, the rangers have to look for them. And they help visitors who have accidents.

Rangers have to be good at doing lots of things. They go hiking with groups of visitors in the forests and they go skiing in the mountains in winter. Rangers go camping in the parks and they often go on boat trips on the lakes and rivers. They watch the wild animals and take photos of America's most beautiful places.

IF YOU WANT TO BECOME A RANGER, VISIT OUR WEBSITE.

3 **A park ranger's mind map**
First draw this mind map in your exercise book.
Then read the text again and finish the mind map.

4 **Remembering**
Close your book and look at your mind map.
What can you remember from the text?
Write it down. Then tell a partner.

Tip:
Mind maps help you to remember main points. Pictures and colours make your mind map more interesting and make it easier to remember.

▸ W 39, 14   ▸ W ⊙

LISTENING Talking about a town

1 Anacortes adverts

2◉5 Look at the pictures. Listen to the CD. You'll hear three adverts for each picture.
Pick the right advert – a), b) or c).

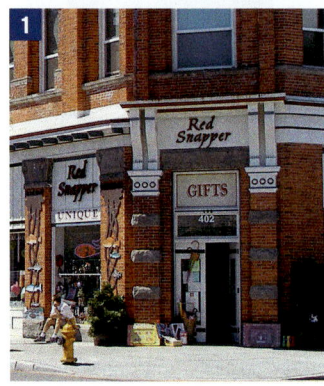
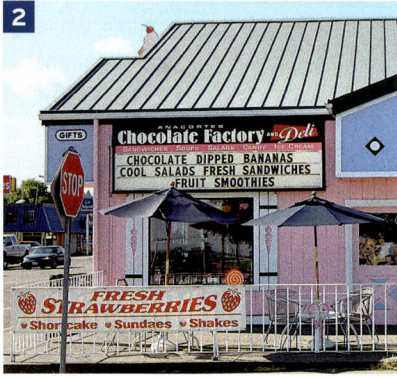

2 A survey about Anacortes

2◉6 Toby Brown has done a survey for the school radio.

a) Listen to the five people. Pick a), b) or c).

1 This boy thinks that Anacortes is ...
   a) OK   **b)** terrible   **c)** cool
2 This girl likes the ...
   a) weather   **b)** people   **c)** food
3 This boy says that Anacortes is busy in ...
   a) spring   **b)** summer   **c)** winter
4 This girl comes to Anacortes for ...
   a) work   **b)** school   **c)** whale watching
5 The teenagers think that Anacortes is ...
   a) boring   **b)** exciting   **c)** beautiful

b) Listen to the survey again.
Pick the right words in the box.

→ good • uncool • nice •
  great • quiet

1 **Boy**   It's ... for water sports.
2 **Girl**   The people here are ...
3 **Boy**   In winter it's ...
4 **Girl**   It's a ... place to make money!
5 **Teens**   Anacortes is ...

3 The story of Fidalgo Island and Anacortes

2◉7 First copy this table in your exercise book. Then listen to the CD and put in the years.

... years ago	Native Americans lived here.
17...	The first Europeans came.
1790 – ...	Hunters came.
187...	The town got a post office and a name.
18...	200 people lived in Anacortes.
19...	4000 people lived here.
1950 – ...	Lots of businesses came to the town.
...	About 15,000 people live here.

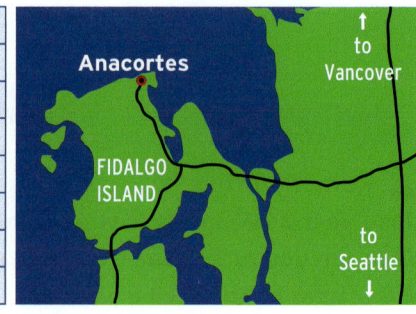

▶ W 40, 15   ▶ W ◉

SPEAKING At the visitor center

1 **Rita works at the Anacortes visitor center.**

a) What are these visitors going to do?

RITA Hi. Can I help you?

GIRL Hi. We're in Anacortes for a day and we'd like to do something interesting. What can you recommend?

RITA Oh, there are lots of things to do.
What about kayaking? It's fun!

BOY That sounds good. Where can you do it?

RITA At San Juan Safaris. They're in Friday Harbor. Here's a brochure.

GIRL Great. Thank you.

b) Practise the dialogue with two partners.

2 **More tourists need help.**

a) Look at the brochure and finish the dialogue.

RITA Hi. Can I …?

BOY Hi. We'd like to do something …
What can you …?

RITA What about …?

GIRL That … good. Where can you …?

RITA At … . They're in … . Here's …

BOY Great. …

b) Act the dialogue with a partner.

3 **INTERPRETING**

You're at the visitor center with your grandma. Help her.

GRANDMA Wir wollen gern etwas Interessantes unternehmen. Was kann die Frau uns empfehlen?

YOU Hi. We'd like to … . What …?

RITA Are you interested in learning about Native Americans? There's a great museum.

YOU Willst du …? Es gibt …

GRANDMA Ja, das klingt sehr interessant. Wo ist das Museum?

YOU That … . Where …?

RITA It's at Neah Bay. There's a bus every day at 10 a.m.

YOU Es ist …

GRANDMA Vielen Dank für die Hilfe. Auf Wiedersehen.

YOU …

MAKAH MUSEUM
P.O. Box 160 • Neah Bay, WA 98357
Phone (360) 645-2711

4 **ROLE PLAY**

PARTNER A: You work at the visitor center. Look at your card on p. 95.

PARTNER B: You're a tourist. Look at your card on p. 95.

▶ W 40, 16–17   ▶ W ⊙

READING A school magazine article

1 Read the article and pick a title.

a) Job adverts   **b)** Job tips for teens   **c)** My dream job

Tip:
Don't worry about new words.
First try to guess them.
Then check in a dictionary.

Lots of students at our school have part-time jobs. This is what some people say:

<u>Hassan</u> (15): "My uncle is a baker and I work part-time for him.
It's hard work."

<u>Britany</u> (15):
"I work as a sales clerk in a clothes shop for teens. The job is cool because I like meeting people.
I work there every Saturday.
<u>Ashley</u> (15): "I work as a cleaner in a movie theater. It's OK. But you have to work fast."
<u>Brad</u> (16): "I'm a part-time babysitter. It's easy and I like children."
<u>Calina</u> (16): "I work in a library. I'm an assistant.
I put books back on the shelves. It's boring, but I only work on Saturdays. And the pay is OK."
<u>Sancha</u> (16): "I work in a coffee shop – I'm a cashier. I have to work every Saturday and Sunday, so I don't have much free time. But the pay is good and there are lots of tips.

Are you thinking of looking for a part-time job? Do you want work experience? Here are some ideas to help you.

1 Pick a job that you like. Maybe you'll find your dream job!
2 You must write a good résumé and cover letter.
3 Before you go to your interview, find out about the business, store or restaurant. And think about why you want that job. The interview is important, so practise it with a friend.
4 If you go to an interview, wear nice clothes. And don't forget to ask the interviewer for information about the job.
5 Don't work too many hours. Remember, your school work is the most important thing, so you shouldn't be too tired for school.

2 Read the first part of the article. Who could say these things?

1 "I love nice clothes, so my job is cool."
2 "Now I know everything about bread!"
3 "I watch TV when the kids are in bed."
4 "I often go early and watch a movie."
5 "When it's quiet I can read."

3 Now read the second part of the article and correct these sentences.

1 There are six job tips.
2 Your résumé isn't so important.
3 Don't worry about the interview.
4 Only the interviewer can ask questions.
5 You should work as much as you can.

4 What do you think? Finish these sentences.

1 I'd like a job as a ... because ...
2 I wouldn't like a job as a ... because ...   ▶ Wordbank 6, p.130

Tip:
Look at the jobs in the magazine article. Think of other jobs too.

▶ W 41, 18

WRITING Applying for a job in the USA

1 A job advert
Read the advert. Would you like this job?

ANACORTES ADVENTURES
933 Commercial Avenue

Anacortes' best outdoor store!

We are looking for a

part-time sales clerk

Saturdays 9 a.m. – 6 p.m.
$8 per hour.
Apply today
to Angela King.

2 A résumé
Read Toby Brown's résumé. Do you think he'll get the job?

FAMILY NAME	Brown
FIRST NAME	Toby
ADDRESS	1241 14th Street
	Anacortes, WA 98221
PHONE	360-555-8441
CELLPHONE	360-555-7712
AGE	16
SCHOOL	Anacortes High School
GRADE	10
HOBBIES	Hiking, camping, music
EXPERIENCE	Junior Rangers (3 years)
	Part-time cashier (1 year)

3 A cover letter
Read Toby's letter. Find the missing words.   Exercises 1 and 2 can help you.

1241 14th Street
Anacortes, WA 98221
April 4th, 20…

Ms Angela King
Anacortes Adventures
933 Commercial Avenue
Anacortes, WA

Dear Ms (1),

I saw your (2) in the newspaper last week and
I would like to apply for the job of (3).
I am (4) years old and I am in grade (5) at
Anacortes High School. I am interested in
outdoor activities like (6) and (7). I have some
work (8) – I was a (9) in a shoe store for one year.
And I was a Junior (10) for three years.
I'm looking forward to hearing from you.

Yours truly,
Toby Brown

4 More job adverts
Which job would you prefer?

I'd prefer the job at … because …

ODEON CINEMA
We are looking for
cleaners
Tuesdays–Sundays,
5–7 p.m.
$8 per hour.
Apply to: Rick Mason

DADDIO'S PIZZA
Part-time cashier
Mondays–Saturdays
from 5 to 10 p.m.
$5 per hour.
Apply to: Janet Seaman

WHALETOURS
ASSISTANT
$7.50 per hour.
Saturdays 9 a.m.–5 p.m.
Apply to: Harold Hughes

5 AND YOU?
Apply for a job in exercise 4.
a) Write your own résumé.
● **b) Then write a cover letter.**
Look at Toby's résumé and cover letter.

▶ W 41, 19   ▶ W ⓒ

WHALE HUNTING

1 **Which of these texts comes from ...**
- a newspaper article?
- an animal rights brochure?
- a book about the Makah people?

A Whale hunting is a very important tradition here. In the past our people hunted in small canoes. After killing a whale, we took it to the beach in Neah Bay. We ate the meat. We used the oil for cooking and for lamps.

B **Stop whale hunting today!**
Whale hunting is wrong.
Some whales are nearly extinct.
We're against whale hunting.
We should stop whale hunting now!

C **Trouble at Neah Bay**

There was lots of activity at Neah Bay, WA last weekend. Whale hunters met at Neah Bay early on Saturday morning. Animal rights people were there too. They protested against whale hunting. They say that whale hunting is wrong. But for the Makah people it's an old tradition. There was some trouble and the police came. The Makah people can go whale hunting again. They can kill four whales every year.

2 **For or against whale hunting?**
a) Put these sentences in two lists: for whale hunting / against whale hunting.

I don't like whale hunting. • Four animals per year is OK. • We don't need whale oil. •
It's OK for the Makah people. • People have always hunted, so hunting is OK. •
There aren't many whales in the world – we have to save them. • All hunting is bad. •
There are lots of grey whales again. • I have no problem with whale hunting. •
It's an old tradition and traditions are important. • Whales are beautiful animals.

b) **What do you think about whale hunting? Talk about this question in your class.**
Use the phrases in a).

3 **SENTENCE SEARCH** Find sentences in the texts on this page for the pictures.

1) The Makah people can go ...

2) After killing ...

3) Stop ...

4 WORD SEARCH

Look at the pictures. Can you guess the missing words? Check on pages 56–57.

1 The teenagers were looking forward to ... out of town. (ll. 5–6)

2 After ... Port Townsend, the boys drove to Port Angeles. (l. 8)

3 Toby loved outdoor activities like ... and ... (l. 11)

4 "What about ... to Neah Bay?" (l. 15)

5 There was lots of great Makah ... and ... . (l. 38)

6 ... was very important. (ll. 46–47)

5 OVER TO YOU!

Look in the unit and find more examples for the rules.

Tip:
Write the checkpoint in your exercise book.

CHECKPOINT

Die *ing*-Form

- kann Subjekt eines Satzes sein und steht oft am Anfang.
  Smoking is dangerous.

- folgt oft auf bestimmte Verben.
  Do you like learning about horses?

- wird häufig nach Wendungen mit Präpositionen gebraucht.
  It's a great place for fishing.

▶ Eine Übersicht über diese Regeln findest du auf der *Summary*-Seite 134.

▶ Extra Practice, pp. 108 ff.

▶ W 42–43

NACH DIESER UNIT KANN ICH ...

über Urlaubspläne sprechen.	▶ *First we want to go to Seattle. Then we ...*
Orte beschreiben.	*Anacortes is busy in summer. It's great for water sports. It's a good place to ...*
über Walfang diskutieren.	▶ *All hunting is bad. / It's OK for the Makah people.*
um Informationen in einem Fremdenverkehrsamt bitten.	▶ *We'd like to do something interesting. What can you recommend?*
über Berufe sprechen.	▶ *I'd like a job as a cashier. I wouldn't like ...*
mich um eine Arbeitsstelle bewerben.	▶ *I'd like to apply for the job as ...*
meinen Lebenslauf schreiben.	
mind maps erstellen.	

Music in Miami

Florida

Miami

A

B

C

D

1 **Match the sentences in the box with the photos.**

Spanish signs in Little Havana
Old men playing games
Crime in Miami
A Miami rapper on stage
MTV music awards in Miami
Miami's famous South Beach
A picture on a wall in Little Havana
The Calle Ocho festival

– photo E
– photo ...

2⊙10

2 **Listen to the radio programme. Match the speakers and the photos.**

Mariela: photo ..., ..., ...
and ...
Ramon: photo ..., ..., ...
and ...

► W 47, 1

3 Work with a partner and pick a), b) or c). Then listen again and check.

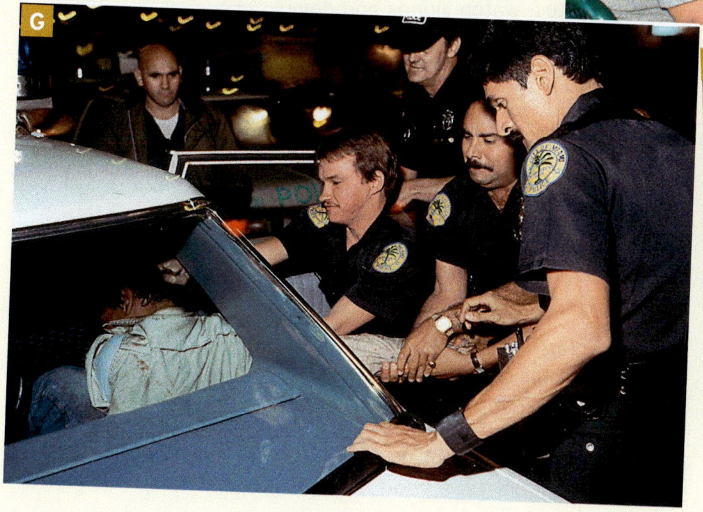

1◉10

1 In Miami   **a)** lots of people   **b)** some people   **c)** not many people speak Spanish.
2 The Hispanic population in Miami is   **a)** 6%   **b)** 16%   **c)** 66%.
3 In Little Havana crime is   **a)** no problem   **b)** a small problem   **c)** a big problem.
4 Miami has a great   **a)** music   **b)** theatre   **c)** film scene.
5 The Calle Ocho festival is a big   **a)** art festival   **b)** street party   **c)** food festival.
6 The MTV awards brought lots of   **a)** film fans   **b)** musicians   **c)** problems to Miami.

> **Tip:**
> % =
> per cent

4 **GAME** Pick a photo. Write a description. Write one wrong thing.
Your partner reads it and says what's wrong.

There are lots of people. I can see two musicians. They're playing instruments. There's a table behind one musician. Five people are sitting under an umbrella. It's nice weather.

> **Tip:**
> Use the present progressive to write about activities in pictures:
> *A boy and a girl are dancing.*
> *The boy is wearing …*

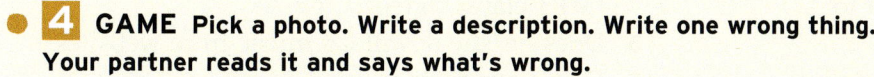

Three people are sitting under the umbrella.

▶ W 47, 2–3

MY MUSIC

1 Look at Ramon's page on a website for friends. Do you have a page like this or use websites for friends?

2 Read about Ramon. What would he like to be when he leaves school?

mypage   HOME   NEWS   BLOGS   GUIDE   LOGOUT

Male
15 years old
Miami, USA

About me
I'm from Colombia, my family moved to Miami when I was 11. I spend lots of my time in front of my computer. I look at music websites, watch videos and download songs. I listen to music on my MP3 player too. I like listening to music when I do my homework. I can work better like that. And I often watch music TV – concerts and the music awards.

Ramon's interests

General Music, dancing, friends, blogging

Music Pop, rap, R & B. I like most music really, but I'm not a big fan of punk or metal. I play the guitar and the piano, and I sing too.

Who I'd like to meet
I'd like to meet Shakira. She's from my country and she sings in Spanish and English. She's a fantastic dancer! I like Justin Timberlake too. He lives in Miami, so maybe I'll meet him!

Ramon's blog
Yesterday I went to an audition for a new boy band. They said I sang really well and I have to go back next week. I hope I'll be in the band. I'd like to be a singer when I finish school. But my parents say most singers have a hard life. They think I should get a good, safe job.

▶ *Hips don't lie*
Shakira and Wyclef Jean

3 What you know about Ramon: Finish the sentences.

1 Ramon's general interests: ..., ..., ... and ...
2 Ramon's favourite music: ..., ... and ...
3 Ramon plays the ... and the ...
4 He uses his computer to ..., ... and ...
5 He listens to music on his ...
6 He listens to music when he does ...
7 He'd like to meet ... because ...
8 He'd like to meet ... too.
9 Yesterday he went to an ...

4 What you know about your partner: Write the answers to the questions. Then check your answers with your partner.

1 What are your partner's interests?
2 What music does he/she like?
3 Does he/she play an instrument or sing?
4 How does he/she listen to music? (MP3 player, videos, ...)
5 Does he/she download music from websites?
6 Does your partner listen to music when he/she does homework?
7 Which musician would he/she like to meet? (Why?)
8 Has your partner been to a concert? (What concert?)

▶ Wordbank 7, p.130

▶ W 48, 4   ▶ Wordbank 8, p.131

5 SONG *Hips don't lie*

a) **Listen to the song.**

b) **What's the song about?** It's about …
1 Spain **2** love **3** dancing **4** violence

c) **How do they sing?** I think he/she sings …

→ sadly • happily • confidently •
angrily • quickly • slowly • wildly

d) **Do you like the song? Why? / Why not?**

I like / don't like the singer / the singer's voice /
the rhythm / the words / …
The music sounds sad / happy / …
The music is good for dancing / singing /
relaxing. ▸ Wordbank 7, p.130

6 **Pick a song that you like. Tell the class about it.**

The title of the song is …
It's by …
It's about …
I like this song because …

Tip:
- Talk about:
  - the title
  - the singer
  - what it's about
  - what you like about the song
  - how the music sounds
  - how the singer sings
- Use the phrases in exercise 5.

PROJECT My page

- **First find a good picture of yourself. Write about yourself:**
  - **male / female**
  - **age**
  - **where you live**
- **Write about your interests:**
  General: friends / football / TV / computers / …
  Music: pop, rap, R & B, metal, …
- **Put in your song from exercise 6.**
  Write two or three sentences about it.
- **Write more about yourself: interesting things, what
  languages you speak, what you do in your free time:**
  I'm from / My parents are from …
  I speak …
  I listen to music / send texts to my friends / …
- **Write who you'd like to meet:**
  I'd like to meet … because …
- **Write your blog for yesterday.**
  Yesterday I went to … / I met … / I watched … / I played …

Tip:
Look at Ramon's page again.
- Make a page that looks like *mypage*. Use the same headings.
- Use Ramon's sentences to help you.
Exercises 4 and 6 can help you too.

Tip:
Write your page and put it on the classroom wall.
OR
Write your page on the computer and put it on a website for friends, or on your school/class website.

▸ W 48, 5–7

1 **What are the most important things and activities in your life?**

My MP3 player / swimming / ...

2 **Read the story. Why is there no music in the girl's life?**

A life without music

2◉12

by Elizabeth Urban

Elizabeth Urban is 16 years old and lives near Cleveland, Ohio. She likes writing stories in her free time.

I wake up suddenly. The moon is high above the trees next to my bedroom window. I get up. Everything is quiet. I don't hear the door when I go to the bathroom. I don't hear the light switch when I turn on the lights. I look in the
5 mirror. I see a tired fifteen-year-old girl. You can't see why I never hear anything: why I can't hear my little sister laugh, why I can't hear my brother read every night, or why I can't hear my own voice.

I wasn't always deaf. I was twelve years old, and I lost my
10 hearing on my birthday. My parents had come into my bedroom to sing happy birthday. They sang loudly, but I didn't wake up. My mother shook me and then I woke up, but I only saw her mouth moving. The most frightening thing was when I tried to talk and heard nothing. I haven't
15 heard my own voice now for three years.

I go back to my bed, but before I sleep, I get up again, open my closet and close its doors. I hear nothing. I sigh. *Maybe I'll have my hearing back tomorrow.* I've been thinking that for three years; I try to hope.

I wake up in the morning to the sound of nothing ... again. My 11-year-old brother, Kyle, is

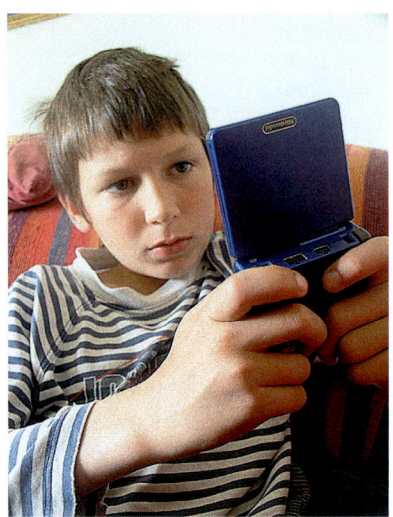

shaking me. I walk down to my little sister's room. She
20 is two years old with blonde hair. When Sophie sees me, she opens her arms and I pick her up. She kisses me and we go to the kitchen. Mom is looking for her keys in the kitchen and Kyle is playing a video game. Mom finds her keys and shouts something at Kyle. He turns off his
25 game and they leave.

Sophie is trying to say something to me. I shake my head, but she doesn't understand. Her mouth is open, her hands are on her ears. I say, "What's wrong?" She doesn't take her hands off her ears. There's a car in the
30 street opposite our house. A woman comes out of her house and pushes a button on something in her hand. *Of course!* I think. *Car alarm. Stupid!* We eat breakfast.

Five minutes later Mom is home and we go out. In the car Mom turns on the radio.
35 I look out the window. I can't listen to music. I can't listen to the talk shows that Mom
listens to. In the street I see people talking on their cellphones. *Can't do that.* I see a

woman running with an MP3 player on her arm. *Can't do that.* I see a man between two young children. They're all talking. I sigh sadly. I close my eyes. Everything is so quiet. I read that in a famous horror movie, a director didn't use any music because people feel nervous when every-thing is quiet. My life is like that movie.

40

45

50

3 **Find the information about the girl in the story.**

Age: ...
She can't hear, she's ...
She lost her hearing when she was ... years old.
Her brother's name and age: ...
Her sister's name and age: ...

4 **Put the sentences in the right order.** 1 d), 2 ..., ...

a) Her little sister isn't happy and the girl doesn't know what's wrong.
b) In the morning her brother shakes her and she wakes up.
c) She sees people in the street: they can all do things that she can't do.
d) At night the girl wakes up and thinks about how she became deaf.
e) The girl's mum and her brother leave. She looks after her little sister.
f) The girl goes out with her mum and sister.

5 **Feelings: Pick a word from the box.**

→ confident • bored • frightened • angry • sad • stupid • uncool

1 When the girl can't hear her voice on her birthday, she feels ...
2 When the girl doesn't know what Sophie wants, she feels ...
3 In the car the girl feels ...

6 **Deaf**
a) What things can't the girl in the story do? Make a list with a partner.

She can't hear ...
She can't listen to ...
She can't talk on a ...
She can't use ...

● **b) Imagine you are deaf like the girl in the story. Write about your day.**
  • **What can you do? (with friends, alone)**
  • **What can't you do?**
  • **How do you feel?**

▶ W 49, 9–11

1 ODD WORD OUT Which word is wrong? These words are in the story on pages 70–71.

1 hand, arm, key, ear
2 happy, deaf, frightened, sad
3 feel, sleep, wake up, get up
4 voice, mouth, talk, shake
5 next to, opposite, loud, above
6 mirror, closet, car alarm, light switch

2 A music fan blog

a) Put in the words in the box.
These words are on pages 66–69.

→ stage • rhythm • awards • musicians • piano • male

Justin Timberlake comes from Tennessee, but he lives in Florida. He's one of the best (**1**) ... singers today and he has won many (**2**) ... He plays the guitar and the (**3**) ... too. Justin has worked with lots of other famous singers and (**4**) ... . I love his songs because they always have a good (**5**) ... . And Justin is fantastic on (**6**) ...

● **b) Write a fan blog about another singer or musician.** Use the text in a) to help you.

3 WORD SEARCH Prepositions

a) Look at the pictures and finish the sentences. Then check on pages 67–71.

b) You're talking about a holiday picture. Use the words in a).

1 There's a table ... one musician. (p. 67)
2 Three people are sitting ... an umbrella. (p. 67)
3 I spend lots of time ... my computer. (p. 68)
4 The moon is high ... the trees. (p. 70, l. 1)
5 There's a car ... our house. (p. 70, ll. 30 – 31)
6 I see a man ... two young children. (p. 71, ll. 39 – 40)

There's a cafe (**1**) ... two trees. The name *Amy's Place* is (**2**) ... the door. There's a big hotel (**3**)... the cafe. There are some tables (**4**)... the cafe. That's me in the pink T-shirt. I'm sitting (**5**) ... my dad. There's a dog (**6**)... one of the tables.

▶ W 50, 12 – 15 ▶ W ◉

1 Jobs

a) Write the music jobs.

1 A … sings songs.
2 A … dances on stage.
3 A … plays music at clubs.
4 A … puts make-up on people.
5 A … plays an instrument.
6 A … makes films or music videos.

**b) What other jobs do you know?
Make a list with the class.**

● **c) Pick three of the jobs in b). Write
short definitions like in a).**

2 Your job

a) What job would you like to do?

- I'd like to be a …
- I'd like to work at an airport /
  a hospital / restaurant / hotel / …
- I'd like to work for *Greenpeace* / …

b) Say why:

- I'd like to work alone / with people /
  with animals / with my hands / outdoors /
  indoors / at night / …
- I'd like to have an interesting job / help people /
  get lots of money / have lots of free time / …

Tip:
Use a dictionary
or ask your
teacher for help.

3 The music business

a) Put the verbs in the article.

→ deal • take • sleep • dream • relax • follow

Do you **(1)** … of a career as a singer or in a band?
The music business is hard. Musicians often
have to travel and **(2)**… in hotels. For many
famous singers and musicians it's hard to **(3)** …:
Photographers often **(4)** … them, so they can
(5) … their photos. And some musicians have to
(6) … with drug and alcohol problems.

● **b) AND YOU? Would you like to be famous?
Why / Why not?**

Yes, because your life is … / you meet lots of … / …
No, because you are never alone / you always have
to look … / …

4 Music websites

a) You're online on your favourite singer's website. You see these links:

Home ｜ News ｜ Photos ｜ Tour ｜ Media ｜ Mobile ｜ Fan Club ｜ Store

Which link do you use if you want to …

1 find out dates for concerts?
2 get a new ringtone for your phone?
3 send the singer a message?
4 look at pictures?
5 go to the first page of the website?
6 buy CDs and other things?
7 find out new information?
8 watch videos and listen to songs?

b) SAY IT IN GERMAN Tell a partner what the links mean.

▶ W 51, 16–18   ▶ W ⊚

LISTENING Useful phrases

 1 Salina is going to Florida. Listen and pick the three topics that Salina talks about.

→ cold winters • warm winters • hurricanes • beaches • theme parks • TV shows

 2 Listen again. Pick the right answers.

1 In winter in Florida it's about …
a) 12° C
b) 20° C
c) 21° C

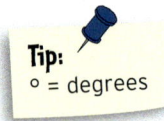
Tip:
° = degrees

2 There are hurricanes …
a) all year
b) from June to November
c) from July to December

3 At Sea World there are …
a) shows with pirates
b) shows with whales
c) lots of boats

4 At Epcot you can learn about …
a) our environment
b) sports
c) food

5 At the Kennedy Space Center you can …
a) go into space
b) find out about planes
c) be an astronaut for a day

Tip:
Don't worry if you can't remember a word or you said something wrong. Use these phrases!

3 Listen again and put in the missing phrases from Salina's talk.

1 So I'm going to tell you something about Florida. *(Er)*, just …
2 But there is a problem with *(er)* – what's … – yes, hurricanes.
3 Hurricanes have hit lots of houses in Florida and killed lots of people. What I'm trying … that Florida has warm weather, but it can be dangerous too.
4 A theme park is *(er)* something … a "Freizeitpark", but much bigger.
5 Epcot is a theme park where you can learn about our environment and "Technologie", sorry, I … technology.

● **4** Put the phrases from exercise 3 in the sentences. Then listen and check.

1 Theme parks are great but they're – … – expensive, very expensive.
2 You can see a shuttle at the Space Center. A shuttle is *(er)*, … a plane that goes into space.
3 Many people in Florida not speak English, … they don't speak English at home.
4 Now I'm going to talk about, *(er)*, …, I'm going to talk about crime in Miami.
5 I didn't explain that very well! … that Miami has a big problem with crime, but it's a fantastic city.

▶ W 52, 19   ▶ W ⊙

SPEAKING Polite phrases

1 **Salina is staying with an exchange family in Miami.**

a) Listen and match the conversations and the pictures.   Picture A is conversation ...

b) What was the problem in conversation 1?

2 **Be polite!**

a) Match the sentences (1–6) and the answers (a–f).

1 Hello, I'm Barbara.
2 Do you mind if I sit here?
3 Could you give me the salad, please?
4 I'm afraid I don't eat meat.
5 Could you tell me where the
   bathroom is, please?
6 Thank you.

a) Go ahead.
b) It's on the right, opposite the
    kitchen.
c) I'm Salina. Nice to meet you.
d) Yes, of course. Here you are.
e) You're welcome.
f) Oh, I'm sorry.

b) Listen to conversation 2 again
and check your answers in a).

c) Practise the sentences
and answers with a partner.

3 **Find the right phrases in 2a).**

What do you say when ...

1 somebody tells you his/her name?
2 you want to do something?
3 you ask for something?
4 you say politely that there's
   a problem?
5 somebody says thank you?

4 **ROLE PLAY**

Partner A: You're at a party.
You sit down at a table and meet
Partner B. Look at your card on
page 96.

Partner B: You're an exchange
student in Miami. You meet
Partner A at a party. Look at your
card on page 96.

Tip:
Be polite! Always
say *please* and
thank you and use
these phrases.

▸W 52, 20–21 ▸W ◉

SKILLS TRAINING

READING Winners!

1 **Read the article. What do the winners get?**

This week in Greatest Hits we're looking at our favorite music awards and TV shows.

MTV Video Music Awards

The MTV Awards for the top artists and music videos of the year started in 1984. Famous Hollywood stars present the nominees and the winners. There are eleven categories (like *Male Artist of the Year*, *Female Artist of the Year*, *Best Group*) and there are usually five nominees in each category. A jury votes for the winners. In one category – *Best New Artist* – MTV viewers can vote. The winners get a statue of a moon man – like the statue in the photo. Madonna has won the most moon men: she has twenty MTV awards!

American Idol

American Idol is the most popular talent contest on American TV. The show tries to find the best young singer (between 16 and 28 years old) in the USA.

First there are auditions with thousands of singers in lots of different states. In the finals, the twelve best singers sing on stage. Viewers vote for the winner who gets a million dollar recording contract. Kelly Clarkson was the winner of the first *American Idol*. The show was the start of her career. After *American Idol* Kelly had lots of number 1 hits and won many important awards. She's a big star now.

2 **Read the article again. Are the sentences true or false or not in the text?**

1 There are five categories of MTV awards.
2 Viewers pick the winner of the *Best New Artist* award.
3 The people who present the awards should look good.
4 There are twelve singers in the finals of *American Idol*.
5 Before *American Idol* Kelly Clarkson worked at a club.
6 Kelly Clarkson has had a terrible career as a singer.

3 **Find words in the article that mean …**

1 a prize
2 a singer or musician
3 a person who could win
4 people who watch TV
5 to pick somebody for a prize
6 a competition for singing and dancing

4 **AND YOU? Tell the class.**

a) **Do you watch music TV? What do you watch?**   I watch concerts, music videos, news, …

b) **Do you watch the music awards? What do you like most?**
   I like finding out the winners / the music / the clothes that the stars wear / …

c) **Would you like to be in a talent contest?**   Yes, I would. / No, I wouldn't (because) …

▶ W 53, 22

WRITING A letter

AWARD COMPETITION

Win concert tickets! Write to *Greatest Hits* magazine.
Tell us which singer or band should win our "Nicest Star" award
and why. Pick one of our musicians or pick your own.

Courtney Long
• gives money to homeless
  young people
• never says no to a fan
  who wants an autograph

Ricky West
• helps young singers to
  start their careers
• took drugs but now tells
  young people about the
  problems of drugs

1 Read about the
competition and then read
Ramon's letter. Answer the
questions.

- What's the award for?
- Who does Ramon think
  should get the award?
  Why? Find three reasons.

1942 SW 8th St.
Miami, FL 33135

April 28th

Tip:
Write your
address and
the date here.

Tip:
Start your
letter with
Dear ...

Dear Greatest Hits,

In my opinion, Shakira should get your award. She's a big star, but she doesn't take
drugs or go to wild parties every night like lots of other singers. She's very nice to
her fans too and she always answers messages on her website. I believe that she's
one of the nicest people in the music business.

Shakira helps children and teenagers in Colombia. She gives money to poor families
and children who have had problems with violence. I think this is fantastic.

I'm sure that she would like to win your award.

Best wishes,

Ramon Ramirez

Tip:
Finish your letter
with *Best wishes*
and your name.

2 Look at the letter again. Find four phrases that Ramon uses to say what he
thinks. (They're all at the start of a sentence.)

 3 Your letter for the competition
a) Write to *Greatest Hits* (60–80 words).

– Write your address and the date.
– Start your letter with the right phrase.
– Say who you think should get the magazine's award and why.
– Finish the letter and write your name.

Tip:
Remember to use the
phrases in exercise 2.
Look at Ramon's
letter for help.

b) Your teacher reads the letters and picks three musicians. The class votes for the winner.

▶ W 53, 23   ▶ W ⊚

1 **Read the website information.**
How many Hispanics are there in the USA?

Facts

The number of Hispanics in the USA is growing fast. There are now about **44** million Hispanics in a population of about **300** million Americans. Experts think there will be about **100** million Hispanics in the USA in 2050.

Hispanics and the economy

About 12 million people in America came to the USA illegally - they have no papers. Most of these illegal immigrants are Hispanic and many come across the border from Mexico. They pay lots of money to get into the USA safely. American employers often pay them badly — but they get more money than in Mexico. Other illegal immigrants come to the USA as tourists and then stay longer. They can easily buy papers on the street.

Some Americans say that all illegal immigrants should go home. Others think differently and say that they should stay because the American economy needs them. Illegal immigrants work hard and they do the worst jobs.

HISPANIC POWER!

Hispanic stars

Some people think that all Hispanics are illegal immigrants, poor and only speak Spanish. Of course that isn't true! Many Hispanics are born in the USA, have good jobs and speak English very well. And some are big stars – like the singers Jennifer Lopez and Marc Anthony (their parents come from Puerto Rico).

2 **WORD SEARCH**

a) **Find these words on this page.**

1 About 12 million people in America came to the USA ...
2 They pay lots of money to get into the USA ...
3 American employers often pay them ...
4 They can ... buy papers on the street.
5 Others think ... and say that they should stay.

b) **Now find these words on this page.**

1 The number of Hispanics is growing ...
2 Illegal immigrants work ...
3 Many Hispanics are born in the USA and speak English very ...

3 **Adjectives and adverbs**

a) **Look at exercise 2a) again and find the adverbs.**

Adjectives	Adverbs
illegal	*illegally*
safe	...
bad	...
easy	...
...	...

Tip:
Be careful with the spelling! See *Summary*, page 137.

b) **Now look at exercise 2b) and find these adverbs.**

Adjectives	Adverbs
fast	...
hard	...
good	...

4 **OVER TO YOU!**
Finish the checkpoint.

Tip:
Write the checkpoint in your exercise book.

CHECKPOINT

Adverbien

- Mit Adverbien kannst du beschreiben, wie man etwas macht.

- Die meisten Adverbien bildest du, indem du ... an das Adjektiv anhängst.

- Achtung! Bei den folgenden Adjektiven gibt es besondere Adverbformen:
  good - ... , fast - ... , hard - ...

▶ Eine Übersicht über diese Regeln findest du auf der *Summary*-Seite 137.

▶ Extra Practice, pp. 112 ff.

▶ W 54–55

NACH DIESER UNIT KANN ICH ...

über meinen Musikgeschmack und meine Musikgewohnheiten sprechen.	▶ *I like R & B and pop music. I play the piano. / I don't play an instrument. I often download songs from websites.*
über Songs sprechen.	▶ *I like the rhythm. I don't like the singer's voice. The music is good for dancing.*
sagen, wo sich etwas oder jemand befindet.	▶ *There's a sign above the door. Our school is opposite the park.*
Gesprächsstrategien anwenden: – um eine Redepause bitten, – mich selbst verbessern, – etwas umschreiben.	▶ *Just a minute. / What's the word? What I'm trying to say is ... / Sorry, I mean ... It's something like ...*
eine höfliche Konversation führen.	*Nice to meet you. Do you mind if I sit here?*
höflich auf ein Problem hinweisen.	*I'm afraid ...*
meine persönliche Meinung äußern.	▶ *In my opinion, ... / I believe ... I think ... / I don't think ...*

Weitere Übungen: www.new-highlight.de   ▶ W 56, Test yourself   ▶ W 57–58, Portfolio   ▶ W ⊙

▶ Extra Reading, pp. 122–125

Unit 6*

Going west

Before 1840 most people lived in the east of the USA. But between 1841 and 1868 more than 300,000 people went west to Oregon. It was a long and difficult trip. It was called the Oregon Trail. And the people were called pioneers.

People sat at the campfires, ate, talked and sang songs.

The pioneers wanted a better life.

1 **On the Oregon Trail**
Look at the pictures, texts and map.

What do you think – why was the Oregon Trail difficult?

2 **The diary of Abi Russell**
2◉16 Listen to the radio programme.
Look at the map.
Which places can you hear?

3 **Listen to the first part of Abi's diary.**
2◉17 Are these sentences true or false?

1 Abi Russell lived in Richmond, Missouri.
2 Abi's brothers and sisters wanted to leave.
3 Abi said goodbye to her parents.
4 First Abi's family went to Independence.
5 On the trail most people were on horses.
6 The pioneers had lots of animals with them.
7 Fort Laramie was a small town.

*Unit 6 ist nur Pflichtstoff für den E-Kurs in Nordrhein-Westfalen.

The wagon trains were often long, with lots of people and animals.

At night the pioneers camped together. It was safer. They were frightened of Indians and wild animals like cougars and buffaloes.

These wagons were very important for the pioneers. They put lots of things in them, like food, clothes and furniture.

4 **Listen to the second part of Abi's diary. Pick the right answer.**

2⊙18

1 Independence Day is on
   a) May 10th **b)** June 20th **c)** July 4th
   d) August 20th.

2 Abi liked Joseph
   a) Dunn **b)** Brown **c)** Russell **d)** Jones.

3 In the mountains things were more
   a) expensive **b)** exciting **c)** different
   d) difficult.

4 Abi didn't like
   a) fish **b)** bread **c)** buffalo meat **d)** vegetables.

5 The Indians were very
   a) friendly **b)** angry **c)** young **d)** frightened.

6 On October 1st, the Russells got to
   a) California **b)** Oregon City **c)** Washington
   d) Chicago.

7 The Russells' new farm was
   a) at Snake River **b)** at Deschutes River
   c) in Oregon City **d)** near Richmond.

▶ W 59, 1–3

A SUMMER IN OREGON

1 **Summer plans**

Scan these e-mails. What can you find out about Laura and Martin?

a) Where are they from?

b) Are they friends?

c) Who's going to travel next summer?

Tip:
When you're looking for information in a text, you "scan" it.

Laura Russell

Martin Maier

From: martin.maier29@wannabe.de
To: laurarussell@xyz.com

Dear Laura,
Thanks for your invitation. If I had enough money, I'd visit you in the USA.
But you know that I have four brothers and sisters. If we all went to the USA, it would be very expensive. So I think that we'll stay here in Bielefeld this summer.
What are your summer plans? Would you like to come to Germany?
Best wishes from your e-pal.
    Martin

From: laurarussell@xyz.com
To: martin.maier29@wannabe.de

Hi Martin,
Thanks for your e-mail and for your invitation. If I had time, I'd love to go to Germany. But summer is busy here on the ranch. I have to help with the horses. And I have to practice for the rodeo at the County Fair. If you came to Bend in August, we'd take you to the fair. It's awesome! And we'd go to the coast. And if you wanted, I'd teach you to ride. So you really should come to the USA. If you came alone, it wouldn't be so expensive. And if you came to Portland, we'd pick you up at the airport. It's only three hours from here.
Bye,
    Laura

From: martin.maier29@wannabe.de
To: laurarussell@xyz.com

Hi again, Laura!
Great news! My grandma is going to give me some money for my birthday. And I have a weekend job. So I can come to the USA in August — alone. I'm really excited. Can you send me some information about Bend and Oregon — or some links?
    Martin

2 **What are these words in German? Guess first. Then check in a dictionary.**

1 enough   2 e-pal   3 fair

4 coast   5 teach   6 excited

3 **Who writes about these things: Martin, Laura or nobody?**

1 a big family   3 riding horses   5 Christmas in Bend   7 a great present

2 a busy summer   4 a part-time job   6 a trip to the coast   8 hiking in Germany

4 **AND YOU?** Finish these sentences.

1 If I went to the USA, I'd visit / try / eat / …

2 If an American friend came to Germany, we'd go to / meet / …

3 If I had lots of money, I'd buy / give / …

5 **An American e-pal**
Imagine that you have an American e-pal. Write an e-mail. Invite him/her to visit you. Say what you'd do.

▶ W 60, 4

6 The history of Bend

Laura sent this brochure to Martin. Read it and finish the "Short history of Bend".

**Deschutes County Historical Society
Bend, Oregon**

The first pioneers came to the Bend area in 1813. But they didn't stay. They were going to California. Then in 1874 the first houses were built near the Deschutes River. More people came and in 1881 the first school was built. It had 5 students. A post office was established in 1886. In 1900 the little town was named Farewell Bend. That was because lots of people said farewell (goodbye) here, before they went to California. But in 1905 the name was changed to Bend.

**A SHORT HISTORY
OF BEND**

1813	The first ... came to the area.
1874	The first ... were built.
1881	The first ... was built.
1886	A ... was established.
1900	Name: ...
1905	New name: ...

PROJECT More about Oregon

a) Work in groups. Each pupil in the group picks one of these topics, looks for information and makes notes.

Tip:
- Use online encyclopedias like *wikipedia.org* or *infoplease.com*
- When you use a search engine, put in two or more words. Examples: *Oregon Bend* or *Oregon activities coast*

1 Bend, Oregon

– What's the population?
– What can you do there?
– What should tourists see?

2 Oregon's geography

– Towns and cities?
– Mountains, lakes and rivers?
– The weather?

Tip:
Scan the texts on the websites. Look only for the information that you need.

3 Oregon's animals

– Oregon's nickname?
– What's a Jackalope?
– What's a skunk?

4 Activities in Oregon

– Activities on the coast?
– Activities in Oregon's schools?
– What's *disc golf*?

Tip:
- Don't worry about new words.
- Pictures and titles can help you to find what you need.

Tip:
The *Presentation Phrases* at the start of the book can help you.

b) Write a paragraph about your topic.   c) Present your topic to your group.

▶ W 60, 5–7

1 **Martin's holiday: Look at the pictures and answer these questions.**

1 How did Martin travel?   **2** What did he see?   **3** Do you think he had a good holiday?

An Oregon diary

2◉19

When Martin was planning his trip to the USA, his English teacher in Bielefeld asked him to write a diary in English. Martin agreed. Here are parts of his Oregon diary.

Monday, August 4th

I'm at Dulles Airport in Washington now. I left Frankfurt today at 9 a.m. The flight to Washington was nine and a half hours. But it's only 12.30 p.m. now! I'm so tired! If I had time, I'd find a quiet
5   place and sleep. But my flight to Portland is soon. Laura's family is picking me up there. I don't know them, so I'm feeling nervous. Everybody here speaks so fast. I can't understand much! And writing my diary in English is difficult.

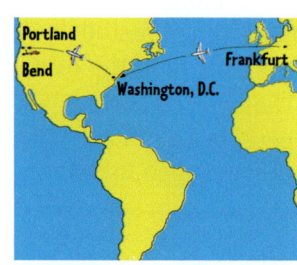

Tuesday, August 5th

10 Yesterday was a long, long day! I got to Portland and the Russells were waiting. Laura is very nice. Her mum and dad are friendly too. And her little brother, Dylan is really funny. He's only seven.
15 First we drove on the highway. That was a big road, but the cars weren't going very fast. The speed limit here is only 65 miles per hour (that's about 100 kilometres per hour). We got to

20 Bend at 11 p.m. and I fell into bed. I was very tired. This morning Laura and Dylan showed me the ranch. It's nice. There are lots of big, old barns. The house is big and modern. The tractors are big too. In fact, everything is big here – bigger than in Germany!

Thursday, August 7th

Yesterday I tried riding Laura's horse. I almost fell off and Laura laughed. But it wasn't
25 funny! Today we're in Bend. It's a very nice town – typical American like in the films! I met some of Laura's friends. They're nice, but I don't understand a word when they talk together. So I stay quiet. We had hot dogs for lunch. But I didn't like them – they're different from German sausages. Laura and her friends are shopping now. But it's too hot for me, so I'm sitting at a diner writing my diary and drinking a soda. You can get refills
30 and they're free! That's great. I think I'll have another soda!

Friday, August 8th

I stayed in my room for a long time today. Laura wanted to go riding again, but I said no. And she wanted to meet friends, but I was too tired. I played some games with Dylan. That was fun – and I can understand Dylan!

35 The food here is different from home. The bread isn't
very nice. People here eat lots of white bread! I miss the
food from home. I miss my family too. In fact, I'm
feeling homesick! If I had a plane ticket, I'd go home
now.

40 **Sunday, August 10th**
I'm feeling much better now. Today was a great day. It
was very hot – hotter than in Bielefeld! So Laura, Dylan
and I went to the Deschutes River, near Bend. We met
some of Laura's friends there. We went *tubing*. We sat in
45 big tubes and went slowly down the river. We laughed all
the time. It was great. Then we made a campfire near
the river and had *s'mores*. That's an American tradition –
marshmallows are grilled on the fire. You can eat them
with chocolate and crackers. They're great!
50 My English is better now and I can understand Laura's
friends. I told them about life in Germany. They were very interested. They told me about
the pioneers and the Oregon Trail.

Friday, August 15th
This week has been awesome! (Laura says "awesome" all the time.)
55 We did so much. We went to the County Fair. Laura was in the rodeo
competition. She didn't win, but she was very good. And the best
news is that I learned to ride. But no rodeo for me! Now I'm in
Portland with all the family. My holiday is almost over. On Sunday
I'm going to go home.
60 So what do I think of Oregon? It's a great place. People are so
friendly and the area is very beautiful. I'm not surprised that the
pioneers wanted to come here. But I'm looking forward to going
home. And I'm really looking forward to eating German food again!

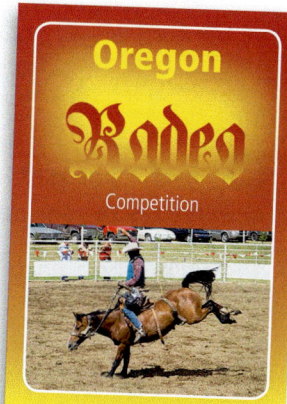

2 **Something is wrong in every sentence. Correct the sentences.**

1 Martin's flight to Washington
was 12 hours.
2 The speed limit on highways is the
same in the USA and in Germany.
3 Martin learned to ride on his third day.
4 Martin's first week in Bend was boring.
5 You need boats for tubing.
6 Martin's second week was terrible.

3 **In Oregon: Finish the sentences.**

1 Martin liked lots of things, for example ...
2 He didn't like some food, for example ...
3 Some things were very different: ...
4 It was a good holiday because ...

● **4** **Home again**
**Imagine that you're Martin. Write an e-mail
to Laura. Say thanks for the holiday.
Say what you learned about Oregon.**
The e-mails on page 82 help you to start and finish.

▶ W 61, 8–10

1 ODD WORD OUT All the words are on pages 84–85.

1 river, highway, speed limit, miles per hour
2 white bread, s'mores, rodeo, hot dogs
3 awesome, typical, great, beautiful
4 marshmallow, ranch, barn, tractor
5 airport, plane ticket, flight, refill
6 nervous, homesick, tube, tired

2 Find the missing words in these sentences.

1 In Germany you say "kilometres per hour", but in America you say "..."
2 In Germany people eat lots of brown bread, but in America people often eat "..."
3 Americans often say "awesome", but British people say "..."
4 In Britain drinks like lemonade are called "fizzy drinks". In America they're called "..."
5 In Germany a big road is called an "Autobahn". In America it's called a "..."
6 In America a small restaurant is often called a "..."

3 Finish these networks in your exercise book.

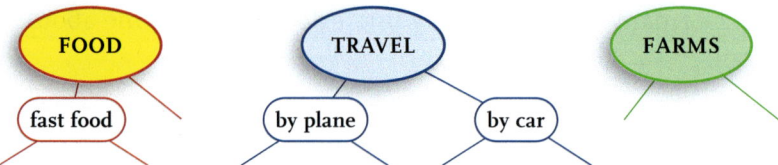

FOOD — fast food

TRAVEL — by plane — by car

FARMS

Tip: Put in words from this unit. Then find more words for the networks.

▸ Wordbank 9, p. 131

4 Useful phrases

a) First try to remember what these phrases are in English.

1 Möchtest du nach Deutschland kommen? (p. 82)
2 Du solltest wirklich in die USA kommen. (p. 82)
3 Ich bin echt begeistert. (p. 82)
4 Ich kann nicht viel verstehen. (p. 84, ll. 7–8)
5 Dylan ist wirklich lustig. (p. 84, l. 14)
6 Typisch amerikanisch! (p. 84, l. 25)
7 Ich freue mich darauf, nach Hause zu fahren. (p. 85, ll. 62–63)

b) Now check your answers to a) on pages 82, 84 and 85.

5 WORD SEARCH The passive

a) Put in _was_ or _were_. Then check your answers in exercise 6 on page 83.

1 In 1874 the first houses ... built.
2 In 1881 the first school ... built.
3 In 1886 a post office ... established.
4 In 1900 the town ... named Farewell Bend.
5 In 1905 the name ... changed to Bend.

b) When do you use the passive? Make the rule.

The passive
You use the passive when
- it is/isn't important who did it
- you know/don't know who did it

▸ W 62, 11–14   ▸ W ⊙

Reading logs

STEP 1 Start a reading log.
When you read a story or a book, you can write a reading log.
It's like a diary. It can help you to understand and remember the story.
Start a reading log for the story *An Oregon Diary* on pages 84/85.

STEP 2 Write notes on the story.

Title: An Oregon Diary		
PAGE	**WHAT HAPPENS**	**WHAT DO THE CHARACTERS FEEL/THINK**
84	Martin leaves Frankfurt. He goes to Portland. He meets the Russells. They drive to Bend. Martin sees the ranch.	Martin is nervous. He thinks that the Russells are nice. He says Dylan is funny. He's tired. Martin likes Laura's friends.

Tip:
- Write the title of the story.
- Write the page numbers.
- Say what happens.
- Say what the characters feel and think.
- You can use the simple present.

Finish these notes about *An Oregon diary*.

STEP 3 Write what YOU think and feel.

What I think/feel about:		
THE CHARACTERS I like … I don't like … I think that the Russells are …	**THE PLACE** I think that the ranch is … Bend sounds … I think that Oregon is …	**THE STORY** I think that the story is … Tubing sounds … I like/ don't like it when …

Tip:
Use:
☺ 😐 ☹

Finish these notes and write what you think about *An Oregon diary*.

STEP 4 Pick one of these activities. Write …

A SHORT SUMMARY This story is about a German boy who goes to Oregon. He visits the Russells in Bend …	A REVIEW I think that this is a good story because … But I don't like it when …	MRS RUSSELL'S E-MAIL Dear Mr and Mrs Maier, Martin is having a nice time here. But he's …
LAURA'S DIARY FOR ONE DAY Monday, August 4th We drove to Portland. We met Martin at the airport. He …	AN ADVERT FOR OREGON Come to Oregon. Visit Bend. It's a beautiful city. Go tubing on the …	MARTIN'S LAST DAY Sunday, August 17th We got up early and went to the airport. I was sad …

STEP 5 Read the story *The Road to Freedom* on pages 122–25.
Write a reading log for that story. Then read other pupils' logs.

▶ W 63, 15–18   ▶ W ⊙

LISTENING A family trip

 1 **Booking a room in a motel**

2◉20 **a)** **Listen and find out:**

1 How many rooms do they need?
2 Does the motel have free rooms?
3 How much is a double room?
4 How many nights do the people want to stay?

b) **Imagine that you work at the Sunset Motel. Copy this form. Listen again and fill it in.**

> SUNSET MOTEL, BANDON, OREGON
> Name: *Amanda*
> Arrive: *Friday,*
> Leave: _____
> Number of rooms: _____
> Double rooms: _____ Single rooms: _____

 2 **On the road**

2◉21 **a)** **Listen to *Radio Cascades*.**
Are these sentences true or false?

1 All the roads are quiet today.
2 Highway 101 is busy.
3 There's a wildfire.
4 Highway 5 is closed.
5 Bend is going to be warm and dry.
6 It's going to be hot on the coast.

b) **Listen again and check.**

 3 **On the coast**

2◉22 **Listen. Pick the right answer.**

1 Now the Russells are — **a)** in the mountains. **b)** at home. **c)** in Bandon.
2 Laura and Martin are — **a)** on the beach. **b)** in a hotel. **c)** in the car.
3 Martin thinks this place is — **a)** busy. **b)** nice. **c)** boring.
4 The weather here is — **a)** hot. **b)** terrible. **c)** cool.
5 Are Martin and Laura talking about sign **a)**, **b)** or **c)**?

 4 **SAY IT IN GERMAN** Pick one sign in exercise 3 and explain it to a partner.

▶ W 64, 19

SPEAKING At a motel

1 **The Russells at Sunset Motel, Bandon**
2⊙23 **a) How much must Mrs Russell pay for two nights?**

MRS RUSSELL	Hi. I've booked three rooms for two nights. My name is Amanda Russell.
RECEPTIONIST	Hello Mrs Russell. You've booked two double rooms and a single room. Is that right?
MRS RUSSELL	Yes, that's right.
RECEPTIONIST	We have a special offer this week. I can give you a family room for four and a single room.
MRS RUSSELL	How much is that?
RECEPTIONIST	It's $120 per night for the family room and $45 for the single room.
MRS RUSSELL	That's fine.
RECEPTIONIST	You have rooms 187 and 188. Enjoy your stay, Mrs Russell.
MRS RUSSELL	Thanks.

b) Practise the dialogue with a partner.

3 **Tom Wilson at Sunset Motel**
a) Make the dialogue with a partner.

MR WILSON	Sage hallo. Sage wie du heißt. Sage, dass du ein Zimmer reserviert hast.
RECEPTIONIST	Begrüße den Gast. Frage, ob er ein Einzel- oder Doppelzimmer möchte.
MR WILSON	Sage, dass du ein Einzelzimmer möchtest. Frage, wie viel das kostet.
RECEPTIONIST	Sage, dass es $90 pro Nacht kostet.
MR WILSON	Sage zu. Frage, wo das Zimmer ist.
RECEPTIONIST	Sage, es ist auf der rechten Seite, neben dem Restaurant. Wünsche dem Gast einen angenehmen Aufenthalt.

b) Write your dialogue and practise it.

2 **Mr and Mrs Brown at Sunset Motel**
2⊙24 **a) Finish the dialogue.**

MRS BROWN	Hello. I'd like a … for one night, please.
RECEPTIONIST	Hello. Do you want a … room or a … room?
MRS BROWN	A double room, please. How … is it?
RECEPTIONIST	It's $85 … night.
MRS BROWN	That's …
RECEPTIONIST	You have room 359. Enjoy your …
MRS BROWN	…

b) Act the dialogue with a partner.

4 **SAY IT IN ENGLISH**
You work at a hotel in Germany. Explain the most important information on this sign to an English tourist.

Hotel Avalon

Lieber Gast,

Wir heißen Sie herzlich willkommen in unserem Hotel.
Hier einige Informationen:

Frühstück: *Von 6 bis 11 Uhr*
Check out: *Bitte räumen Sie Ihr Zimmer am Abreisetag vor 11 Uhr.*

Stadtrundfahrten:
Karten sind an der Rezeption erhältlich.

▶ W 64, 20–21   ▶ W ⊙

READING Heroes of the Wild West

1 **Scan texts A and B and find out:**
- **Who are the two texts about?**
- **Which text is a song?**

A

THE STORY OF AN OUTLAW

Jesse James was born in Missouri in 1847. He had an older brother, Frank. The two boys joined a gang in 1866, when Jesse was only 19, they robbed a bank. A young man in the bank was killed.
After that the James brothers robbed banks and trains. Lots of people were killed. Jesse and Frank were often in the newspapers. They were famous.
Jesse changed his name to Thomas Howard. There was a reward of $10,000 for the person who helped to catch Frank or Jesse James. Then in 1882 Jesse was shot by a friend – Robbert Ford. Jesse James died and Ford got the reward.
Some people thought that the James boys robbed the rich and gave to the poor – like Robin Hood. But this wasn't true. They weren't heroes. They were just outlaws who robbed and killed people.

B

Jesse James

Jesse James was a lad
That killed many a man
He robbed the Glendale train
He stole from the rich
And he gave to the poor
He had a hand and a heart and a brain.

Well it was Robert Ford
That dirty little coward
I wonder now how he feels
For he ate of Jesse's bread
And he slept in Jesse's bed
And he laid poor Jesse in his grave.

Well Jesse had a wife
To mourn for his life
Three children
Now they were brave
Well that dirty little coward
That shot Mr Howard
He laid poor Jesse in his grave.

2 **Work with a partner.**
a) **Partner A reads text A, Partner B reads text B.**
b) **Now try to answer all the questions together.**

1 When was Jesse James born?
2 Who robbed the Glendale train?
3 Who was Frank James?
4 Was Jesse James married?
5 Did he have children?
6 Who was Mr Howard?
7 When did Jesse James die?
8 Who shot Jesse James?

3 **Words in the text**
a) **Pick one of the texts. Find the words in the text and guess what they are in German.**

Text A
1 outlaw (*noun*)
2 robbed (*verb*)
3 reward (*noun*)
4 catch (*verb*)
5 rich (*noun*)
6 hero (*noun*)

Text B
1 lad (*noun*)
2 robbed (*verb*)
3 rich (*noun*)
4 coward (*noun*)
5 slept (*verb*)
6 wife (*noun*)

b) **Check your words in a dictionary.**

4 **Listen to the song. Then talk about these questions in your class.**
2⊙25 **Do you like the song? Do you think that Jesse James was a hero? Why?**

▶ W 65, 22

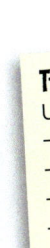

WRITING   A Wild West story

Imagine that you're writing a Wild West story for TV.
Look at the pictures and write the story (about 100 words). Think of an interesting ending.

1866 – cowboys – come to
small town – Oregon

gang – bank – leave – horses
in front of – go in

Tip:
Use phrases like:
- The year was …
- It was 12 o'clock.
- At five past twelve
- After ten minutes
- Then
- Later
- Suddenly

cashier – give – money
put in bags – people
stand – next to wall

gang – leave – bank
run into street

Tip:
Describe the scene
with phrases like:
- It was hot.
- The town was quiet.
- People were frightened/
  nervous/surprised.

no horses – in street
cowboys – surprised

horses – shop – eat vegetables
sheriff – surprised

Tip:
Use words like:
- because
- and
- but
- so
- when

▶ W 65, 23   ▶ W ⊚

DREAMING ABOUT AMERICA

1 If you won a trip to the USA where would you go? Why?
Look at the pictures and tell a partner.

New York

Chicago

Los Angeles

If I won a trip to the USA, I'd go to ... because ...

Washington

Miami

Oregon

Tip:
Look in Units 1–6 for more ideas.

2 More dreams!
If you went to New York, Oregon or the other places, what would you do there?

| If I went to New York, LA, Oregon, Chicago, Washington, Miami, ... | I'd ... | visit see
go   play
try   eat
ride   meet | Ground Zero • Disneyland • Hollywood • Bend
surfing • a Segway • basketball • bears
tubing • whale watching • Neah Bay • a rodeo
shopping • rangers • a horse • famous people
kayaking • hot dogs • s'mores • a rodeo |

3 WORD SEARCH

a) Look at the pictures. Guess what the missing words are. Check the e-mails on page 82.

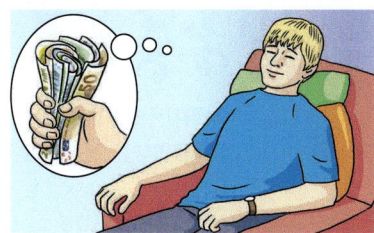

If I ... enough money,
I'd visit you in the USA.

If we all ... to the USA,
it would be very expensive.

If I ... time,
I'd love to go to Germany.

b) Now guess these missing words. You can check them on page 82.

If you came to Bend,
we'... ... you to the fair.

If you wanted,
I'... ... you to ride.

If you came to Portland,
we'... ... you up.

4 OVER TO YOU!

Write the checkpoint in your exercise book and put in:

– would / 'd
– the simple past

CHECKPOINT

If-Sätze (Typ II) verwendest du, wenn du sagen willst, was wäre wenn ...

Die Situation ist eher unwahrscheinlich.	*if*-Satz	Hauptsatz
	if + ...	... + verb

▶ Eine Übersicht über diese Regeln findest du auf der *Summary*-Seite 138.

▶ Extra Practice, pp. 116 ff.

▶ W 66–67

NACH DIESER UNIT KANN ICH ...

sagen, was gemacht wurde oder passiert ist.	▶ *The first houses were built in 1874. A post office was established.*
ein Lesetagebuch führen.	▶ *The title of the story is ... . Martin goes by plane from ...*
	▶ *I think that the story is ... . I like ... . I don't like ...*
ein Zimmer im Hotel reservieren.	▶ *I'd like to book a room for one night, please.*
in einem Hotel einchecken.	▶ *Hello. My name is ... . I've booked a room for one night.*
eine Geschichte schreiben.	▶ *The year was 1866. Six cowboys were in a small town ...*
sagen, was wäre wenn ...	▶ *If I won a trip to the USA, I'd go to New York.*

Unit 1   (page 19)

Card A
You invite a friend.

A Do you have any plans for Sunday afternoon?

B ...

A I'm having a party. Do you want to come?

B ...

A About 4 o'clock. There'll be some sausages and bread.

B ...

A Yeah, can you bring some fruit or cake?

B ...

Card B
A friend invites you.

A ...

B No, not really.

A ...

B That sounds great, thanks. When should I be there?

A ...

B That sounds good. Can I bring anything?

A ...

B OK. Thanks for the invitation. See you then.

Unit 2   (page 33)

Card A
You phone a friend.

B ...

A Hello. Can I speak to ..., please?

B ...

A When will he/she be back?

B ...

A Can he/she phone me back? I'm ... . And my number is ...

B ...

A Yes, that's right. Thanks. Bye.

Card B
You answer the phone.

B Hello.

A ...

B Oh, he/she isn't here. He/She's in ...

A ...

B After ... p.m. Can I take a message?

A ...

B No problem. I'll write your name and message. So you're ... . And your number is ...

A ...

B Bye.

Card A

You know about school.

A What do you want to know about school?

B ...

A You must / mustn't wear shorts ...

B ...

A You can bring ... / but you mustn't bring ...

B ...

A No, you mustn't bring ... / That's OK. You can bring ...

Card B

You ask about school.

A ...

B What about clothes? What / must / wear?

A ...

B Can / bring / mobile / MP3 player / beer / ...?

A ...

B What about my ...?

Card A

You're a tourist.

– We'd like to do **something interesting**. **What** can you **recommend**?

– That sounds **interesting/nice/**... **Where** is it?

– **What** can you **buy** there?

– **What day** is it open?

– **What time** is it open?

– Is there a **market every month**?

Card B

You work at the visitor center.

Anacortes Farmers Market
7th Street in Old Town

Fruit & vegetables
Cakes • Cheese • Bread
Saturdays 9–2
May–October
Remember ... come hungry!

Unit 5   (page 75)

Card A

You say "hello" to Partner B.

A Hello, I'm ...
B ...
A mind / sit here?
B ...
A give / bread / please
B ...
A Thank you.
B ...

Card B

You meet Partner A at a party.

A ...
B pleased / meet / you
A ...
B Go ahead.
A ...
B yes / here / are
A ...
B You're welcome.

REVISION Simple present → Summary, p. 132

1 Famous New Yorkers
Put in the verbs.

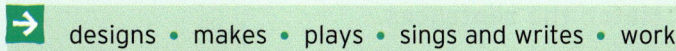

designs • makes • plays • sings and writes • works

Scarlett Johansson | Eddie Murphy | Calvin Klein | Alicia Keys | Carmelo Anthony

She ...
in Hollywood. | He ... funny
films. | He ... cool
clothes. | She ... songs. | He ... basketball.

2 Jazmin's day

a) Write Tyrell's mum's questions for Jazmin.

1 When (**you / go**) to school? *When do you ...?*
2 When (**your parents / start**) work?
3 (**you / have**) lunch at school?
4 When (**your mom / come**) home?
5 What (**you / do**) after school?
6 (**your dad / work**) late?

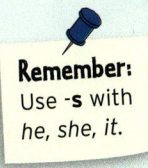

Tip:
Sometimes you can have
two **do**s in a question.
Example: What **do** you
do at the weekend?

b) Tyrell is telling a friend about Jazmin. Finish his sentences.

My cousin Jazmin (**live**) in Greenville in South Carolina.
She has three brothers and they (**play**) lots of sports together.
They (**not have**) a TV, but they (**listen to**) music all the time.
Jazmin (**not like**) pop, but she (**love**) rap. She always (**know**) the
best songs. She (**want**) to be a DJ when she's older.

Remember:
Use **-s** with
he, she, it.

3 Your day

a) Write five sentences about your day.

| I | always
usually
sometimes
never | get up
go to school
have lunch
do sport
watch TV
meet friends
go to bed | at ...
early.
late.
in the morning.
in the afternoon.
in the evening. |

**b) Now use your own
ideas. Write 5–10 more
sentences about your
day.**

Comparisons → Summary, p. 136

○ **4** Match the sentences.

Spiderman helps people in New York! He's great!

1	He's faster than other people.	a	He's never frightened.
2	He has better eyes than most people.	b	But not everybody likes his jokes.
3	He's braver than other people.	c	Be careful!
4	He's more dangerous than other people.	d	He can see at night.
5	He's funnier than other people.	e	He can climb very quickly.

○ **5** Travel

a) Travel in New York: Compare the New York subway and taxis. Pick words from the box.

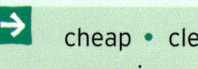
cheap • clean • dangerous • easy • expensive • fast • nice • popular • safe

Tip: Check your spelling!

1 The subway is ... than taxis.
2 It's ... than taxis.
3 It's ...

4 Taxis are ... than the subway.
5 They're ... than the subway.
6 They're ...

b) Travel in your area: Write three sentences in your exercise book.

In my area you can go by ... . Bikes/Buses/Trams/Cars/ ... are ... than ...

○ **6** Finish the text about the World Trade Center.

The two towers of the World Trade Center were (high) **the highest** skyscrapers in New York. But on September 11th, 2001, one of (terrible) ... and (sad) ... things in New York's history happened: two planes flew into the towers in (busy) ... part of New York. One of (famous) ... skyscrapers in the world fell to the ground. It made (big) ... hole in New York: Ground Zero. Soon there will be new skyscrapers there. The Freedom Tower will be (exciting) ... tower in New York. It's one of the city's (expensive) ... projects.

7 Work with a partner. What's wrong with these sentences? Write new sentences.

> ### Eat at Sam's.
>
> ## It's the dirtiest deli in the city!
>
> Our sandwiches are worse than the sandwiches in other delis!
> We have the highest prices in NYC!
> We have the most terrible cooks in the neighborhood!

8 An advert for your school deli

a) Work with a partner. Look at exercise 7 again and write an advert for your deli. Write about:

- The place
- The food
- The prices
- The cooks

> → cheap • clean • cool • early • exciting • friendly • good • great • healthy • hungry • late • new • nice • polite • romantic

b) Compare your adverts with other pupils. Who has the best advert?

TEST PRACTICE

9 A New York postcard

a) Talk about the picture with a partner. What can you see? What's the place like?

> **Tip:**
> - Use *There is …/There are …* to talk about things and people.
> - Say what the place is like:
>   *It's big/small/…*,
>   *It's bigger/busier/more … than …*
> - Use these phrases to say where they are:
>   *in the background, in the foreground, on the right/on the left.*

b) AND YOU? Compare your town or village with New York. Which is busier/nicer/…?

 10 You want to send a postcard from New York to an English friend. Write the postcard (40–50 words). Write:

– where you are and why you are there
– what the weather is like
– what you did yesterday
– what you are doing today

> **Tip:**
> - Start your postcard with *Dear …*, or *Hi …*,
>   Finish with *Love, …* or *Best wishes, …*
> - Check your postcard.

REVISION Present progressive → Summary, p. 132

1 **What's happening?**

○ **a) Describe the picture in eight sentences.**

A girl		working	in the park.
A boy		playing	bikes.
A man		riding	a chat.
A woman	is	walking	on a mobile.
Some girls	are	having	baseball.
Some boys		reading	with his dog.
Some men		sitting	a book.
Some women		talking	on the grass.

○ **b) Look at the picture again.**
Write five more sentences.

100

one hundred

● **2** **What's happening?**
Pick a picture on pages 24–36 of this book. Write five things. Tell your partner.
Can your partner guess which photo you picked?

Who / That → Summary, p. 138

○ **3** **Who's who and what's what? Put the parts together and make the sentences.**

1 Richard Bailey is a man ...   that has lots of smog.
2 Caitlin is a student ...   who often surf.
3 Nina and Lee are teens ...   that's very popular in Los Angeles.
4 Surfing is a sport ...   who goes to Santa Monica High School.
5 Los Angeles is a city ...   that makes famous films.
6 Warner Brothers is a studio ...   who wants the best for his daughter.

○ **4** **A man in Hollywood**
Put in *who* or *that*.

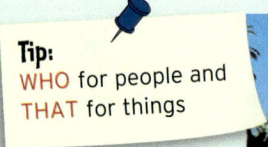

Tip:
WHO for people and
THAT for things

1 I watched a DVD ... I thought
   was very funny.
2 It's about an English man ... goes to Hollywood.
3 He stays with some people ... have a nice house.
4 He visits a museum ... has lots of famous pictures.
5 This man does some things ... are very stupid.
6 What's the name of the man ... is the star of this
   film? – It's Mr Bean!

● **5** **AND YOU?** Finish these sentences with more information.

1 I know a girl who likes ...
2 I know a boy who hates ...
3 I go to a school that ...

4 I have friends ...
5 Maths is a subject ...
6 I have a mobile ...

Past progressive → Summary, p. 133

○ **6** **The Herrmann family in Los Angeles: Pick the right word.**

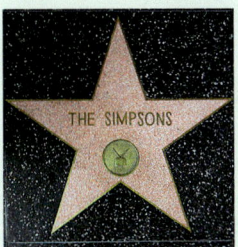

When the Herrmanns from Berlin (**1**) was/were visiting LA last summer, they did lots of interesting things. They (**2**) was/were staying in a hotel in Santa Monica and every day they went to different places. When they visited Hollywood, they saw lots of people who (**3**) was/were walking along Hollywood Boulevard. Nora (**4**) was/were looking for famous stars, but she didn't see any. Andi (**5**) was/were reading the names of famous people on the pavement – and he saw the Simpsons!

The next day the Herrmanns went to Warner Brothers Studios. When they (**6**) was/were visiting the studios, the tour guide told them lots of interesting stories. They (**7**) was/were going past a film scene, when Andi and Nora saw Sean Penn. He was with other actors and they (**8**) was/were wearing cowboy gear. They (**9**) was/were making a new cowboy film. Nora (**10**) was/were feeling very happy now – she loves Sean Penn!

○ **7** **At a TV show: Put the verbs in the past progressive form.**

That evening the Herrmanns were at *Teen Talk*, the new chat show. Nora was happy again.
1 "When we got to the KABC Studios, lots of people (**wait**).
2 A young woman (**check**) the tickets.
3 When I looked behind the scene, the camera people (**talk**) to the director.
4 The director (**shout**) all evening.
5 Nobody (**listen**) to the director.
6 The star of *Teen Talk* (**look**) very nervous.
7 I couldn't see everything because I (**sit**) at the back.
8 When everybody (**leave**), I looked into another studio."

● **8** **In another studio**
When Nora looked into another studio, lots of things were happening. Look at the picture and write some sentences.

Some actors were ...   One cowboy was ...
Another cowboy ...   The director ...

9 **An accident in Santa Monica**
Officer Kennedy has lots of questions.
Put in the verbs.

→ buying • talking • jogging • driving • walking • riding

Who was ... the car?

Who was ... the bike?

Were you ... on your cellphone?

Was the boy ... across the street?

Were the joggers ... in the street?

Were the shoppers ... vegetables?

10 **We weren't doing anything! What are the teenagers saying to Officer Kennedy?**

1 I wasn't driving ...!

5 We ...!

2 We weren't using ...!

3 I wasn't ...!

4 We ..!

11 **INTERPRETING** A German tourist saw something on the beach.
He's talking to Officer Kennedy. Can you help?

OFFICER	Where were you sitting?
YOU	Wo saßen Sie ...?
TOURIST	Ich saß gerade am Strand.
YOU	He was sitting on ...
OFFICER	What happened then?
YOU	Was ...?
TOURIST	Ich sah zwei Männer. Sie waren gerade dabei, Taschen zu stehlen.

YOU	He saw two men. They were ...
OFFICER	What were they wearing?
YOU	Was ...?
TOURIST	Sie hatten schwarze Kleidung an.
YOU	They ...
OFFICER	Thank you for your help.
YOU	Danke ...

TEST PRACTICE

12 **At Disneyland with Peter Pan: What can you see in the picture?**

1 What does the picture show?
The picture shows ...
2 What are the people doing?
The children are ...
3 How do you think the people are feeling?
I think that ...
4 What are the people wearing?
One boy is wearing ...
A girl ...
A woman ...
Peter Pan ...

13 **Who can teach me?**

a) Sarah Greene (15) can't surf. So she has put this advert in her school newspaper:

> I can ride a bike and a quad!
> I can drive a car and I can swim like a fish.
> I have a surfboard and I live near the beach.
> But I can't surf!
> **So who can teach me?** **Help!**
> Phone number: 310-555-7383
> Please call after 8 p.m.

b) Now write Brad's advert.

Brad Wilson (15) can't surf. But he has a new surfboard and surfing gear. He isn't a very good swimmer.
He doesn't live near the sea, but he has a car. He has a mobile (310-555-6534), but you can't call him between 8 a.m. and 4 p.m. on school days. He works on Saturday mornings – he's a photo model!

14 **An e-mail to an American friend**
You were in LA last month for a holiday. Your friend Mike has sent you an e-mail.
a) First read Mike's questions.
b) Write an e-mail to Mike. Write 50–80 words.

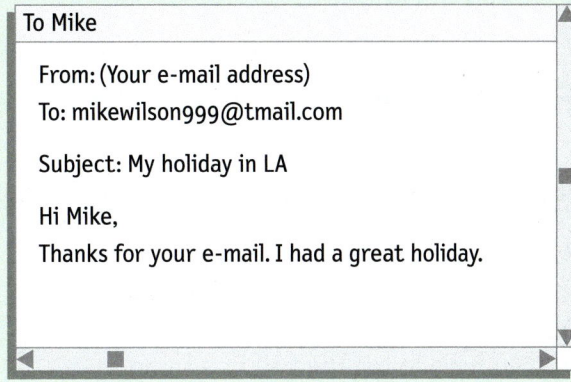

REVISION *Can/Can't* → Summary, page 135

1 In Chicago: Match the sentences with the pictures.

1 You can go on a boat trip on the Chicago River.
2 You can go shopping at one of the biggest department stores in the world.
3 You can visit the funfair on Navy Pier.
4 You can relax by Lake Michigan.
5 You can look at the city from the top of Sears Tower.
6 You can go to a concert in Millennium Park.

2 Sightseeing

a) Read the advert. Finish the sentences with *can* or *can't*.

> Go on a tour of Chicago's greatest landmarks and neighborhoods on our double-decker buses. Buy tickets and get on the bus at all our bus stops. Tours start at 9 a.m. All day tickets mean that you can jump on and off any of our vehicles. It's the only tour in Chicago that goes to Chinatown, Greektown and Little Italy.

1 You ... go sightseeing in Chicago by bus.
2 You ... start the tour at different bus stops.
3 You ... travel without tickets.
4 You ... go on a tour at 8 a.m.
5 You ... use different buses.
6 You ... visit immigrant neighbourhoods.

b) What can or can't you do in your area? Compare it with Chicago. Write 5–8 sentences.
You can use words and phrases from exercise 1.

In my area you can ...
But you can't ...

see • visit • go • go on • go to • take • look at • ...

REVISION *Have to/Don't have to* → Summary, page 135

3 Put these sentences in two lists: basketball or American football.

1 You have to wear a helmet.
2 You have to play on a special field.
3 You don't have to play outdoors.
4 You have to get the ball in a hoop.
5 You don't have to wear protectors.
6 You don't have to jump.
7 You have to have five players in a team.
8 You have to play for sixty minutes.

4 The Chicago Bulls: Finish the sentences with *you have to / you don't have to.*

If you're in Chicago, ... see a Chicago Bulls game! But ... buy tickets early because they sell quickly. ... pay lots of money for tickets – the cheapest tickets are only $10. And ... go to the United Center for tickets, you can buy them online. The United Center is always busy, so ... get there early before the game starts. And remember: ... take your own food – you can buy hot dogs and potato chips there.

Ben Gordon

5 Write about Ben Gordon and the Chicago Bulls players. Use *have to / don't have to / doesn't have to.*
Ben Gordon doesn't have to ..., but he ... . The players ...

Ben:	✘ get up early
	✔ go to the gym every day
	✔ relax between games
	✘ play in every game

The players:	✔ stay healthy
	✘ eat special food
	✔ play together as a team
	✘ practise together every day

Imperative → **Summary, page 134**

6 What adults say to pupils at school
Match the sentences with the places.

→ music room • classroom • gym • playground • library • swimming pool

1 Don't forget to do your homework.
2 Go back to your classrooms! Break has finished.
3 Throw the ball to your partner.
4 Don't run or you'll fall! It's wet.
5 Practise that song again, please.
6 Please be quiet and don't write in that book.

7 Classroom phrases
a) What pupils say to other pupils: Make five sentences.

| Please | (don't) | talk to me
give me
look at
kick | in English • in German • now • ...
the dictionary • the book • that pen • ...
my answers • the exercise • the map • ...
my bag • my foot • the table • ... |

b) Work with a partner. Write more classroom phrases. Collect the phrases on the board and write them in your exercise book.

 be • help me • do • explain • take • write

Should / Shouldn't → Summary, page 135

○ **8** **Candice's advice**

a) **April has a problem. Read Candice's advice.**

You should get help, you shouldn't wait. Maybe you should talk to your aunt – or a teacher. You should explain what's happening at home. And you should stay with us tonight. You shouldn't worry, April.

What should I do, Candice?

b) **Pick the right answer.**

April has a problem with ...
1 her homework
2 bullies
3 her parents

○ **9** **The school yearbook**

Every year a team of students makes a yearbook. Candice is giving advice to a younger student. Put in the words in the box.

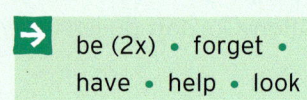

→ be (2x) • forget • have • help • look

You know the yearbook should ... students to remember their school days. So the yearbook should ... everybody's photos and names in it. And of course you shouldn't ... the teachers! There should ... something about sports, special school activities and parties. The book should ... good but it shouldn't ... expensive.

● **10** **Advice for Candice**

Pick one of Candice's problems. Give her advice.

I don't like the food at school.

I can't sleep.

I need new clothes.

My mom has lost her job.

You should ...
You shouldn't ...

Must / Mustn't → Summary, page 135

○ **11** **Match the school rules with the pictures.**

1 You mustn't use cellphones.
2 You must have the right books and pens.
3 You mustn't eat or drink in class.
4 You must listen when others speak.
5 You mustn't be late.
6 You must turn off the lights when you leave.

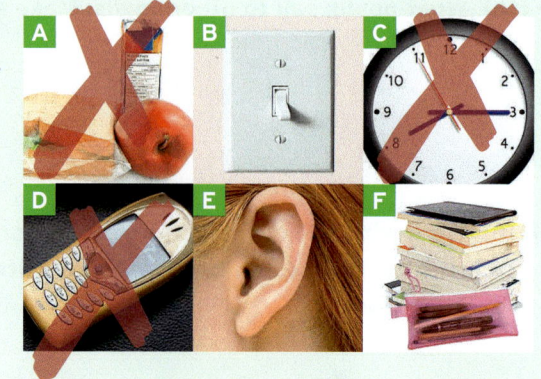

12 **Homecoming**

a) Read this report by an exchange student about homecoming. Put in *must* or *mustn't*.

In homecoming week, old students visit their school. Students at the school ... do lots of activities. At Sullivan High students wear different clothes: one day girls ... wear boys' clothes and boys ... wear girls' clothes. On another day students ... come to school in the school colours: blue and gold. This is the day of the big homecoming game. You ... miss it!

b) Finish the report about the homecoming dance. Use the notes.

*   students decorate school in school colours
    Students must decorate the school in the school colours.
*   students pick homecoming king or queen
*   students wear nice clothes
*   not wear jeans
*   teachers and parents be there too
*   students from other schools not come

TEST PRACTICE

13 **Sport and me**

a) Find an object for a sport that you do or that you like watching on TV: a football, a helmet, ...

b) Make notes:

- Say what your object is and what it's like.

> **Tip:**
> Use colours and words like *new*, *expensive*, ...

- Talk about when/where you do this sport or when/where you watch it.

> **Tip:**
> Use the simple present for activities that you often do.

- Say why you picked this sport.

> **Tip:**
> Use *because*.

c) Show a partner your object and talk about it. Use your notes.

– football shirt
– red, number 7
– play every Saturday
– school team
– watch matches on TV
– like football, fast and exciting

> **Tip:**
> Talk in complete sentences.

> I'm going to talk about football. This is my football shirt. It's red with the number 7. I play football every Saturday with the school team. I watch matches on TV too. I like football because it's fast and exciting.

REVISION Simple past → Summary, page 133

1 Natalie's first trip to America

a) What two things did Natalie like?

NATALIE: My aunt moved to Seattle in America many years ago. Last June she wrote an e-mail and she invited me to visit her. Of course I said yes! On July 10th, I went by plane from Frankfurt to Seattle. The trip took 13 hours. That evening my aunt picked me up at the airport in Seattle and we drove to her house. It was only 7 p.m., but I was very tired and I fell into bed! The next day we visited the centre of Seattle. It was beautiful. I ate my first American hamburger and it was great!

b) Draw this table in your exercise book. Put in all the simple past forms in the text. Then put in the infinitives.

Simple past	Infinitive
moved	move
wrote	...

c) Now find the time words.
Many years ago, ...

2 Natalie's work experience: Put the infinitives in the simple past.

Last summer, when I (**be**) in Seattle, I (**work**) in my aunt's German restaurant. I (**get**) up very early every morning. I (**take**) the bus to the centre and then I (**walk**) ten minutes to the restaurant. First I (**go**) to the supermarket with my aunt and we (**buy**) lots of vegetables and fruit. Then I (**help**) in the kitchen. We (**eat**) lunch at 12 o'clock. The restaurant (**be**) very busy at lunchtime, so we only (**have**) ten minutes. In the afternoon we (**make**) the food for the evening. At 5 o'clock I (**finish**) work.

List of irregular verbs p. 197

3 NOW YOU Pick a) or b) and write a paragraph (60–80 words).

a) Think of a special trip. When was it? Where? How did you travel? Who went with you? What happened?

b) Have you had a part-time job? Where was it? What was the job? What did you have to do? Did you like the work?

REVISION Adjectives → Summary, page 136

4 All about Seattle
Pick the right adjectives and finish the paragraph about Seattle.

Seattle isn't the capital of Washington (that's Olympia), but it's the biggest/smallest city in the state. There are lots of new buildings, so the city looks very old/modern. There are lots of shops, people and traffic in the centre, so it's always very busy/quiet. And it's a very boring/interesting city because it has great museums, restaurants and clubs. The area near Seattle is beautiful/bad with its mountains, sea, islands and lake.

5 All about Anacortes
Put some of the adjectives into the text.

→ beautiful • busy • clean • cold • exciting • friendly • interesting • long • modern • new • nice • old • quiet • small

I live in Anacortes. It's a ... town in Washington State. It's on a ... island – Fidalgo Island. There are lots of ... buildings from the 1880s here. Only 15,000 people live in Anacortes, so it's very ... in winter. But in summer there are lots of visitors, so the town is very ... There's a ... supermarket here, where you can get everything. But there are lots of ..., ... shops too. Come to Anacortes – it's a ... town!

6 All about your town or village
Now write about a place that you know (60–80 words).

Tip:
Use lots of adjectives and make your text interesting. Exercise 5 can help you.

ing-form   → Summary, page 134

7 Leavenworth, Washington
a) Write the text in your exercise book. Put the verbs in the *ing*-form.

(**Live**) in Leavenworth in the 1960s wasn't easy. (**Find**) a job was a problem then. So people started (**leave**) the town and (**look**) for work in other places. Then some people had an idea – they thought of (**make**) Leavenworth a German town! So they started (**change**) the shops, hotels, cafes and houses. Today Leavenworth looks like a town in Bavaria! So if you're interested in (**visit**) a German town in the USA, you should go to Leavenworth. If you like (**listen**) to the music of Bavaria – Leavenworth is the place for you! And if you like (**ski**), (**hike**) in the mountains, (**eat**) German food and (**sing**) German songs, visit Leavenworth.

b) Joel and Leanne have no plans for the weekend. Finish their dialogue.

LEANNE
Hey, Joel, do you want to go 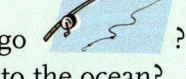 ?
What about 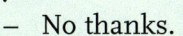 to the ocean?

Well, are you interested in  Leavenworth?
You can go 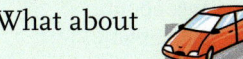 !
It's a great place for  .

JOEL
– No thanks. 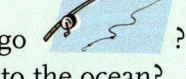 is boring!
– It's too far! And I hate 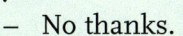 when it's hot!

– Leavenworth? What can you do there?

– No thanks!!!
– OK, let's go! I love  .

c) Make an advert for Leavenworth. Use phrases like:
Do you like ...? Are you interested in ...? Do you want to try ...? What about ...?

8 A Native American story

Telling stories is an important tradition for Native Americans. Their stories are often about animals. Here's a popular Native American story from Washington. It's about two birds – a raven and a crow.

a) Can you guess what kind of birds a *raven* and a *crow* are?

> **Tip:**
> Think of the names of birds in German. Then check in a dictionary.

"Looking for food isn't my favourite activity," Raven thought. "Working is stupid. I prefer sitting here in my tree, doing nothing. I love watching all the other animals when they collect food for the winter." But winter came and Raven had no food. He was hungry. So he went to his friend, Crow. Crow had lots of food for the winter. "Crow, you like singing! Right?" Raven asked. "Er, yes," Crow answered. "But I'm not very good at singing," he said. "Oh, that isn't true," Raven said. "You're famous for your great singing!" "Really?" Crow said. He was very happy. "Yes," Raven said. "So what about having a big winter party, with lots of nice food? And you can sing." "OK," said Crow and he started making the food. Raven went to all the other animals in the forest and he invited them to 'his' party. Lots of animals arrived and Crow started singing. Raven and the other animals started eating. "Another song!" Raven shouted. So Crow sang lots of songs. But when everybody had finished eating, poor Crow could only sing "caw, caw." And today crows can't sing. They can only say "caw, caw."

b) Read the story and put these pictures in the right order.

a   b   c   d   e

c) Answer these questions about the text.

1 What's an important tradition for Native Americans?
2 What activities didn't Raven like?
3 What did Crow like doing?
4 What did the other animals do when Crow started singing?

> **Tip:**
> We often use *ing*-forms when we talk about hobbies and activities.
> Example: singing, reading, playing football, …

9 What about your hobbies? Finish these sentences.

1 Playing … is my favourite sport.
2 I think … is stupid!
3 I like reading, …
4 I love …
5 I often go …
6 I'm not very good at …
7 I never go …
8 I hate …

TEST PRACTICE

10 SAY IT IN GERMAN

Pick one of the brochures and tell your partner about it – in German, of course.

A
Anacortes
A natural destination for your North-West vacation

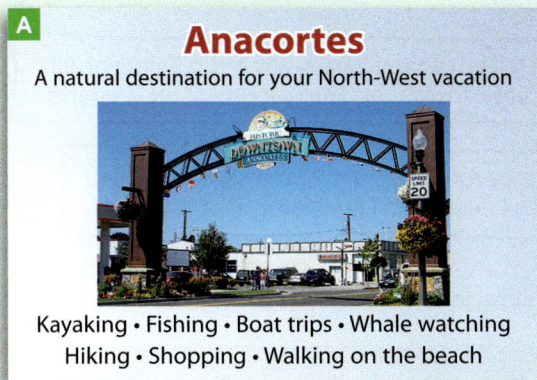

Kayaking • Fishing • Boat trips • Whale watching
Hiking • Shopping • Walking on the beach

Tip:
Only talk about the main points.
You can use a dictionary.

B
Hobuck Beach
Campground and Resort
Come see the beaches!

– Relax
– Watch wild animals
– Hike
– Fish
– Surf
– Swim

Visit us at the Hobuck Campground & Resort in Neah Bay, Washington, along the coast of the Pacific North-West.

11 Port Townsend: Pick a) or b).

a) Write an advert for Port Townsend (30–40 words).

b) Write a short article about Port Townsend for a tourist magazine (60–80 words).

PORT TOWNSEND

State	Washington
Population	8800
Activities	Boat trips, fishing, shopping, swimming, hiking, whale watching, kayaking, cycling
Visitor Center	2437 E Sims Way, Port Townsend, WA 98368
Internet	ptguide.com

12 An e-mail to a visitor centre

You want to visit Port Townsend next summer. Write an e-mail to the visitor centre there (60–80 words). Write about these points:

Are you travelling with your family or with friends?
How many people are going to travel to Port Townsend?
How long do you want to stay?
What activities do you want to do?

You have questions about:

the weather in June / Port Townsend /
a campground in Port Townsend

To: ptguide.com   Date: May 1st
Subject: a holiday in Port Townsend

Dear Sir/Madam,

I'm planning a holiday in Port Townsend next month. I'm travelling with my ...

REVISION *Will*-future → Summary, p. 134

1 Fourth of July hopes

a) Look at the weather for July 4th and read what Ramon and his mum say. Who will be right?

> **The Fourth of July** is **Independence Day**, an important day in America. On July 4th, 1776, the USA became free from Britain. Most cities and towns have Fourth of July festivals.

RAMON — I hope it'll be really hot and sunny on the Fourth of July. And I hope it won't rain later because of the fireworks.

RAMON'S MOM — I hope it won't be wet, of course. But I hope it won't be too hot, I like it best when it's cloudy.

b) Finish the advert for Miami's Fourth of July celebrations with *will*, *'ll* or *won't*.

MIAMI BEACH

At 7 p.m. on the Fourth of July, there will be a special celebration: children from other countries who live in Miami **(1)** ... become Americans. Later there **(2)** ... be a free concert by Carlos Oliva. Fireworks **(3)** ... start at 10 p.m. There **(4)** ... be a better place to be on the Fourth of July! The celebrations **(5)** ... be on the beach at 10th Street and Ocean Drive.

TROPICAL PARK

There **(6)** ... be lots of Fourth of July activities. But there **(7)** ... be food, so bring a picnic. And make other plans for the evening: there **(8)** ... be fireworks here in Tropical Park.

2 A Fourth of July picnic: Put in the right words.

→ cook • ask • look • take • buy • wear

1 Dad: I'll ... some drinks at the supermarket.
2 Ramon: I'll ... my guitar with me.
3 Mom: I'll ... some chicken.
4 Grandma: I'll ... my new shoes.
5 Ramon: I'll ... for the camera.
6 Ana: I'll ... my friend to come.

3 Future hopes

a) For a Fourth of July project, Ramon is writing about his hopes for his country and family for the next year. Look at Ramon's notes. Write his sentences.

I hope mom will ... . I hope dad won't ...

— mom find better job
— dad not have another accident
— mom and dad win some money
— not be any more problems with hurricanes
— the Miami Heat win all their games
— I learn to play the guitar better
— I not have any problems at school
— I get a girlfriend

b) Write 5–8 sentences about your hopes for the future.

REVISION Prepositions of place → **Summary, p. 137**

○ **4** **Look at the pictures. Pick the right word.**

1 The guitar is between / opposite the chair and the bed.
2 The two women are behind / in front of the man.
3 The CDs are on / under the table.
4 The piano is above / opposite the door.
5 The photographer is in front of / between the band.
6 The club is next to / above the cafe.

○ **5** **Eight things are different. Write them in your exercise book.**
In picture 1, KC is standing between BB and TJ. In picture 2, TJ is standing ...

● **6** **An interesting picture**
a) Find a picture from a magazine or the Internet with lots of things on it. Write about it. Say where things are and why the picture is interesting. Don't say people's names!

b) Put the pictures on the board. Read out your description. Can the class guess the picture?

Adverbs → **Summary, p. 137**

○ **7** **Match the pictures with the sentences.**

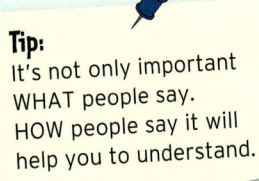

Tip:
It's not only important WHAT people say. HOW people say it will help you to understand.

1 She's speaking loudly.
2 She's speaking sadly.
3 She's speaking happily.
4 She's speaking nervously.
5 She's speaking angrily.
6 She's speaking politely.

8 Downloading music

a) Finish the text. Use adverbs.

Lots of people download music on the Internet. In my opinion, downloading music is great. You can get songs (**fast**) and very (**cheap**). Some musicians say they work (**hard**) and we take their songs (**illegal**). But some musicians think (**different**): they don't make CDs, they put their songs on the Internet.
I think things will change (**complete**) soon. Everybody will download music and not buy expensive CDs.

b) What do you think?

I think downloading music is ... because ... . In the future I think / don't think that ...

9 Rewrite the sentences for an article about a concert.

1 Bobbie sang his new song. He was confident.
Bobbie sang his new song confidently.
2 The fans sang. They were very loud.
3 Bobbie danced. His dancing was good.
4 The fans screamed. They were wild.
5 Bobbie smiled. He was happy.
6 He walked off the stage. He was tired.

10 AND YOU?

a) Say what you think your partner does ...

– well   – dangerously
– confidently   – loudly
– carefully   – nervously
– easily   – badly

b) If your partner agrees with your sentences, you can read them to the class.

Alex plays football well.
He plays his guitar loudly.

11 SAY IT IN ENGLISH Your American friend Pauline has a letter in German, but she doesn't understand everything. Tell her in English what it means.

Klara says thanks for your letter. The concert sounds ... . She'd like to ...

Liebe Pauline!

Danke für deinen Brief. Der Konzert klingt super, ich würde auch gern Gwen Stefani auf der Bühne sehen. Ich finde, sie singt wirklich gut auf ihrer letzten CD. Waren die Karten teuer? Letzte Woche habe ich Karten für "Tokio Hotel" gekauft – das ist eine deutsche Band, aber die Jungs singen auch auf Englisch. Und sie singen toll. Du kannst Lieder von ihrer Website billig herunterladen.

Ich schreibe dir bald wieder.

Viele Grüße von Klara

Tip:
Read the letter and pick the main points. Say these in English – you don't have to translate everything.

TEST PRACTICE

12 **INTERPRETING** **You and your American friend have been to dinner with your grandma. Practise the dialogue with two partners.**

FRIEND Could you say thank you for dinner, please?

YOU Er sagt, ...

GRANDMA Keine Ursache.

YOU She says ...

GRANDMA Darf ich ein Bild von euch machen?

YOU Do you mind if she ...

FRIEND Go ahead.

YOU ...

GRANDMA Ich kann leider nicht so gut fotografieren, aber ich werde dir das Bild schicken.

YOU ...

13 **Partner A: Look at the information about Beyoncé's concert. Answer your partner's questions. Then ask Partner B about Gwen Stefani's concert.**

Partner B: Ask Partner A about Beyoncé's concert. Then look at the information about Gwen Stefani's concert and answer your partner's questions.

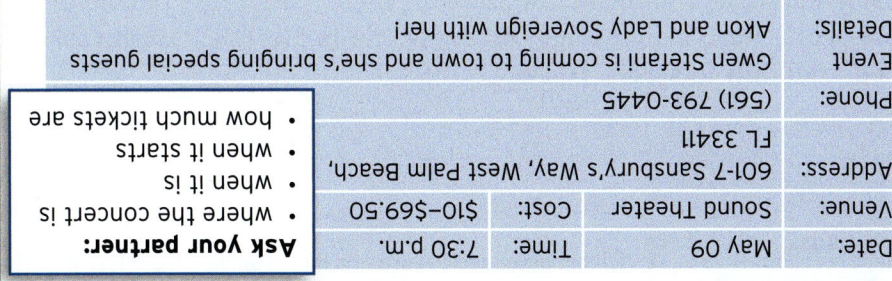

A Beyoncé

Date:	May 22	Time:	8:00 p.m.
Venue:	Bank Center	Cost:	$69
Address:	One Panther Parkway, Fort Lauderdale, FL 33323		
Phone:	(954) 835-8000		
Event Details:	Beyoncé, with opening act Robin Thicke, will be live in concert at the Bank Center		

Ask your partner:
- where the concert is
- when it is
- when it starts
- how much tickets are

B Gwen Stefani

Date:	May 09	Time:	7:30 p.m.
Venue:	Sound Theater	Cost:	$10–$69.50
Address:	601-7 Sansbury's Way, West Palm Beach, FL 33411		
Phone:	(561) 793-0445		
Event Details:	Gwen Stefani is coming to town and she's bringing special guests Akon and Lady Sovereign with her!		

Ask your partner:
- where the concert is
- when it is
- when it starts
- how much tickets are

14 **Write a letter to Ramon (about 100 words). Tell him about:**

- **what kind of music you like and your favourite singers and bands**
- **how often you listen to music and how:** MP3 player / Internet / CDs or music TV / ...
- **what you think of downloading free music on the Internet:** great / not fair to musicians / ...
- **if you watch music awards and talent contests and what you think of them:** OK / boring / ...

Tip:
Use phrases like
I believe, I think ...

REVISION Simple present / Simple past → Summary, pp. 132, 133

1 On the Oregon coast: Pick the right form – simple present or simple past.

Every summer lots of tourists (go/went) to the Oregon coast. It ('s/was) beautiful. There (are/were) beaches, rocks and forests. Last August Laura's family (take/took) Martin there for a weekend. The first day (is/was) sunny, so they (spend/spent) lots of time on the beach. But on Saturday morning the weather (changes/changed). "The weather often (changes/changed) suddenly here," the receptionist at the Sunset Motel (tells/told) them. "I (have/had) an idea," Laura (says/said). "I (want/wanted) to show Martin the Oregon dunes." "Where are they?" Martin (asks/asked). "You'll see," Laura (answers/answered).

REVISION Simple past / Past progressive → Summary, p. 133

2 Fun in the dunes

a) Put the verbs in the simple past.

The Russells (**leave**) the motel at 2 o'clock on Saturday afternoon. While they were driving along Highway 101, Laura (**see**) a sign: SPINREEL DUNES. They (**turn**) left. They were going along a small road when Martin (**shout**), "Wow!" The dunes (**look**) fantastic – they're more than 100 metres high! While they were walking in the dunes, they (**hear**) a noise. It was getting nearer when suddenly they (**see**) it. "It's a dune buggy," Dylan (**say**).

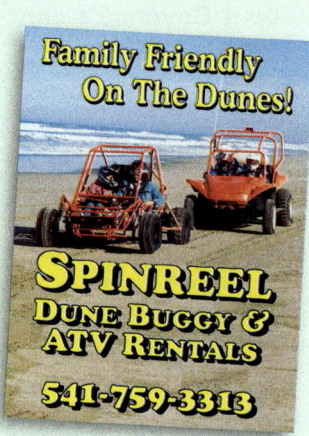

b) Now put these verbs in the past progressive.

It was a very big dune buggy and it (**go**) very fast. Six people (**sit**) in it and they (**have**) a great time. They (**shout**) and (**laugh**). While Martin (**take**) a photo, the Russels ran out of the dunes quickly. "Those people (**ride**) a dune buggy on the beach! Is that OK?" Martin asked. "Yes," Laura answered. "But only in special places."

3 Martin's e-mail
Martin is writing an e-mail to his family. He's telling Laura what's in the e-mail. Pick the main points and explain them in English.

> I'm writing that I'm on the Oregon coast with you and …
> It's fantastic …
> We're staying …
> From my room …

> Hallo zu Hause,
>
> ich bin gerade mit Laura und ihrer Familie an der Küste in Oregon. Es ist toll hier. Wir übernachten in einem kleinen Hotel. Von meinem Zimmer kann ich das Meer sehen. Und am Strand gibt es riesige Dünen! Als wir durch die Dünen liefen, haben wir "dune buggies" gesehen. Das sind so kleine Wagen, die durch die Dünen fahren. Die fuhren vielleicht schnell! Heute ist mein letzter Tag.

REVISION *Mustn't* → Summary, p. 135

4 Beach rules

a) Look at the sign. Find six things that you mustn't do:

You mustn't make …
You mustn't bring …
You mustn't use …
You mustn't …

b) SAY IT IN GERMAN
Pick three rules on the sign. Tell a partner what they mean.

Tip: Use a dictionary.

WELCOME
Have fun and enjoy your beaches.

No fires or fireworks on the beach.
Dogs not permitted on the beach.
Ball playing in designated areas only.
No dressing or undressing on the beach.
No tents, camping or sleeping.
Place all trash in trash cans.
No alcoholic beverages.
No drums or percussion instruments.
No playing of audio or electronic devices
before 8 a.m. or after 10 p.m.
No driving on the beach.

Passive → Summary, p. 138

5 Native American history
Put in *is, are, was, were*.

When Europeans first came to America, other people were living there. In the past they … called *Indians* by the Europeans. Today these people … called *Native Americans*. But sometimes the name *Indians* … used today too. In the 1860s the east part of America … taken by the Europeans. The Native Americans … sent west. Then more Europeans came to America. So more land … needed. In the end, reservations … established. The Native Americans … sent to these reservations.

Indian land 1492

Indian land 1890

6 A famous Native American
Put in *was/were* and these verbs:

 killed (2x) • born • shown • called (2x) • changed

In 1829 a baby … in Arizona. He … Goyathlay. He was Native American. As a boy, he … how to hunt, ride horses and swim. One day, when Goyathlay was away, white people came to his village and his family … . On that day, Goyathlay's life … . Later people gave him a new name – now he … *Geronimo*. He was angry with the white people because they took Native American land. So the Indian Wars started and many people … . Geronimo became very famous.

If-clauses (type II) → Summary, p. 138

7 **City dreams: Laura Russell lives in the country.**
But she often dreams of living in the city. Finish her dreams.

1 If I could live anywhere, I'd live in the city.
2 If I lived in the city, I'd go ...
3 But if I went out with friends every evening, I ...
4 And if I was tired, ...
5 If I wasn't good at school, ...
6 If I didn't get a good job, ...
7 If I didn't make enough money, ...
8 If I didn't go out often, life in the city ...
9 If life in the city wasn't interesting, I'd prefer ...
   So I think I'll stay in the country!!!

8 **Country dreams: Martin Maier dreams of living in the country – in America.**
Look at the pictures and write about some of his dreams.

MARTIN: If I lived
in America, I'd ... /
I wouldn't ...

9 **Your dreams: Pick a) or b) and write a paragraph.**
a) Imagine that you could live where you wanted.

Where would you live? Would you live in a city or in the country?
What would you do there? What kind of a house or flat would
you live in? What hobbies would you have?

b) Imagine that you won a million euros.

What would you do with the money? What would you buy?
Who would you give money to? Where would you live?
What countries would you visit? Would you help people? Who?

TEST PRACTICE

10 **Instructions in English**
Your neighbour has bought a new photocopier and a laptop for his office.
a) Which instructions (A/B) are for the photocopier, which are for the laptop?

A

Xpect user's guide

1 Insert the battery pack.
2 Connect the cable to the telephone line.
3 Plug in the power cord.
4 Open.
5 Turn on by pressing the power button.

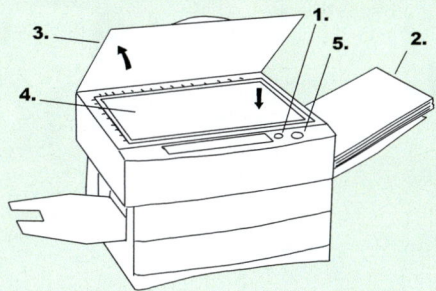

B

PIXON MT 500

Press button (**1**) to turn on.
Put paper in the auto feeder (**2**).
Lift the cover (**3**).
Put in your document (**4**).
Close the cover and press the "copy" button (**5**).

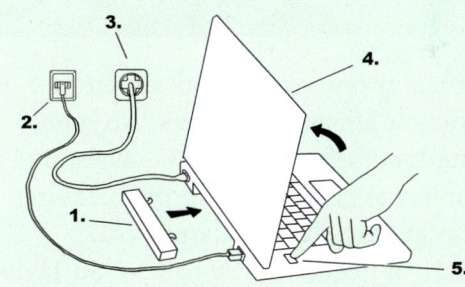

b) **SAY IT IN GERMAN** Help your neighbour and explain the instructions.

11 **SPEAKING**
a) **Talk about the picture.**
– **What can you see?**
– **What are the people doing?**

b) **AND YOU?**
– **Would you like to work here?**
– **Why?/Why not?**
– **Where would you like to work?**

12 **WRITING Life in Germany**

Your American penfriend wants to know all about your life in Germany. Write a letter (about 100 words) and tell him/her: where you live; what it's like there; the food you like; about your flat/house; your hobbies; your family; your school and if Germany is different from the USA.

Tip:
Don't forget
- your address,
- the date,
- how you start a letter,
- how you finish a letter.
Look at page 77 for help.

EXTRA READING

ISN'T TECHNOLOGY AWESOME?

2◉26

> **Read the story. Then make a comic: ask your teacher for a copy of the story. Write what Taylor and Alexa say or think in the pictures.**

Taylor had two weeks of work experience in the office at Ellison and Peters. No school and homework for two weeks – awesome! But he had to get up early in the morning. And on his first day his alarm clock stopped – it needed a new battery. So Taylor got to the office late.

Alexa showed Taylor the office. She was doing work experience too and she was really nice. She explained Taylor's jobs for the morning. First he had to make some copies and put them in the right files. It sounded very easy. "Yeah, no problem," Taylor said. Alexa smiled.

The photocopier in the office was bigger than the photocopier at school. Taylor tried different buttons for ten minutes: nothing happened. He read the instructions in the book near the photocopier and found the problem. But then the photocopier made 20 copies and Taylor only wanted one! "Dumb machine," he said.

Then Taylor had to find some information on the Internet. He loved the Internet. It was so easy to find information! Taylor found the website that he needed. But before he could print out the pages, the dumb computer crashed. "No problem," Taylor said to Alexa. He restarted the computer and found the information. The computer crashed again.

▶ You can find new words in the *Dictionary* (pages 160–179).

At lunch Taylor ate his sandwiches alone. The others read e-mails or played computer games. Nobody talked. After lunch Taylor went to the drinks machine to
35 get a hot chocolate. But there was a big sign: "Out of order". "Why do these dumb machines never work?" thought Taylor. He got a glass of water from the kitchen.

In the afternoon Taylor had to scan in some pictures. Easy! His parents had a scanner at 40 home, so he knew how to scan in things. But this machine used different software and Taylor didn't understand it. He looked at it for a long time and then saw Alexa. "Er, Alexa," he said. "I have a problem. Can you 45 help me?"

After his first day, Taylor wasn't very happy. Alexa felt sorry for him. She asked if he wanted to meet her later. Of course Taylor
50 wanted to see her! He really liked Alexa and he wanted to know her better. He felt happier now. Alexa put his number in her cellphone. "I'll send you a text message when I've been shopping," she said.
55 "I need about an hour."

Taylor went to an Internet cafe and waited for Alexa's text message. He read the sports news and wrote an e-mail. After an hour he looked at his cellphone. It wasn't charged up! And he didn't have Alexa's number ... 60 Another phone beeped. "A text from my daughter in England," a man at the next computer said to him. He smiled. "Isn't technology awesome?"

THE ROAD TO FREEDOM

The true story of Harriet Tubman

Harriet sat on the floor with a baby in her arms. The house was quiet. Her mother and brothers were working in the tobacco fields. Her father was working in the forest. And Harriet was looking after this little white baby.

The year was 1827 and the place was Maryland, on the east coast of America. It was a nice spring day – a day for running and playing in the fields. But Harriet was a black girl and a slave. She was the daughter of slaves and the granddaughter of slaves. A hundred years earlier, white people had taken her great-grandmother from her home in Africa. They had brought her to America and had sold her to a tobacco farmer. Harriet and her family "belonged" to a white farmer, Mr Brodess. They called him "Master". So Harriet never played in the fields. She was only a child – 8 years old – but she had to work.

White farmers could buy and sell slaves.

People said that things were different in the northern states like Pennsylvania, New York and New Jersey. Some people said that there were no slaves there. They said that black people were free. They said that black children didn't have to work. All children went to school.

Harriet lived in a small cabin.

But Harriet didn't go to school. Her days were always the same. She got up before the sun. She had to make fires in the big house. She swept the floors. Then she helped in the kitchen. And sometimes she looked after Mr and Mrs Brodess's baby. She worked for 14 hours every day. At night she went back to the cabin where her family lived.

READING LOG 1 Write notes when you're reading the story.

Tip:
Write what happens on each page.
Write the most important things.
You can use the *simple present*.

Page 122: Harriet lives in a cabin with ...
　　　　　She works in ...
　　　　　She gets up ...
　　　　　She makes ... / helps ... / looks after ...
Page 123: One day Harriet takes ...
　　　　　Mrs Brodess ...
　　　　　...

Page 124: Harriet leaves ...
　　　　　She walks ...
　　　　　...
Page 125: Harriet finds ...
　　　　　She remembers ...
　　　　　...

▶ You can find new words in the *Dictionary* (pages 160–179).

Harriet was often hungry. She saw the nice food that the Brodess family ate, but she couldn't eat it. One day she

30 took some sugar. But Mrs Brodess saw her and was angry. She hit Harriet. Harriet lost her job in the big house. So she had to work in the fields. And that was very hard work. In the summer it

35 was hot. In the winter it was cold and it often rained. But Harriet didn't complain – she was always a happy girl. She sang in the fields every day and the other workers liked listening to

40 her. She made them feel happy too.

Slaves had to work hard in the fields.

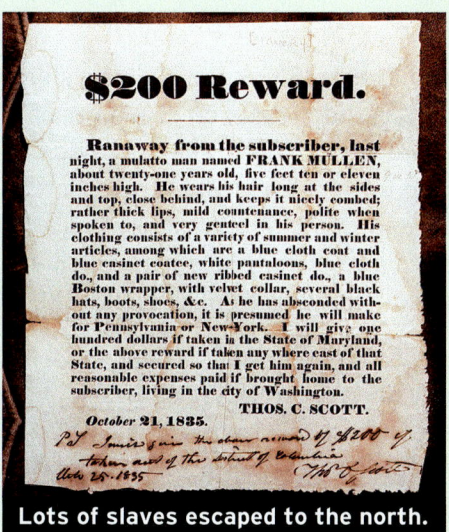

$200 Reward.

Ranaway from the subscriber, last night, a mulatto man named FRANK MULLEN, about twenty-one years old, five feet ten or eleven inches high. He wears his hair long at the sides and top, close behind, and keeps it nicely combed; rather thick lips, mild countenance, polite when spoken to, and very genteel in his person. His clothing consists of a variety of summer and winter articles, among which are a blue cloth coat and blue casinet coatee, white pantaloons, blue cloth do., and a pair of new ribbed casinet do., a blue Boston wrapper, with velvet collar, several black hats, boots, shoes, &c. As he has absconded without any provocation, it is presumed he will make for Pennsylvania or New-York. I will give one hundred dollars if taken in the State of Maryland, or the above reward if taken any where east of that State, and secured so that I get him again, and all reasonable expenses paid if brought home to the subscriber, living in the city of Washington.

THOS. C. SCOTT.

October 21, 1835.

Lots of slaves escaped to the north.

News came to the farm that the slaves in other states in the north of America were free now. But it was different in Maryland and in the states in the south. Slaves were important there on the tobacco and cotton farms. Harriet heard that slaves were escaping 45 to the north. She heard that in some places they were fighting against their masters. Harriet listened to these stories and she dreamed of a better future.

Years passed. Harriet worked in the fields every day. She became very strong and fit. But she didn't want 50 to be a slave. She dreamed of escaping to the north and living as a free woman. But how? She "belonged" to the master. He had lots of men who watched the slaves. He had dogs too!

One day a little boy came to Harriet in the fields. He was crying. He had some bad news. 55 The Brodess family planned to sell their slaves to a cotton farm in the south. Harriet knew that she had to do something.

READING LOG 2 Say what you think about:

HARRIET	– I think she's …
MR AND MRS BRODESS	– I think they're …
BRODESS'S HOUSE	– I think …
HARRIET'S CABIN	– …
THE STORY OF HARRIET'S	
GREAT-GRANDMOTHER	– …
HARRIET'S LIFE AS A SLAVE	– …

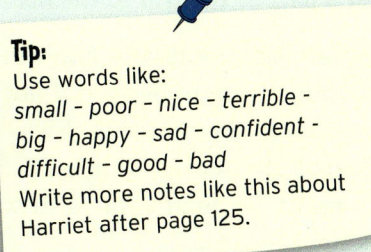

Tip:
Use words like:
small - poor - nice - terrible - big - happy - sad - confident - difficult - good - bad
Write more notes like this about Harriet after page 125.

2 ● 29

That night Harriet got a bag and some
food. She waited till everybody was in
60 bed. Then she left her parents' cabin
quietly. She didn't say goodbye to her
mother and father because she knew
that they would be too sad. But she
knew that she'd come back for them
65 one day.

Work on the cotton farms was very hard.

Harriet waited, watched and listened.
The farm was quiet. Then she walked
across the fields. She went into the
forest. She followed the North Star. She was excited because she was on the *Road to*
70 *Freedom*. But she was frightened too. She knew that if the Master's men found her, they'd
beat her. So she was very careful. Before the morning she stopped near a small river and
slept for two or three hours.

Harriet's *Road to Freedom*

In the morning she looked at the trees. She knew that the side
with moss was the north side. She didn't walk on roads because
that was dangerous. On the third day, at night, she heard dogs. 75
The Master's men were looking for her. Then she remembered
something that her father had told her. If you go across a river,
dogs can't find you. She came to a big river and she jumped
into the cold, black water. She waited behind some rocks. She
could see the men and their dogs, but they couldn't see her. 80

For six days and nights Harriet walked across the country.
When she saw a farm or a town, she went around them.
Sometimes she heard men on horses, so she stayed in the
forest. At last she came to the city of Philadelphia in
Pennsylvania. This was a state with no slaves. Harriet was now 85
a free woman.

READING LOG 3 Harriet's diary

**Imagine you're Harriet. Pick one day and write
your diary for a part of the trip to the north.**

DAY 1 It was very late. Mom and pop were in bed.
My brothers were in bed too. I got my bag and ...

DAY 2 It was early in the morning. I was tired.
I looked at the trees. The moss ...

DAY 3 It was night. I was in a forest. It was quiet.
Suddenly I heard ...

DAY 6 At last I was in ...

Tip:
Say how you felt. Use words like:
frightened – happy – sad – terrible –
nervous – cold – hungry – lonely –
tired – excited – safe.
Use your own ideas for the diary:
– I saw some slaves in a field. They ...
– The weather was ...
– I found some apples and I ...
– The city was ...

2●30

Harriet found a job and an apartment in
Philadelphia. Now she got $2 per week for
her work. This was new for her. It was
90 exciting too. But she didn't forget the people
at home in Maryland. She wanted to help
them to escape too, so she started to make
plans. After a year in Philadelphia she had
some money and lots of friends. So she
95 went back to Maryland and started to help
other slaves to escape – on the *Road to
Freedom*. She guided them through the

She helped other slaves to escape.

fields and forests at night. She knew that this was dangerous for her. But Harriet was very
brave. She helped hundreds of black men, women and children – her own family too.
100 There were posters with her picture everywhere: "$10,000 reward for Harriet Tubman!"
Harriet was famous.

In 1861 a terrible war started between the states of the north and
the states of the south.
When the war was over, all slaves were free.

105

Now things were better for black people.
But there were lots of other problems.
Black people were very poor. Many didn't
have good jobs or houses. Many were
110 hungry. Harriet Tubman helped these poor
black people. She got money from the
government. She built hospitals, schools
and homes. She helped people all her life.

READING LOG 4 **Pick one of these activities:**
You can use ideas from reading log 1.

- **Write a short summary of Harriet's story.**
  This story is about a girl. She lives in Maryland in ...
  Her family ... . She works ...

- **Write a review of the story.**
  I think that this is a good/interesting/sad/ ... story
  because ... . I like it when ... . I don't like it when ...

- **Design a cover for a book about Harriet Tubman.**
  Think of a title. Find some photos on the Internet.
  Write a short text for the back of the book.

- **Imagine you can do an interview with Harriet for an American newspaper.**
  What questions would you ask? What do you think she'd answer?

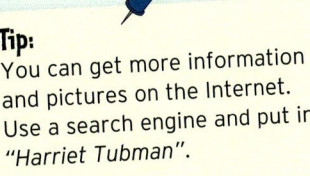
Tip:
You can get more information
and pictures on the Internet.
Use a search engine and put in
"Harriet Tubman".

WORDBANKS

Wordbank 1

Unit 1

Meat and fish

beef, chicken, ham, salmon, sausage

pork   lamb   squid   bacon   tuna

Fruit

apples, bananas, oranges

plums   strawberries   pears   cherries   melon

Vegetables

leeks, lettuce, potatoes, tomatoes

cauliflower   beans   pepper   mushrooms   broccoli

Other food

bread/roll, cheese, chips, eggs, hamburger, pizza

rice   pasta   soup   stew   biscuits

Wordbank 2 Unit 2

Photo A
surfers, walk along the beach, carry surfboards, wear wetsuits, blue sky, sunny

Photo B
stalls, bags, T-shirts, buy clothes, sit on a chair, look at the stall, nice weather

Photo C
drive on the highway, lots of cars and buses, traffic jam, road signs, busy, hot

Photo D
walk along the street, busy, carry shopping bags, wear sunglasses, no cars

Photo E
ride a bike, go in-line skating, mountains, blue sky, sunny weather, palm trees along the boardwalk

Photo F
famous Hollywood sign, cars, drive along street, trees, mountain, nice day

Photo G
ask for money, hold a sign and a cup, long grey beard, blanket round his shoulders, look cold

Photo H
city with skyscrapers, grey sky, lots of trees, smog, pollution

Photo I
lots of people, busy, nice day, blue sky, castle, bridge, flags

beard *Bart*; blanket round his shoulders *Decke um die Schultern*; carry *tragen*; grey *grau*; highway (AE) *Fernstraße*; palm tree *Palme*; pollution *Umweltverschmutzung*; sunglasses *Sonnenbrille*; sky *Himmel*; skyscraper *Wolkenkratzer, Hochhaus*; tree *Baum*; traffic jam *(Verkehrs-)Stau*; wetsuit *Surf-/Tauch(schutz)anzug*

Wordbank 3 Unit 2

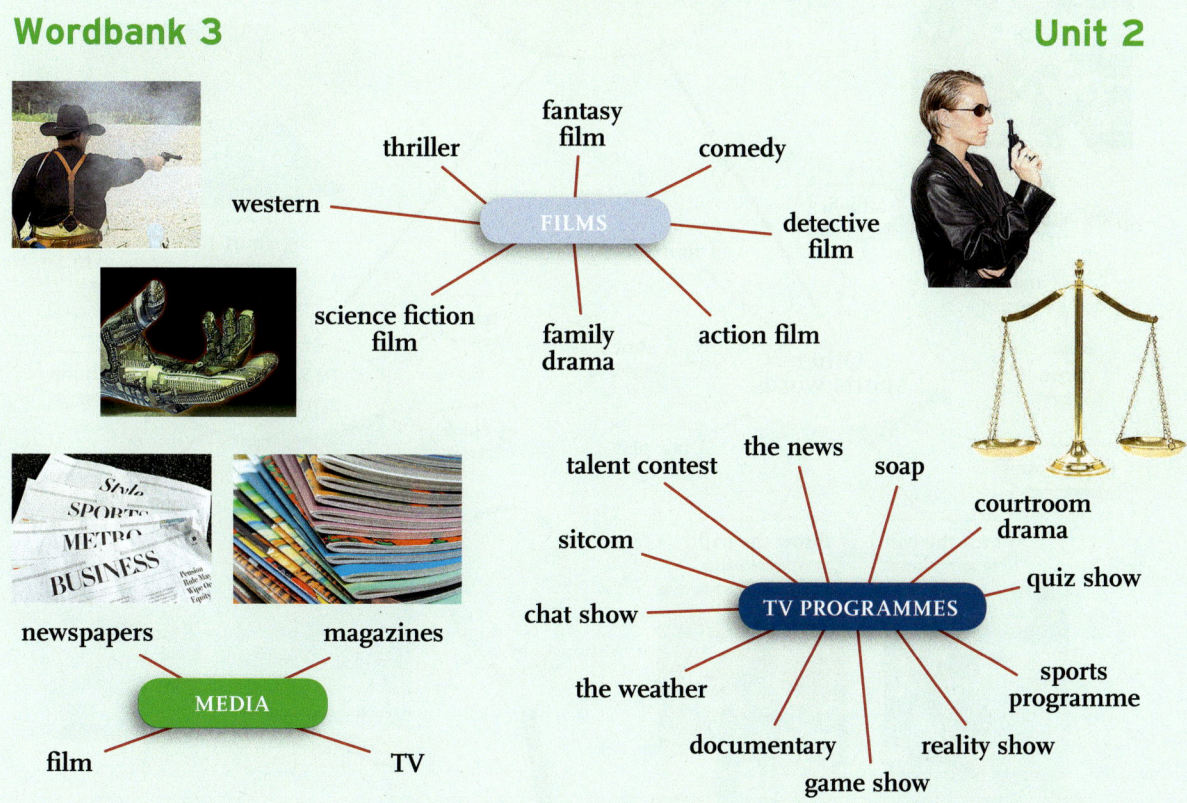

FILMS — western, thriller, fantasy film, comedy, detective film, science fiction film, family drama, action film

newspapers, magazines

MEDIA — film, TV

TV PROGRAMMES — talent contest, the news, soap, courtroom drama, quiz show, sitcom, chat show, sports programme, the weather, reality show, documentary, game show

family drama *Familienfilm*; soap *Seifenoper, Unterhaltungsserie*; courtroom drama *Gerichtsshow, -sendung*; documentary *Dokumentarfilm*; sitcom „*Situationskomödie", Comedy-Serie*; talent contest *Talentwettbewerb*

Sports gear
- jogging trousers
- shorts
- glove
- T-shirt
- trainers
- helmet
- boots

People in sport
- referee
- cheerleader
- player
- trainer
- team
- captain
- goalkeeper

SPORT

Other sports words
- athletics
- foul
- match
- shot
- game
- free throw
- kick the ball
- throw the ball
- fair play

Places and equipment
- track
- court
- gym
- clock
- hoop
- racket
- swimming pool
- net

Wordbank 5   Unit 3

School subjects

English (Englisch)
maths (Mathematik)
German (Deutsch)
history (Geschichte)
PE = physical education (Sport)

biology (Biologie)
geography (Geografie)
art (Kunst)

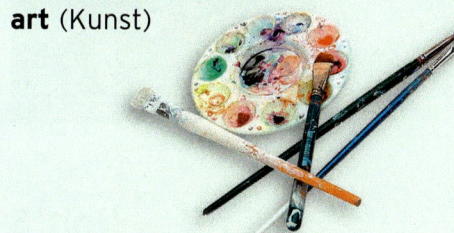

music (Musik)
science (Naturwissenschaften)
RE = religious education (Religionslehre)
social studies (Gesellschaftslehre)
textile technology (Textilgestaltung)

**ICT = information and communication
technology** (Informatik)
home economics (Hauswirtschaftslehre)
environmental studies (Umweltlehre)

Clubs and activities

school band (Schulorchester)
choir (Chor)
school garden
(Schulgarten)
school magazine
(Schülerzeitung)
school cafe
(Schülercafe)
computer club
(Computer-AG)
chess club
(Schach-AG)
drama club
(Theater-AG)
**arts and crafts
club** (Bastel-AG)

in-line skating club
(Inlineskating-AG)
volleyball club
(Volleyball-AG)
table tennis club
(Tischtennis-AG)
judo club
(Judo-AG)

Special classes and activities

homework club (Hausaufgabenbetreuung)
extra classes (Förderunterricht)
school council (Schülermitverwaltung)
peer mediation (Streitschlichtung)

Wordbank 6   Unit 4

Part-time job?

babysitter, cashier, cleaner, courier
assistant (Assistent/-in)
builder's helper (Baugehilfe/-gehilfin)
kitchen help (Küchenhilfe)
porter (Gepäckträger/in)
shop assistant (Verkäufer/in)
waiter/waitress (Kellner/in)

Where?

cafe, garden, hotel, hospital, office,
restaurant, shop, supermarket
building site (Baustelle)
garage (Autowerkstatt)
petrol station (Tankstelle)
retirement home
(Seniorenheim)

Do what?

clear tables (Tische abräumen)
deliver newspapers (Zeitungen austragen)
hand out flyers (Handzettel verteilen)
make beds (Betten machen)
mow lawns (Rasen mähen)
run errands
(Besorgungen machen)
serve food and drinks
(Essen und Getränke servieren)
stack shelves (Regale auffüllen)
walk dogs (Hunde ausführen)

Wordbank 7   Unit 5

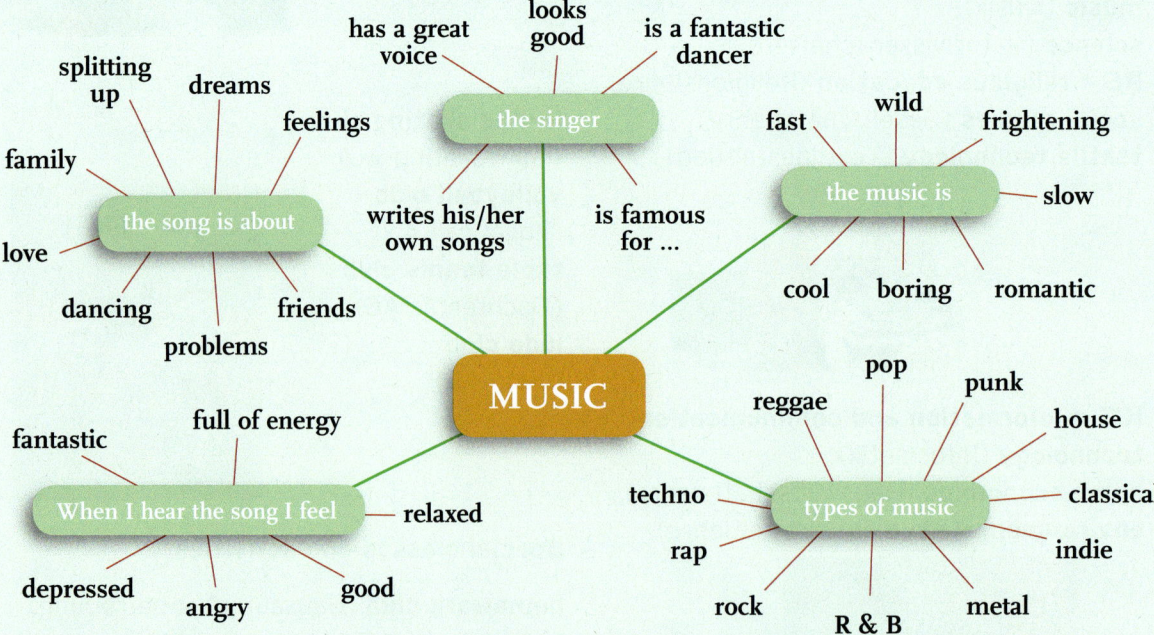

splitting up *Trennung*; feelings *Gefühle*; frightening *beängstigend, Furcht erregend*; slow *langsam*;
full of energy *energiegeladen*; relaxed *entspannt*; depressed *deprimiert*; types of music *Musikrichtungen*;
classical *klassisch*

Wordbank 8

Musical instruments

Unit 5

accordion   bass guitar   clarinet   drums   electric guitar

keyboard   piano   recorder   saxophone   trumpet

Wordbank 9

Unit 6

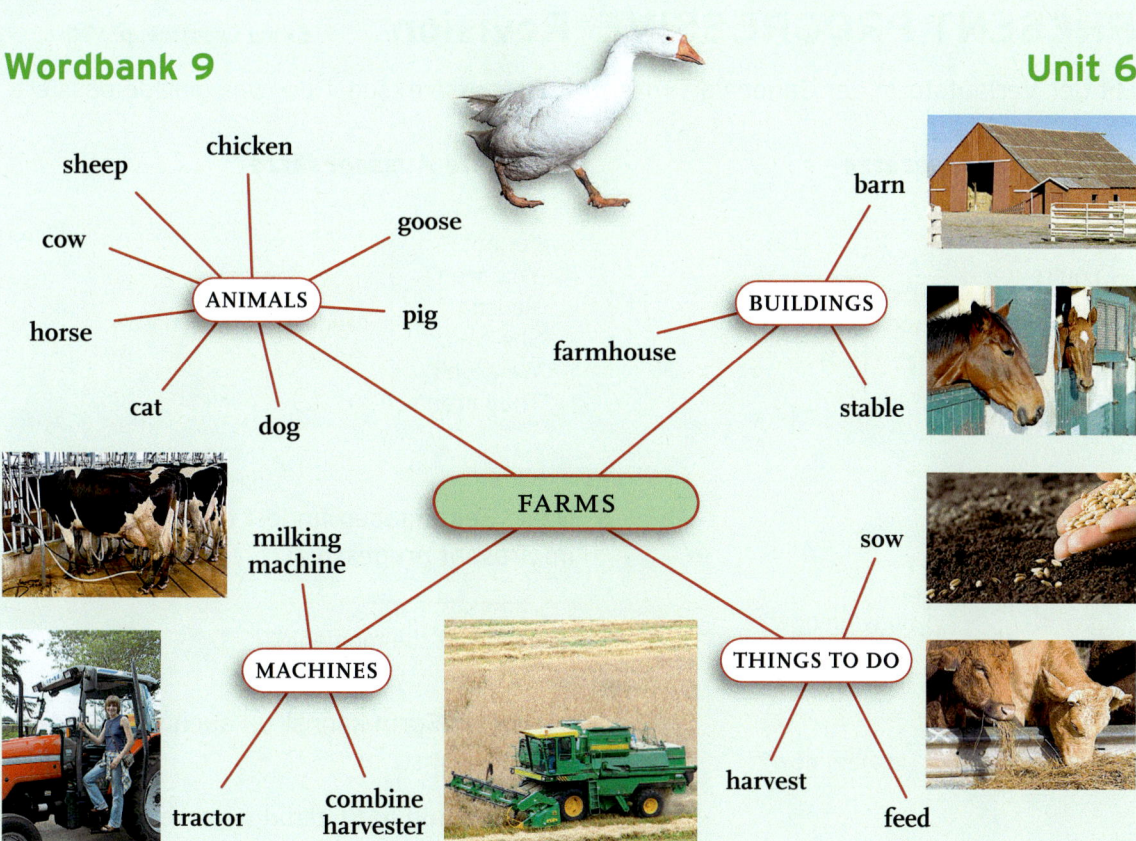

ANIMALS: sheep, chicken, cow, goose, horse, pig, cat, dog

BUILDINGS: barn, farmhouse, stable

MACHINES: milking machine, tractor, combine harvester

THINGS TO DO: sow, harvest, feed

FARMS

SIMPLE PRESENT Revision → Extra Practice, pp. 97, 116

Mit der einfachen Gegenwart (*simple present*) sagst du, was jemand immer wieder oder regelmäßig tut.

Bejahte Aussagesätze	*Verneinte Aussagesätze*	*Fragen*

I We You	play.

I We You	don't	play.

Do	I we you	play?

He She	plays.

He She	doesn't	play.

Does	he she	play?

❗ Diese Zeitangaben findest du oft in Sätzen im *simple present*:

> every day • every Monday • every week •
> every month • every year • on Mondays •
> always • usually • often • sometimes • never

PRESENT PROGRESSIVE Revision → Extra Practice, p. 100

Mit der Verlaufsform der Gegenwart (*present progressive*) sagst du, was gerade passiert.

Bejahte Aussagesätze	*Verneinte Aussagesätze*

I'm You're He's She's We're They're	reading	English now.

I'm not You aren't He isn't She isn't We aren't They aren't	reading	French now.

Fragen	

Is	he she	leaving now?

Are	we you they	leaving now?

❗ Diese Zeitangaben findest du oft in Sätzen im *present progessive*:

> now • at the moment

Mit dieser Form kannst du auch sagen, was du planst:

I'm travelling to England next week.

SIMPLE PAST Revision → Extra Practice, pp. 108, 116

Mit der einfachen Vergangenheit (*simple past*) sagst du, was in der Vergangenheit geschah.

Bejahte Aussagesätze	*Verneinte Aussagesätze*	*Fragen*

I You He She We They	went to school yesterday.

I You He She We They	didn't go to school yesterday.

Did	I you he she we they	go to school yesterday?

! Regelmäßige Verben haben die Endung -*ed*:

answer**ed**	jump**ed**
arriv**ed**	miss**ed**
danc**ed**	need**ed**
finish**ed**	organiz**ed**
happen**ed**	visit**ed**
invit**ed**	work**ed**

! Unregelmäßige Verben haben besondere Vergangenheitsformen:

bring – brought
do – did
drink – drank
eat – ate
forget – forgot
put – put

! Diese Zeitangaben findest du oft in Sätzen im *simple past*:

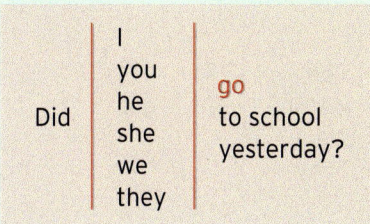

last year/month/week/Friday
in July/2007
on February 14th
at 3 o'clock

PAST PROGRESSIVE → Extra Practice, pp. 101–102, 116

Mit der Verlaufsform der Vergangenheit (*past progressive*) sagst du, was in der Vergangenheit gerade im Gange war.

Bejahte Aussagesätze	*Verneinte Aussagesätze*	*Fragen*

I He She	was	reading.

I He She	wasn't	reading.

Was	I he she	reading?

You We they	were	reading.

You We they	weren't	reading.

Were	you we they	reading?

! Ein stummes e am Ende des Verbs fällt bei der *ing*-Form weg:
arriv**e** – arri**v**ing   com**e** – co**m**ing

 ! Bei manchen Verben wird der letzte Buchstabe verdoppelt:
sto**p** – sto**pp**ing   ru**n** – ru**nn**ing

WILL-FUTURE Revision → **Extra Practice, p. 112**

Wenn du voraussagen willst, was in der Zukunft geschehen wird, benutzt du *will* oder die Kurzform *'ll*.

	Bejahte Aussagesätze			*Verneinte Aussagesätze*			*Fragen*		

I You He/She We They	'll	go.

I You He/She We They	won't	go.

Will	I you he/she we they	go?

ING-FORM → **Extra Practice, pp. 109–110**

Mit der *ing*-Form kannst du über Tätigkeiten und Hobbys sprechen.

Die *ing*-Form kann Subjekt eines Satzes sein.

Camping is great.

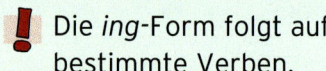 Die *ing*-Form folgt auf bestimmte Verben.

finish	prohibit
hate	start
like	stop
love	try

Die *ing*-Form wird häufig nach Ausdrücken mit Präpositionen gebraucht.

She's good at dancing.

I'm against …	It's famous for …
I'm interested in …	It's great for …
I don't have a problem with …	It's popular for …
I look forward to …	She's good at …
After …	Thanks for …
Before …	What about …?

IMPERATIVE → **Extra Practice, p. 105**

Mit der Befehlsform (*imperative*) forderst du jemanden auf, etwas zu tun oder nicht zu tun. Du benutzt die Grundform des Verbs.

In einem verneinten Befehlssatz benutzt du *don't* und die Grundform des Verbs.

Close the door, please. Come here.

Don't	worry! run!

CAN/CAN'T Revision → Extra Practice, p. 104

Mit *can/can't* sagst du, was jemand (nicht) tun kann oder darf.

I You He/She We They	can can't	play football.

Can I use your mobile?

HAVE TO/DON'T HAVE TO Revision → Extra Practice, pp. 104–105

Mit *have to* sagst du, was jemand tun muss.
Mit *don't have to* sagst du, was jemand nicht zu tun braucht.

I You We They	have to don't have to	be quiet.

He She	has to doesn't have to	be quiet.

SHOULD/SHOULDN'T → Extra Practice, p. 106

Mit *should/shouldn't* rätst du jemandem, etwas zu tun oder nicht zu tun.

I You He/She We They	should shouldn't	help him.

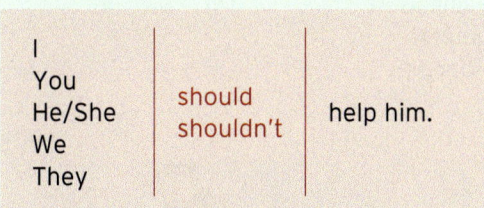

MUST/MUSTN'T → Extra Practice, pp. 106–107, 117

Mit *must* sagst du,
was jemand tun muss.

I You He/She We They	must	go home.

Mit *mustn't* verbietest du jemandem,
etwas zu tun.

I You He/She We They	mustn't	go into the water.

 you don't have to = du musst nicht

 you mustn't = du darfst nicht

SUMMARY

ADJECTIVES Revision → Extra Practice, pp. 108–109

Adjektive (*adjectives*) geben Informationen über eine Person oder eine Sache.

Adjektive können nach dem Verb *be* stehen.

The weather was terrible.

Adjektive stehen oft vor einem Nomen.

Our new neighbour has a big dog.

Wenn mehr als ein Adjektiv vor einem Nomen steht, kannst du ein Komma verwenden.

Mum bought a big, old house.

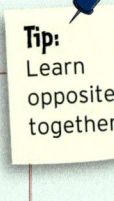

big – small
nice – terrible
clean – dirty
English – German
white – black
cheap – expensive
early – late
narrow – wide

Tip: Learn opposites together.

COMPARISONS Revision → Extra Practice, pp. 98–99

Personen, Dinge, Tiere oder Orte kann man miteinander vergleichen.

Bei einsilbigen und den meisten zweisilbigen Adjektiven auf -*y* hängst du -*er*, bzw. -*est* an das Adjektiv, um die Vergleichsformen zu bilden.

fast – faster – fastest
cheap – cheaper – cheapest
quiet – quieter – quietest
happy – happier – happiest

 Manchmal musst du bei der Schreibweise aufpassen.

hot – hotter – hottest
busy – busier – busiest
safe – safer – safest

 Diese Formen musst du auswendig lernen:

good – better – best
bad – worse – worst

Bei dreisilbigen und manchen zweisilbigen Adjektiven setzt du *more* bzw. *most* vor das Adjektiv.

interesting – more interesting – most interesting
beautiful – more beautiful – most beautiful
expensive – more expensive – most expensive
famous – more famous – most famous

ADVERBS → Extra Practice, pp. 113–114

Adverbien (*adverbs*) benutzt du, um zu beschreiben WIE man etwas macht.
Die meisten Adverbien bildest du, indem du -*ly* an das Adjektiv anhängst.

Adjektiv	Adverb
quick	quickly
careful	carefully
safe	safely

! Bei Adjektiven, die auf -y enden, musst du bei der Schreibweise aufpassen.

easy	easily
angry	angrily

! Diese Formen musst du auswendig lernen:

good	well
hard	hard
fast	fast

PREPOSITIONS OF PLACE Revision → Extra Practice, p. 113

Räumliche Präpositionen (*prepositions of place*) sagen dir, wo etwas ist oder in welche Richtung sich etwas bewegt.

on the chair

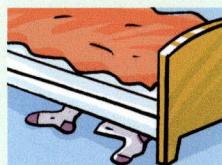
under the bed

in the cupboard

next to the bag

behind the door

between the table and the bed

at the top of the window

above the computer

opposite the chair

in front of the computer

through the door

out of the window

into the bed

down the TV

past the window

WHO / THAT → Extra Practice, pp. 100–101

Mit den Relativpronomen *who* und *that* kannst du zusätzliche Informationen über eine Person oder eine Sache geben.

Who verwendest du nur nach Personen.

Brad Pitt is an actor who comes from Santa Monica.
They are the boys who live in Manhattan.

Ansonsten benutzt du *that*.

Surfing is a sport that is very popular in Los Angeles.
This is a day that you'll remember.

*IF-CLAUSES (Type II) → Extra Practice, p. 118

Mit *if*-Sätzen (Typ II) sagst du, was unter bestimmten Bedingungen geschehen würde. Es ist aber ziemlich unwahrscheinlich, dass die Bedingungen erfüllt werden.

If-Sätze bestehen aus zwei Teilen:

– einem Nebensatz (mit *if*) im *simple past*	– einem Hauptsatz mit *would* oder der Kurzform *'d* und einem Infinitiv
If I lived in the USA,	I'd speak lots of English.
If I went to New York,	I'd visit Chinatown.

Der if-Satz kann auch hinter dem Hauptsatz stehen:

I'd go to the USA if I had the money.

*PASSIVE → Extra Practice, p. 117

Mit dem Passiv *(passive)* sagst du, dass etwas mit einem Gegenstand oder einer Person gemacht wird oder wurde. Wichtig ist, **was** passiert ist, nicht wer es gemacht hat.

Das Passiv wird mit einer Form von *be* und dem Partizip Perfekt des Verbs gebildet.

These cars are made in Germany.
Our house was built in 2007.

Das Partizip Perfekt von regelmäßigen Verben endet auf *-ed:*
finish – finished
start – started
play – played
answer – answered

 Das Partizip Perfekt von unregelmäßigen Verben musst du auswendig lernen. Du brauchst diese Form auch für das *present perfect* und kannst sie in der *List of irregular verbs*, (dritte Spalte) auf S. 197–198 finden.

*Nur Pflichtstoff für den EK in Nordrhein-Westfalen

NUMBERS, SOUNDS, ABC

ENGLISH NUMBERS

1	one [wʌn]		1st	first [fɜːst]
2	two [tuː]		2nd	second ['sekənd]
3	three [θriː]		3rd	third [θɜːd]
4	four [fɔː]		4th	fourth [fɔːθ]
5	five [faɪv]		5th	fifth [fɪfθ]
6	six [sɪks]		6th	sixth [sɪksθ]
7	seven ['sevn]		7th	seventh ['sevnθ]
8	eight [eɪt]		8th	eighth [eɪtθ]
9	nine [naɪn]		9th	ninth [naɪnθ]
10	ten [ten]		10th	tenth [tenθ]

11	eleven [ɪ'levn]	11th	eleventh [ɪ'levnθ]
12	twelve [twelv]	12th	twelfth [twelfθ]
13	thirteen ['θɜː'tiːn]	13th	thirteenth ['θɜː'tiːnθ]
14	fourteen ['fɔː'tiːn]	14th	fourteenth ['fɔː'tiːnθ]
15	fifteen ['fɪf'tiːn]	15th	fifteenth ['fɪf'tiːnθ]
16	sixteen ['sɪks'tiːn]	16th	sixteenth ['sɪks'tiːnθ]
17	seventeen ['sevn'tiːn]	17th	seventeenth ['sevn'tiːnθ]
18	eighteen ['eɪ'tiːn]	18th	eighteenth ['eɪ'tiːnθ]
19	nineteen ['naɪn'tiːn]	19th	nineteenth ['naɪn'tiːnθ]
20	twenty ['twenti]	20th	twentieth ['twentiəθ]

21	twenty-one ['twenti'wʌn]	21st	twenty-first ['twenti'fɜːst]
...		...	
30	thirty ['θɜːti]	30th	thirtieth ['θɜːtiəθ]
40	forty ['fɔːti]	40th	fortieth ['fɔːtiəθ]
50	fifty ['fɪfti]	50th	fiftieth ['fɪftiəθ]
60	sixty ['sɪksti]	60th	sixtieth ['sɪkstiəθ]
70	seventy ['sevnti]	70th	seventieth ['sevntiəθ]
80	eighty ['eɪti]	80th	eightieth ['eɪtiəθ]
90	ninety ['naɪnti]	90th	ninetieth ['naɪntiəθ]
100	a hundred [ə'hʌndrəd]	100th	hundredth ['hʌndrədθ]
	one hundred ['wʌn'hʌndrəd]		

101	one hundred and one [wʌnhʌndrədn'wʌn]	101st	one hundred and first [wʌnhʌndrədn'fɜːst]
...		...	
1000	a thousand [ə'θaʊznd]	1000th	thousandth ['θaʊznθ]
	one thousand ['wʌn'θaʊznd]		

THE ENGLISH ALPHABET

a	[eɪ]	n	[en]
b	[biː]	o	[əʊ]
c	[siː]	p	[piː]
d	[diː]	q	[kjuː]
e	[iː]	r	[ɑː]
f	[ef]	s	[es]
g	[dʒiː]	t	[tiː]
h	[eɪtʃ]	u	[juː]
i	[aɪ]	v	[viː]
j	[dʒeɪ]	w	['dʌbljuː]
k	[keɪ]	x	[eks]
l	[el]	y	[waɪ]
m	[em]	z	[zed]

ENGLISH SOUNDS

[iː]	eat, see, he
[ɑː]	ask, class, car
[ɔː]	or, ball, door, four
[uː]	ruler, blue, too, two, you
[ɜː]	early, her, girl, work
[ɪ]	in, big, England
[e]	yes, bed, again, breakfast
[æ]	animal, cat, black
[ʌ]	us, but, tough, colour
[ɒ]	on, dog, what, across
[ʊ]	put, good, could
[ə]	again, sister, today
[i]	radio, video, happy
[u]	July, museum, usually
[eɪ]	eight, name, play, great
[aɪ]	I, time, right, my
[ɔɪ]	boy, join, voice
[əʊ]	old, no, road, yellow
[aʊ]	our, house, now
[ɪə]	near, here, we're
[eə]	airport, share, there, their
[ʊə]	poor, you're, sure
[b]	bike, table, verb
[p]	pen, pupil, shop
[d]	day, window, good
[t]	ten, matter, at
[k]	kitchen, car, back, book
[g]	go, again, bag
[ŋ]	wrong, morning, bank
[l]	like, old, small
[r]	ruler, friend, sorry
[v]	very, seven, have
[w]	we, where, quarter
[s]	six, poster, yes
[z]	present, quiz, his, please
[ʃ]	she, station, English
[tʃ]	child, teacher, match
[dʒ]	job, German, orange
[ʒ]	usually, treasure hunt
[j]	yes, you, young
[θ]	thing, bathroom, month
[ð]	the, father, with

[iː] [ɑː] [ɔː]

Dieses Wörterverzeichnis enthält neue Wörter des Buches in der Reihenfolge, in der sie im Buch zum ersten Mal vorkommen.

In der eckigen Klammer steht, wie die Wörter ausgesprochen werden.

Ein **blauer/roter** Pfeil heißt: Schau dir den **blauen/roten** Kasten rechts an.

Der graue Pfeil heißt: Schau in die rechte Spalte.

In den **roten** Kästen stehen wichtige Hinweise.

Diese Zahl gibt die Seite an, auf der die Wörter zum ersten Mal vorkommen.

Fette Wörter sind besonders wichtig.

Schräg gestellte Wörter gehören nicht zum Pflichtwortschatz.

Das **rote** Sternchen kennzeichnet unregelmäßige Verben (vgl. unten).

download [ˌdaʊn'ləʊd]	herunterladen	
fantastic [fæn'tæstɪk]	fantastisch	
69 he sings **sadly** ['sædli]	er singt traurig →	
slow [sləʊ]	langsam	
voice [vɔɪs]	Stimme	
rhythm ['rɪðəm]	Rhythmus	
female ['fiːmeɪl]	weiblich →	

Write about **yourself.** — Schreibe über dich (selbst).

Story

70 *wake up [weɪk'ʌp]	aufwachen	
moon [muːn]	Mond	
above [ə'bʌv]	über →	
light switch ['laɪtswɪtʃ]	Lichtschalter	
mirror ['mɪrə]	Spiegel	
deaf [def]	taub	
hearing ['hɪərɪŋ]	Gehör	
they had come	sie waren gekommen	
loud [laʊd]	laut	
*shake: she shook me [ʃeɪk, ʃʊk]	schütteln: sie schüttelte mich	
I see her mouth moving	ich sehe, wie sich ihr Mund bewegt	
mouth [maʊθ]	Mund	
frightening ['fraɪtnɪŋ]	beängstigend, furchterregend →	
closet ['klɒzɪt]	(AE) Wandschrank	
sigh [saɪ]	seufzen	

The song isn't really sad, but they sing it so *sadly*.
→ Please drive *slowly*.
→ I heard two different *voices*.

→ a *female* cook/teacher/trainer/… [eine Köchin/Lehrerin/Trainerin/…]

→ My flat is *above* the shop.

(1) We *shook* the tree, so the apples fell down.
(2) She *shook her head*. [Sie schüttelte den Kopf.]

→ That's the most *frightening* story that I've ever heard!

Tim sighed because he didn't kn…

→ -ly
fight brave**ly**
smoke nervous**ly**
ask polite**ly**
smile shy**ly**

→
man
woman
male
female

Die **blauen** Kästen fassen Wörter in Gruppen zusammen. So lernst du sie besser.

→ über
above the shop
across the can…
about the stor…

→ I'm frightened.
It's frightening.

(AE) heißt, dass dieses Wort vor allem im amerikanischen Englisch verwendet wird.

Dieses Zeichen bedeutet: Aufgepasst!

the *tomatoes*.
‖ In British English *'potato'* [pə'teɪtəʊ] doesn't rhyme with 'tomato' [tə'mɑːtəʊ].

I'll have a hamburger and a cola, please.

Am Ende jeder Unit …

American English vocabulary ★ ★

AE (American English)	BE (British Englis…
grade [greɪd]	year
sneaker ['sniːkə]	trainer

… siehst du, welche Wörter im amerikanischen/britischen Englisch bevorzugt werden und wie die drei Formen der neuen unregelmäßigen Verben aus der Unit lauten.

*Irregular verbs

Infinitive form	Simple past for…
hit [hɪt]	I hit [hɪt]
leave [liːv]	I left [left]
shoot [ʃuːt]	I shot [ʃɒt]

… kannst du auch überprüfen, wie gut du die neuen Wörter schon beherrschst – und wie gut du dich an bekannte Wörter erinnerst.

Test yourself
1 Find the three missing letters and finis…
financ - - -, sal - - -, lett - - -, pri - -…

2 Find the opposites and write them in y…
true - … • quiet - … • white bread…

Do you remember?
Write two lists in your exercise book: a) Pla…
amusement arcade • block • brochure • chur…
holiday • hospital • museum • post office • …

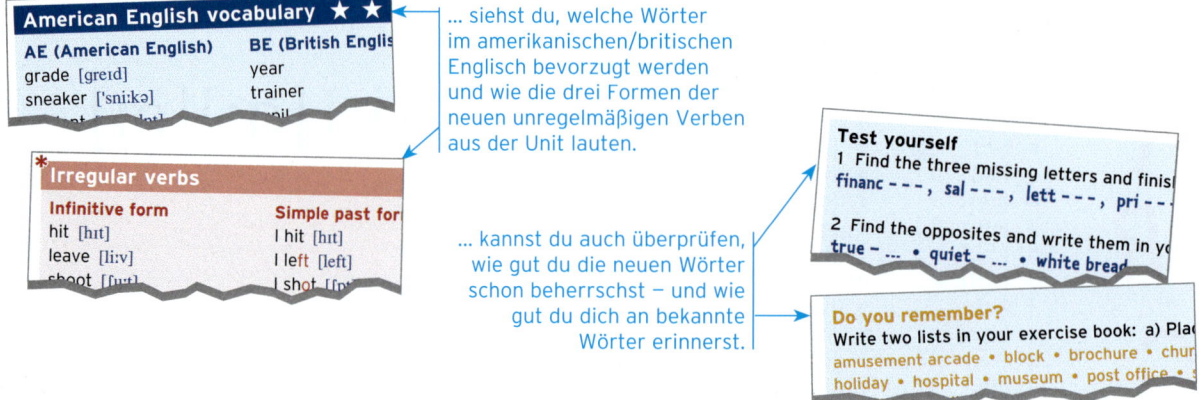

Next stop: USA

Bus Stop

6	**stop** [stɒp]	Halt; Haltestelle →
	Put up your hand.	Heb(t) die Hand.
7	**state** [steɪt]	(Bundes-)Staat, Land
	population [pɒpju'leɪʃn]	Bevölkerung(szahl)

→ Germany has a *population* of more than 80 million.

far [fɑː]	weit 
lake [leɪk]	(Binnen-)See
fact [fækt]	Tatsache

→ The park isn't *far* from here. → near – far

8 **American** [ə'merɪkən]	amerikanisch; Amerikaner/in

→ My friend Joe is *American*, so he speaks *American* English.

pronunciation [prənʌnsi'eɪʃn]	Aussprache
British ['brɪtɪʃ]	britisch; Brite/Britin
conversation [kɒnvə'seɪʃn]	Unterhaltung, Gespräch
Hi you guys. [gaɪz]	(AE) Hallo Leute.
Gimme five! [gɪmi'faɪv]	(AE) *Aufforderung dazu, die (erhobenen) Hände aneinander zu klatschen*
How ya doin'? [haʊjə'duːɪn]	(AE) Wie geht's?
Have a nice day!	(AE) (Einen) Schönen Tag noch!

→ I met lots of *British* people on holiday in Spain.

awesome ['ɔːsəm]	(AE) irre, toll
9 **apartment** [ə'pɑːtmənt]	(AE) Wohnung
store [stɔː]	(AE) Laden, Geschäft
sidewalk ['saɪdwɔːk]	(AE) Bürgersteig
cellphone ['selfəʊn]	(AE) Handy, Mobiltelefon
subway ['sʌbweɪ]	(AE) U-Bahn

→ Billy's new CD is really *awesome*!

→ The New York *subway* is as famous as the London underground.

mix the cards **up** [mɪks]	die Karten durcheinander bringen, mischen
spelling ['spelɪŋ]	Rechtschreibung 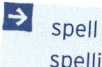

→ spell
spelling

American English vocabulary ★ ★ ★ ★ ★ ★ ★ ★ ★ ★

AE (American English)	BE (British English)	
apartment [ə'pɑːtmənt]	flat	Wohnung
cellphone ['selfəʊn]	mobile	Handy, Mobiltelefon
sidewalk ['saɪdwɔːk]	pavement	Bürgersteig
store [stɔː]	shop	Laden, Geschäft
subway ['sʌbweɪ]	underground	U-Bahn

Can I borrow your mobile, please? – My mobile? Oh, you mean my cellphone!

Unit 1

Lerntipp 1: So lernst du englische Wörter – und behältst sie!

- Fertige ein **Wortbild** an:

- Finde ein **Reimwort** und denke dir etwas dazu: *"cheese – please* = Käse, bitte!"

- Markiere **Unterschiede** zu ähnlichen deutschen Wörtern: Adresse – *address* .

- **Stelle** dir irgend etwas **vor:** *high* [haɪ] (= hoch)

10	**Little Italy** [lɪtl'ɪtəli]	„Klein-Italien"
	financial [faɪ'nænʃl]	finanziell, Finanz-
	district ['dɪstrɪkt]	Bezirk, Gebiet
	Statue of Liberty ['stætʃuːəv'lɪbəti]	Freiheitsstatue
	at the top [tɒp]	ganz oben (auf), auf der Spitze
11	**tour** [tʊə]	Führung, Rundgang
	false [fɔːls]	falsch, unwahr →
	immigrant ['ɪmɪɡrənt]	Immigrant/in, Einwanderer/Einwanderin
	neighbourhood ['neɪbəhʊd]	Viertel, Gegend
	theatre ['θɪətə]	Theater
	busy ['bɪzi]	**1** hektisch, belebt; **2** beschäftigt
	sightseeing ['saɪtsiːɪŋ]	Besichtigungen
12	**dinner** ['dɪnə]	Abendessen →
	pocket money ['pɒkɪtmʌni]	Taschengeld
	deli ['deli]	(AE) Feinkostgeschäft und -imbiss
	menu ['menjuː]	Speisekarte
	white bread ['waɪtbred]	Weißbrot
	brown bread ['braʊnbred]	Graubrot
	beef [biːf]	Rindfleisch
	smoked salmon [sməʊkt'sæmən]	Räucherlachs
	egg [eɡ]	Ei
	lettuce ['letɪs]	(Kopf-)Salat
	tomato, tomatoes [tə'mɑːtəʊ, tə'mɑːtəʊz]	Tomate, Tomaten
	potato, potatoes [pə'teɪtəʊ, pə'teɪtəʊz]	Kartoffel, Kartoffeln
	potato chips [pə'teɪtəʊtʃɪps]	(AE) Kartoffelchips
	I'll have ...	Ich nehme ...
13	**line** [laɪn]	Linie
	end [end]	Ende
	change at 42nd Street **to** line 7	an der 42. Straße in die Linie 7 umsteigen
	block [blɒk]	Häuserblock

→ Kenn is a nice *little* village. [nettes kleines Dorf]

→

→ We had a picnic *at the top* of the hill.

→ **right – wrong
true – false**

→ My mother works in a *busy* place: She's *busy* from 10 to 5 every day.

→ We did some *sightseeing* in Rome.

→ **breakfast
lunch
dinner**

→ Take your hand out of your *pocket*, please. [Tasche]

→ Let's look at the *menu* first.

→ I'm not keen on *beef*, but I like chicken.

→ We bought some *salmon* for dinner. [Lachs]
❗ Aussprache: ['sæmən]

→ I love sandwiches with *egg* salad.

→ Let's make a salad with the lettuce and the *tomatoes*.

→ ❗ In British English 'potato' [pə'teɪtəʊ] doesn't rhyme with 'tomato' [tə'mɑːtəʊ].

I'll have a hamburger and a cola, please.

→ Where do I have to *change*? – At Times Square.

Story

14	**quote** [kwəʊt]	Zitat
	America [əˈmerɪkə]	Amerika 
	skin [skɪn]	Haut
	in prison [ˈprɪzn]	im Gefängnis
	black people, white people	Schwarze, Weiße

→ Most of the *black people* in New York City live in Brooklyn.

	kill [kɪl]	töten, umbringen
	children's home	Kinderheim
	lawyer [ˈlɔːjə]	Rechtsanwalt, -anwältin
	at that time	damals
	***steal** [stiːl]	stehlen

→ Somebody *stole* my bike!

Ohne 'the'
go to church
go to hospital
go to prison
go to school
go to town

	go to prison	ins Gefängnis kommen
	education [edʒuˈkeɪʃn]	Bildung, Ausbildung
	Muslim [ˈmʊzlɪm]	Muslim, Muslimin
	change his name to ...	seinen Namen ändern in ...
	slave [sleɪv]	Sklave, Sklavin
	***fight** [faɪt]	kämpfen; sich streiten
	right [raɪt]	Recht
	freedom [ˈfriːdəm]	Freiheit
	violence [ˈvaɪələns]	Gewalt, Gewalttätigkeit
	use violence **to** change things	Gewalt anwenden, um Dinge zu verändern
	speaker [ˈspiːkə]	Redner, Rednerin
	bring about [brɪŋəˈbaʊt]	herbeiführen
	change [tʃeɪndʒ]	Veränderung
15	*Mecca* [ˈmekə]	Mekka
	***lose: I lost** [luːz, lɒst]	verlieren: ich verlor

→ My little brothers often *fight*.
→ We have the *right* to say what we think.

→ Most tourists visit New York *to* see Manhattan.

→ Here's my phone number. Don't *lose* it!

Wordpower

16	**meat** [miːt]	Fleisch
	boyfriend [ˈbɔɪfrend]	(fester) Freund
	out [aʊt]	hinaus/heraus; aus
	say/read/explain the dates **to her**	ihr die Daten sagen/vorlesen/erklären

→ I like fish and vegetables, but I don't eat *meat*.

Revision

17	**opposite** [ˈɒpəzɪt]	Gegenteil
	travel [ˈtrævl]	Reise-, Reisen

→ The *opposite* of 'cold' is 'hot'.
→ *Travel brochures* are interesting (and often free).

Skills training

18	**appointment** (card) [əˈpɔɪntmənt]	Termin(kärtchen)
	mall [mɔːl]	(AE) Einkaufszentrum
	concert [ˈkɒnsət]	Konzert
	dentist [ˈdentɪst]	Zahnarzt, Zahnärztin
	any [ˈeni]	irgendwelche
19	When **should** I ...?	Wann soll ich ...?
	movie [ˈmuːvi]	(AE) Film
21	**copy** [ˈkɒpi]	abschreiben; kopieren
	RSVP [ɑːresviːˈpiː]	u.A.w.g. (= um Antwort wird gebeten)

→ Now, do you have *any* questions?
→ *Should* I wear the red or the green T-shirt?

→ ❗ he cop**ies**; he's copying; he copied

by October 15th	bis zum 15. Oktober
message [ˈmesɪdʒ]	Mitteilung, Nachricht

→ I need an answer *by* Monday.

Look at language

22	*way of life*	Lebensweise
	I love living here.	Ich lebe sehr gern hier.
	win a lottery [ˈlɒtəri]	in einer Lotterie gewinnen
	mom [mɒm]	(AE) Mama, Mutti
	What **would** you like/miss?	Was würdest du mögen/ vermissen?

→ Pam *loves reading*, but I *love listening* to music.

→ I*'d* (I *would*) miss healthy food. Jill *wouldn't* like the bread.

American English vocabulary ★ ★ ★ ★ ★ ★ ★ ★ ★ ★

AE (American English)	BE (British English)	
mall [mɔːl]	shopping centre	Einkaufszentrum
mom [mɒm]	mum	Mama, Mutti
movie [ˈmuːvi]	film	Film
potato chips [pəˈteɪtəʊtʃɪps]	crisps	Kartoffelchips

144

*Irregular verbs

Infinitive form	Simple past form	Present perfect form
fight [faɪt]	I fought [fɔːt]	I've fought [fɔːt]
lose [luːz]	I lost [lɒst]	I've lost [lɒst]
steal [stiːl]	I stole [stəʊl]	I've stolen [ˈstəʊlən]

Test yourself

1 Find the three missing letters and finish the words in your exercise book.
financ - - -, sal - - -, lett - - -, pri - - -, viole - - -, oppos - - -, mess - - -

2 Find the opposites and write them in your exercise book.
true – ... • quiet – ... • white bread – ... • find – ...

> **Tipp:**
> Schau dir die vorangegangenen Wortlisten gut an.

3 Find and write in your exercise book:
1 a word for 'highest point'	3 an evening meal	5 a fish
2 a place where actors work	4 a list of food and drinks	6 a green vegetable

4 Make sentences with these words and write them in your exercise book.
1 I'll – some – sandwich – water, – a – beef – have – please. – and
2 Most – to – here – tourists – skiing. – come – go
3 I – Thursday. – have – by – to – article – finish – the

Do you remember?
Write two lists in your exercise book: a) Places in the city; b) Travel words.
amusement arcade • block • brochure • church • cinema • district • guide • holiday • hospital • museum • post office • sightseeing • theatre • tour • tourist • traveller • trip

Are your answers right? Check on page 198.

Unit 2

Lerntipp 2: Planvoll lernen

Um erfolgreich Vokabeln zu lernen, solltest du bestimmte Voraussetzungen schaffen. Du brauchst:

- **Ruhe**: Keine Ablenkung durch andere Menschen, laute Musik, Fernseher oder SMS.
- **Zeit**: Keinen Termindruck und keine anderen dringenden Arbeiten.
- **Pausen**: Finde deinen Rhythmus, z.B. 10 Minuten Lernen – 3 Minuten Pause usw.
- **ein Ziel**: Lege jeden Tag fest, was du schaffen willst, z.B. einen bestimmten Abschnitt, eine bestimmte Menge *irregular verbs*, Wiederholung bestimmter Wörter.
- **einen Weg**: Überlege dir, wie du am besten vorgehst, um dein heutiges Ziel zu erreichen (vgl. auch Lerntipp 1 auf S. 142).

24	**surfer** ['sɜːfə]	Surfer, Surferin	
	stall [stɔːl]	(Verkaufs-)Stand	→ I like the food *stalls* at the pier.
25	**boardwalk** ['bɔːdwɔːk]	(hölzerne) Strandpromenade	→
	homeless ['həʊmləs]	heimatlos; obdachlos	
27	**the media** ['miːdiə]	die Medien →	
	less [les]	weniger	→ I'd like to have more free time and *less* homework.
	What kind of programmes? [kaɪnd]	Was für Sendungen?	→ *What kind of* music do you like best? – Hip hop.
	prefer [prɪ'fɜː]	vorziehen	→ ❗ I prefe**rr**ed
	chat show ['tʃætʃəʊ]	Talkshow	
	series ['sɪəriːz]	Serie; Reihe	→ There's a new family *series* on TV.
	comedy ['kɒmədi]	Komödie, humorvoller Film/Roman	
	romance [rəʊ'mæns]	Liebesfilm, Liebesroman	
	between [bɪ'twiːn]	zwischen	

→ **The media**
newspapers
radio
the Internet
TV

Story

28	**Lucky thing!** ['lʌki'θɪŋ]	Der/Die Glückliche! Du Glückliche/r!	
	he was waiting	er wartete (gerade) →	→ When Tim arrived, his friends *were watching* TV.
	freeway ['friːweɪ]	Autobahn *(in den USA)*	
	remember [rɪ'membə]	daran denken	→ *Remember:* You must drive on the left in England!
	role [rəʊl]	Rolle	
	it **could** be [kʊd]	es könnte sein	→ If you like, we *could* go to Spain this summer.
	career (in TV) [kə'rɪə]	(Fernseh-)Karriere, berufliche Laufbahn (im Fernsehen)	
	audition [ɔː'dɪʃn]	Vorsprechen, Vorsingen	→ About 500 actors queued for the *audition*.
	studio ['stjuːdiəʊ]	Studio	
	it had sent	es hatte geschickt	
	jog [dʒɒg]	joggen	→ I *jogged* through the park in one hour.
	grass [grɑːs]	Gras, Rasen	
	wait in line [ɪn'laɪn]	(AE) Schlange stehen	→ I hate long *lines*. [(AE) Warteschlangen]
	(for) a long time	lange	→ We danced together *for a long time*.
	director [də'rektə]	Regisseur, Regisseurin	

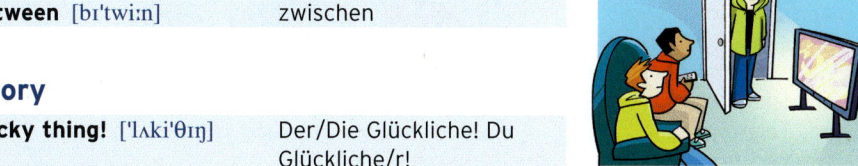

→ **was/were -ing**
I was listening
you were reading
he/she was eating
we were drawing
they were talking

	photo shoot ['fəʊtəʃuːt]	Fotosession, Fotoshooting
29	**wave** [weɪv]	Welle
	wetsuit ['wetsuːt]	Surf-/Tauch(schutz)anzug
	(surfing) gear ['sɜːfɪŋɡɪə]	**1** (Surf-)Kleidung, Klamotten; **2** (Surf-)Ausrüstung
	surf [sɜːf]	surfen
	photographer [fə'tɒɡrəfə]	Fotograf, Fotografin
	make-up artist ['meɪkʌpɑːtɪst]	Visagist, Visagistin
	take photos [teɪk'fəʊtəʊz]	Fotos machen, fotografieren
	turn to the left	sich nach links drehen
	on the beach	am Strand
	model ['mɒdl]	(Foto-)Modell →
	a job like that	so ein Job

(1) Tina is wearing her disco *gear*. (2) We bought some camping *gear* for the holidays.

→ Can you *take a photo* of me and my sister, please?

→ Look! I'd like a car *like that*.

→ **Careers in TV**
actor
director
make-up artist
model
photographer

Wordpower

30	**definition** [defɪ'nɪʃn]	Definition
	What do you call ...? [kɔːl]	Wie nennt/bezeichnet man ...?

→ *What do you call* somebody who reads? – A reader!

Training

31	**context** ['kɒntekst]	Zusammenhang, Kontext
	meaning ['miːnɪŋ]	Bedeutung
	entry ['entri]	Eintrag

→ What are the two *meanings* of the word "gear"?

→ Find the *entry* for "gear" in a dictionary.

Skills training

32	**phone message** ['fəʊnmesɪdʒ]	Telefonnotiz; telefonische Nachricht
	phone call ['fəʊnkɔːl]	Anruf
	call [kɔːl]	anrufen
	Can I take a message?	Kann ich (ihm/ihr) etwas ausrichten?
	answer the phone	ans Telefon gehen
33	**call/phone back**	zurückrufen
35	**against** [ə'genst]	gegen
	drug [drʌg]	Droge
	relax [rɪ'læks]	(sich) entspannen
	main point ['meɪn'pɔɪnt]	Schwerpunkt
	useful ['juːsfl]	nützlich
	On the one hand, ... On the other hand, ...	Einerseits ... Andererseits ...
	all in all	insgesamt

→ Can you *answer the phone*, please? I'm busy.

→ Lots of people are *against* the new airport.

→ After work Sue *relaxes* with a cup of tea.

→ If you live in the country, a car is very *useful*.

→ *On the one hand,* I'd like to have a job.
On the other hand, I like my free time too. ...

→ ... *All in all* I need the money. So I'll look for a weekend job!

Look at language

36	**uncool** [ʌn'kuːl]	nicht cool, uncool
	ride [raɪd]	**1** „Fahrattraktion", Fahrgeschäft; **2** Fahrt
	pirate ['paɪrət]	Pirat, Piratin
	camera ['kæmərə]	Fotoapparat, Kamera →
	fireworks ['faɪəwɜːks]	Feuerwerk

→ There are some cool *rides* at the funfair this year.

→ camera
film
photo
photographer
take photos

American English vocabulary ★ ★ ★ ★ ★ ★ ★ ★ ★ ★

AE (American English)	BE (British English)	
line [laɪn]	queue [kjuː]	(Warte-)Schlange
wait in line	queue (up)	Schlange stehen

Test yourself

1 Write the plural forms of these words in your exercise book.

movie – ... • comedy – ... • model – ... • message – ... • drug – ...

2 Odd word out: One word isn't OK. Write it in your exercise book.

1 wetsuit • stall • wave • surfer
2 comedy • action film • romance • camera
3 phone message • audition • mobile • phone call
4 entry • film • series • programme

> **Tipp:**
> Schau dir die vorangegangenen Wortlisten gut an.

3 Word families: Find the new words in this unit and write them in your exercise book.

1 home (noun) – homeless (adjective)
2 romantic (adjective) – ... (noun)
3 jogger (noun) – ... (verb)
4 mean (verb) – ... (noun)
5 use (verb) – ... (adjective)
6 cool (adjective) – ... (the opposite)

4 Make sentences with these words and write them in your exercise book.

1 you – kind – like – of – what – do – films – best
2 for – jogged – a – through – time – we – field – long – a
3 on – took – we – of – holiday – lots – photos

Do you remember?

Write the answers in your exercise book. What do you call …

a) something that you write in every day?
b) something that you write to invite people?
c) a time to relax between lessons or appointments?
d) a conversation between two people?

Are your answers right? Check on page 198.

Unit 3

Lerntipp 3: Englische Rechtschreibung (1)

In der englischen Rechtschreibung gibt es einige Besonderheiten. Zwei Beispiele:

● **-el** und **-le**: Wörter wie *travel* oder *model* enden auf -el, das ist einfach. Aber du kennst viel mehr englische Wörter, die mit -le am Ende geschrieben werden, wie *table* oder *article*. Denke z.B. an die englischen Wörter für ‚Apfel‘, ‚Titel‘ oder ‚schrecklich, furchtbar‘. Fallen dir noch mehr Beispiele ein?

● **-er** und **-re**: Das einfache -er am Ende kennst du vor allem für Personen, z.B. *reader*, *photographer* oder *sister*. Es gibt aber auch einige (nicht sehr viele!) Fälle, in denen es -re heißen muss, wie bei *centre*, *metre* oder *theatre*. (Nur im amerikanischen Englisch werden auch diese Wörter mit -er am Ende geschrieben.)

Tipp: Führe Listen über Wörter mit besonderen Schreibweisen!

38	**high school** ['haɪskuːl]	Oberschule (in den USA)
	student ['stjuːdnt]	(AE) Schüler, Schülerin
	grade 9 [greɪd]	(AE) 9. Klasse
	as [əz]	als
	English as a Second Language	Englisch als Zweitsprache
	extra classes ['klɑːsɪz]	Förderunterricht
	medical ['medɪkl]	Medizin-; medizinisch
	locker ['lɒkə]	Schließfach, Spind
	cheerleader ['tʃɪəliːdə]	Person, die das Publikum bei einem Wettkampf zum Beifall anfeuert
	security check [sɪ'kjʊərətitʃek]	Sicherheitskontrolle
39	**first aid** [fɜːst'eɪd]	erste Hilfe
40	**court** [kɔːt]	Spielfeld, Platz
	hoop [huːp]	(Basketball-)Korb
	equipment [ɪ'kwɪpmənt]	Ausstattung, Ausrüstung
	shorts [ʃɔːts]	Shorts, kurze Hosen →
	free throw [friː'θrəʊ]	Freiwurf
	shot [ʃɒt]	Korbwurf
	touch [tʌtʃ]	berühren, anfassen
	kick [kɪk]	kicken, treten
	YMCA [waɪemsiː'eɪ]	CVJM
	happy ending [hæpi'endɪŋ]	Happy End
	I spent [spent]	ich verbrachte
	I have no clue [kluː]	ich habe keine Ahnung
	I got [gɒt]	(AE) ich habe
	gotta find me a place ['gɒtə]	(ich) muss einen Ort finden
	***shoot** [ʃuːt]	schießen; werfen
	dreams of being like … ['biːɪŋ]	Träume, in denen ich wie … bin
	a ball's no good	ein Ball nützt nichts
	till [tɪl]	bis
	(it) so happened to be …	zufälligerweise war es …
	score [skɔː]	Spielstand, Punktzahl
	it was tied [taɪd]	es war unentschieden
	*three on the **clock** [klɒk]*	drei (Minuten) auf der Uhr
	it's (= it was) up to me	es lag an mir
	sky-high [skaɪ'haɪ]	himmelhoch
	release [rɪ'liːs]	loslassen
	everything for young men to enjoy [ɪn'dʒɔɪ]	alles, was jungen Männern gefällt
	hang out [hæŋ'aʊt]	herumhängen
	you can get yourself clean	du kannst dich waschen
	meal [miːl]	Mahlzeit, Essen
	you can do whatever you feel [wɒt'evə]	du kannst tun, wonach dir gerade ist
41	**sneaker** ['sniːkə]	(AE) Sportschuh
	brand [brænd]	Marke
	each [iːtʃ]	jede, jeder, jedes
	soccer ['sɒkə]	Fußball

→ "Sullivan High" means "Sullivan *High School*".

→ My sister works *as* a courier.
→ We speak French at home, but I learn *English as a Second Language* at school.

→ We always put our things in *lockers* before sport.

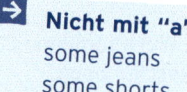

→ **Nicht mit "a"**
some jeans
some shorts

→ I need some new *shorts* for the summer!

→ She didn't hear me, so I *touched* her arm.

→ I like love stories with a *happy ending*.

→ Before I could *shoot*, I lost the ball.

→ What's the *score* now? [Wie steht's jetzt?]

→ Sorry I'm late. The kitchen *clock* isn't working.

basketball   American football   baseball

→ We all know lots of *brand* names from TV.
→ Grandad gave *each* child a little present.
→ *Soccer* (or football) is the most popular sport in Germany.

expert ['ekspɜːt]	Fachmann/-frau, Experte/Expertin	
print out [prɪnt'aʊt]	ausdrucken	

Story

42	she felt **confident** ['kɒnfɪdənt]	sie war zuversichtlich	
	move [muːv]	(sich) bewegen	→ Don't *move* now!
	***throw (at): I threw (at)** [θrəʊ, thruː]	werfen (auf): ich warf (auf)	→ Basketball players don't kick the ball, they *throw* it.
	cheer [tʃɪə]	jubeln, hurra rufen →	
	half-time [hɑːf'taɪm]	Halbzeit	
	score [skɔː]	(Punkte) erzielen, (Tor) schießen	→ I tried, but I didn't *score*.
	it was 24–18 to North ['twenti'fɔːreɪtiːn]	es stand 24:18 für North	→ What's the score? – *It's 2–1 to* England.
	Too bad! ['tuː'bæd]	Schade!	→ Sorry, I can't come tonight. – *Too bad!*
	Well done! ['wel'dʌn]	Gut gemacht!	
	Good luck! ['gʊd'lʌk]	Viel Glück!	
	***hit: I hit** [hɪt, hɪt]	schlagen: ich schlug →	
43	**referee** [refə'riː]	Schiedsrichter, -richterin	
	miss [mɪs]	daneben treffen; daneben gehen	→ I threw the ball, but it *missed* the hoop.
	play by the rules	sich an die Spielregeln halten	→ You can join us if you *play by the rules*.
	self-control [selfkən'trəʊl]	Selbstbeherrschung	→ I lost my *self-control* and I hit her – in my dream.

→ cheer
cheerleader

→ hit
kick
shoot
throw

Wordpower

44	**imperative** [ɪm'perətɪv]	Befehlsform, Imperativ	❗ Aussprache: [ɪm'perətɪv]

Skills training

46	**Giving orders** [gɪvɪŋ'ɔːdəz]	Anweisungen geben, Befehle erteilen	
	in the school car park	auf dem Schulparkplatz	
	tray [treɪ]	Tablett	
	***leave** [liːv]	(liegen) lassen, vergessen	→ Oh no! I *left* my mobile in the cafe!
	over there [əʊvə'ðeə]	da/dort drüben (hin)	→ Let's sit *over there* and have a chat.
	exchange [ɪks'tʃeɪndʒ]	Austausch-; Tausch-	
49	**fix** [fɪks]	reparieren	
	if [ɪf]	ob	→ Ask Pam *if* she can come to my party, please.

Look at language

50	**paramedic** [pærə'medɪk]	Rettungssanitäter/in	→ The *paramedics* took my father to hospital.
	academy [ə'kædəmi]	Akademie	
	give first aid	erste Hilfe leisten	
	become sick [sɪk]	(AE) krank werden	
	on the weekend	(AE) am Wochenende	
	panic ['pænɪk]	durchdrehen, in Panik geraten	→ ❗ he panics, but: he's pani**ck**ing, he pani**ck**ed
	difficult ['dɪfɪkəlt]	schwierig, schwer	→ Swimming isn't *difficult*. It's really easy!
	emotional [ɪ'məʊʃənl]	gefühlsbetont	
	earn [ɜːn]	verdienen	

American English vocabulary ★ ★ ★ ★ ★ ★ ★ ★ ★ ★ ★

AE (American English)	BE (British English)	
grade [greɪd]	year	Klasse
sneaker ['sniːkə]	trainer	Sportschuh
student ['stjuːdnt]	pupil	Schüler, Schülerin

*Irregular verbs

Infinitive form	Simple past form	Present perfect form
hit [hɪt]	I hit [hɪt]	I've hit [hɪt]
leave [liːv]	I left [left]	I've left [left]
shoot [ʃuːt]	I shot [ʃɒt]	I've shot [ʃɒt]
throw [θrəʊ]	I threw [θruː]	I've thrown [θrəʊn]

Test yourself

1 *Schreibe die Grundform dieser Verben in dein Heft.*
I cheered – cheer • I fixed – … • I hit – … • I kicked – … • I left – … •
I missed – … • I panicked – … • I shot – … • I threw – … • I touched – …

2 *Bilde Kommentare aus den Wörtern und schreibe die Dialoge in dein Heft.*
bad • done • good • luck • too • well
1 I scored lots of points in the game. – … …!
2 I'll try to score lots of points in the game. – … …!
3 I didn't score lots of points in the game. – … …!

Tipp:
Schau dir die vorangegangenen Wortlisten gut an.

Do you remember?
Pick the right word and finish the sentences in your exercise book.
gear • point • rules • sign
1 I don't know softball. What are the …?
2 You get one … for each right answer.
3 Give me a … when you're ready.
4 I can't surf – I don't have the right …

Are your answers right? Check on page 198.

Unit 4

Lerntipp 4: Englische Rechtschreibung (2)
Hier sind zwei weitere Beispiele für Besonderheiten der englischen Rechtschreibung.

• **-ea-** und **-ee-**: Diese beiden Buchstabenpaare im Wort werden zwar oft gleich ausgesprochen *(mean, meet)*, aber eben unterschiedlich geschrieben. Sammle Beispiele!

• **-gh und -ght**: Einige englische Wörter hören mit den Buchstaben -gh *(laugh, through)* oder -ght *(right, fight)* auf. Fertige eine Liste an!

52	*evergreen* ['evəgriːn]	immergrün
	Washington State [wɒʃɪŋtən'steɪt]	der Bundesstaat Washington
	forest ['fɒrɪst]	Wald, Waldgebiet

bear [beə]	Bär	
deer [dɪə]	Hirsch, Hirsche	→ We saw lots of *deer* in the national park.
cougar ['kuːgə]	(AE) Puma	
reservation [rezə'veɪʃn]	(Indianer-)Reservation, Reservat	→ We stayed in a hotel *on the reservation*. [in der Reservation]
festival ['festɪvl]	Festival; Fest	
tree [triː]	Baum	

53 | **go whale watching** ['weɪlwɒtʃɪŋ] | auf Walbeobachtungstour gehen | → We went *whale watching* in Canada. *Whale watching* is very popular there. [Walbeobachtung] |
| **island** ['aɪlənd] | Insel | |
| **hike; hiking** [haɪk, 'haɪkɪŋ] | wandern; (das) Wandern → | → *Hiking* is great. I *hiked* all weekend. |

> **-ing**
> Read**ing** is fun.
> I've finished draw**ing**.
> He's good at sing**ing**.

54 | **fire** ['faɪə] | Feuer; Brand | |
smoke; smoking [sməʊk, 'sməʊkɪŋ]	rauchen; (das) Rauchen	→ I don't *smoke*. I think *smoking* is stupid.
campfire ['kæmpfaɪə]	Lagerfeuer	
campground ['kæmpgraʊnd]	(AE) Campingplatz, Zeltplatz	
noise [nɔɪz]	Lärm; Geräusch	
***keep** [kiːp]	halten, behalten	
prohibited [prə'hɪbɪtɪd]	verboten	→ Look, swimming is *prohibited* here.
as many **as**	so viele wie	→ I think Mike isn't *as* nice *as* his brother.

55 | **wall** [wɔːl] | Wand; Mauer | |
beaver ['biːvə]	Biber	
entrance fee ['entrənsfiː]	Eintrittspreis	
person ['pɜːsn]	Person, Mensch	→ All the people were quiet. Only one *person* was talking. ❗Aussprache: ['pɜːsn]

Story

56 | **root** [ruːt] | Wurzel | |
tent [tent]	Zelt	
they were looking forward to getting out of town ['fɔːwəd]	sie freuten sich darauf, aus der Stadt herauszukommen	→ *I'm* really *looking forward to seeing* you again.
After leaving Port Townsend, they drove ...	Nachdem sie Port Townsend verlassen hatten, fuhren sie ...	→ *After finishing* my homework, I went to bed.
***drive: I drove** [drəʊv]	fahren: ich fuhr	→ I love driving. Last week I *drove* to London.
***put up a tent** [pʊt'ʌp]	ein Zelt aufstellen	
***eat: I ate** [et]	essen: ich aß	
Native American ['neɪtɪvə'merɪkən]	amerik. Ureinwohner/in, Indianer/in	→ About 100 *Native Americans* live on the reservation that we visited.
grandparents ['grænpeərənts]	Großeltern →	

> grandparents
> grandma
> grandad

> aunt
> uncle
> cousin

57 | *the Makah people* [mə'kɑː] | das Volk der Makah | |
tepee ['tiːpiː]	Tipi	
longhouse ['lɒŋhaʊs]	Langhaus	
uncle ['ʌŋkl]	Onkel →	
hunt; hunting [hʌnt, 'hʌntɪŋ]	jagen; (das) Jagen	→ For some people, *hunting* is a sport.
***bring: I brought** [brɔːt]	bringen: ich brachte	
illness ['ɪlnəs]	Krankheit	
prohibit [prə'hɪbɪt]	verbieten	
fish [fɪʃ]	fischen, angeln	→ 
ocean ['əʊʃn]	Ozean; Meer	
***forget: I forgot** [fə'gɒt]	vergessen: ich vergaß	→ Where's Ben? – Oh sorry, I *forgot* to phone him.

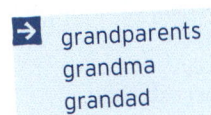
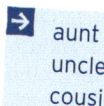

Wordpower

58	**adjective** [ˈædʒɪktɪv]	Adjektiv, Eigenschafts-wort →	→	An alphabet of *adjectives*: angry, big, cheap, dirty, easy, fast, ...

→ noun
verb
adjective

Training

59	**mind map** [ˈmaɪndmæp]	Mindmap (*eine Art Gedan-kenkarte*)	→	A *mind map* can help you to remember things.
	look after [lʊkˈɑːftə]	sich kümmern um, auf-passen auf	→	I can't come tomorrow. I have to *look after* my little brother.
	***lead** [liːd]	führen	→	This road *leads* to the beach.
	get lost [getˈlɒst]	sich verirren	→	We *got lost* on our way to the hotel in London.

Skills training

60	**European** [jʊərəˈpiːən]	europäisch; Europäer, Europäerin →		
61	**Can I help you?**	Kann ich Ihnen behilflich sein?	→	*Can I help you?*

→ American
Asian
European

	recommend [rekəˈmend]	empfehlen	→	For French food I can *recommend* the 'Café Paris'.
	kayaking [ˈkaɪækɪŋ]	Kajakfahren		
63	**apply (for/to)** [əˈplaɪ]	sich bewerben (um/bei)	→	I *applied for* a job as a courier, but I didn't get it.
	part-time [pɑːˈtaɪm]	Teilzeit, Teilzeit-	→	Pat works *part-time* in a disco.
	sales clerk [ˈseɪlzklɑːk]	(AE) Verkäufer/in	→	⚠ Aussprache: BE [klɑːk], AE [klɜːrk]
	per [pɜː]	pro	→	We spent about 10 pounds *per* person for drinks.
	résumé [ˈrezjumeɪ]	(AE) Lebenslauf	→	⚠ Aussprache: BE [ˈrezjumeɪ], AE [ˈrezəmeɪ]
	family name	Nachname, Familienname	→	Sorry, Martin is my *family name* –
	first name	Vorname	→	my *first name* is Richard.
	(work) experience [ɪkˈspɪərɪəns]	(Berufs-)Erfahrung		
	cashier [kæˈʃɪə]	Kassierer, Kassiererin →	→	My mum works as a *cashier*.
	cover letter [ˈkʌvəletə]	(AE) Anschreiben, Begleit-brief		
	Yours truly, ... [jɔːzˈtruːli]	(AE) Mit freundlichen Grüßen ...		
	cleaner [ˈkliːnə]	Putzhilfe, Raumpfleger/in	→	My uncle is a *cleaner*.
	assistant [əˈsɪstənt]	Assistent, Assistentin		

→ **In a shop**
cashier
customer
detective
shop assistant
shopper
shoplifter

Look at language

64	**animal rights** [ˈænɪmlˈraɪts]	Tierrechte, Tierschutz-	→	I love my pets, so I joined an *animal rights* group.
	tradition [trəˈdɪʃn]	Tradition		
	oil [ɔɪl]	Öl		
	cook; cooking [kʊk, ˈkʊkɪŋ]	kochen; (das) Kochen	→	I'm not a good cook. In fact, I hate *cooking*.
	lamp [læmp]	Lampe		
	nearly [ˈnɪəli]	fast		
	extinct [ɪkˈstɪŋkt]	ausgestorben		
	trouble [ˈtrʌbl]	Unruhe		
	there was lots of activity	es war viel los, es gab viel Trubel		
	protest [prəˈtest]	protestieren		
	save [seɪv]	retten		
	grey whale [ˈgreɪˈweɪl]	Grauwal		

→ The paramedics *saved* my friend's life.

American English vocabulary ★ ★ ★ ★ ★ ★ ★ ★ ★ ★ ★ ★

AE (American English)	BE (British English)	
campground ['kæmpgraʊnd]	campsite ['kæmpsaɪt]	Campingplatz, Zeltplatz
cougar ['kuːgə]	puma ['pjuːmə]	Puma
cover letter ['kʌvəletə]	covering letter ['kʌvərɪŋletə]	Anschreiben, Begleitbrief
résumé ['rezjumeɪ]	CV ['siː'viː]	Lebenslauf
sales clerk ['seɪlzklɑːk]	shop assistant	Verkäufer/in
Yours truly [jɔːz'truːli]	Yours sincerely [jɔːzsɪn'sɪəli]	Mit freundlichen Grüßen

*Irregular verbs

Infinitive form	Simple past form	Present perfect form
bring [brɪŋ]	I brought [brɔːt]	I've brought [brɔːt]
drive [draɪv]	I drove [drəʊv]	I've driven ['drɪvn]
eat [iːt]	I ate [et]	I've eaten ['iːtn]
forget [fə'get]	I forgot [fə'gɒt]	I've forgotten [fə'gɒtn]
keep [kiːp]	I kept [kept]	I've kept [kept]
lead [liːd]	I led [led]	I've led [led]
put [pʊt]	I put [pʊt]	I've put [pʊt]

Test yourself

1 Word families: Find the new words and write them in your exercise book.

1 **aunt** (woman) – **uncle** (man)
2 **ill** (adjective) – ... (noun)
3 **fishing** (noun) – ... (verb)
4 **Europe** (noun) – ... (adjective)
5 **clean** (adjective) – ... (noun/job)
6 **cook** (noun) – ... (verb)

Tipp:
Schau dir die vorangegangenen Wortlisten gut an.

2 Make sentences with these words and write them in your exercise book.

1 looking – is – mum – forward – you – my – meeting – to
2 to – after – really – was – I – driving – London, – tired
3 have – after – I – little – my – to – cousins – look

Do you remember?

Write two lists in your exercise book: a) The environment; b) Outdoor activities.

camping • cycling • fishing • forest • hiking • hunting • island • kayaking • lake • mountain • ocean • river • sea • skiing • swimming • walking

Are your answers right? Check on page 198.

Unit 5

Lerntipp 5: The alphabet game

Am meisten Spaß macht das Spiel zu dritt oder zu viert!

Spielablauf: In jeder Runde wird ein Buchstabe genannt. Alle schreiben so schnell wie möglich 5 englische Wörter auf, die mit diesem Buchstaben beginnen. Wer zuerst fertig ist, ruft „Stop!" und erhält 5 Extrapunkte. Alle anderen erhalten pro Wort 5 Punkte. Dann wird gemeinsam im **Dictionary** (S.160–179) überprüft, ob die Wörter richtig geschrieben sind; für jeden Fehler wird wieder ein Punkt abgezogen. Wer hat nach 5 Runden die meisten Punkte?

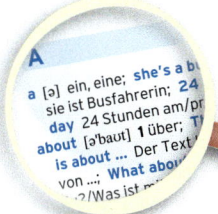

66 **Spanish** ['spænɪʃ] — spanisch; Spanisch; Spanier, Spanierin(nen) ➡

→ Britain – British
Spain – Spanish

→ Luis and Maria live in Spain, but they aren't *Spanish*.

Little Havana [hə'vænə] — „Klein-Havanna"
men playing games — Männer, die Spiele spielen
crime [kraɪm] — Verbrechen ➡
on stage [steɪdʒ] — auf der Bühne
award [ə'wɔːd] — Preis, Auszeichnung

→ The band won many *awards*.

➡ crime
violence
steal
fight
kill
police officer
prison

67 **Hispanic** [hɪ'spænɪk] — Hispano-Amerikaner/in; hispanisch; spanisch-sprachig
% = per cent [pə'sent] — Prozent
musician [mjuː'zɪʃn] — Musiker, Musikerin
umbrella [ʌm'brelə] — Schirm

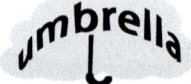

→

68 **male** [meɪl] — männlich

→ My favourite *male* actor is Daniel Radcliffe.

general ['dʒenrəl] — allgemein
piano [pi'ænəʊ] — Klavier

→ I can't play the *piano*, but I can play the guitar.

hip [hɪp] — Hüfte
lie [laɪ] — lügen

→ That wasn't true. He *lied*. ❗ he *lies*, he's *lying*

Colombia [kə'lɒmbiə] — Kolumbien
*spend [spend] — verbringen
in front of [frʌnt] — vor

→ Tim spends all his free time *in front of* the TV.

download [daʊn'ləʊd] — herunterladen
fantastic [fæn'tæstɪk] — fantastisch

69 **he sings sadly** ['sædli] — er singt traurig ➡

→ The song isn't really sad, but they sing it so *sadly*.

➡ -ly
fight brave**ly**
smoke nervous**ly**
ask polite**ly**
smile shy**ly**

slow [sləʊ] — langsam

→ Please drive *slowly*.

voice [vɔɪs] — Stimme

→ I heard two different *voices*.

rhythm ['rɪðəm] — Rhythmus
female ['fiːmeɪl] — weiblich ➡

→ a *female* cook/teacher/trainer/... [eine Köchin/Lehrerin/Trainerin/...]

➡ man
woman
male
female

Write about yourself. — Schreibe über dich (selbst).

Story

70 ***wake up** [weɪk'ʌp] — aufwachen
moon [muːn] — Mond
above [ə'bʌv] — über ➡

→ My flat is *above* the shop.

light switch ['laɪtswɪtʃ] — Lichtschalter
mirror ['mɪrə] — Spiegel
deaf [def] — taub
hearing ['hɪərɪŋ] — Gehör
they had come — sie waren gekommen
loud [laʊd] — laut

➡ über
above the shop
across the canal
about the story

*shake: she shook me — schütteln: sie schüttelte mich
[ʃeɪk, ʃʊk]

→ (1) We *shook* the tree, so the apples fell down.
(2) She *shook* her head. [Sie schüttelte den Kopf.]

I see her mouth moving — ich sehe, wie sich ihr Mund bewegt
mouth [maʊθ] — Mund
frightening ['fraɪtnɪŋ] — beängstigend, furcht-erregend ➡

→ That's the most *frightening* story that I've ever heard!

➡ I'm frightened.
It's frightening.

closet ['klɒzɪt] — (AE) Wandschrank
sigh [saɪ] — seufzen

→ Tim *sighed* because he didn't know what he should do.

I've been thinking that — ich habe das (immer wieder) gedacht

kiss [kɪs]	(sich) küssen
key [kiː]	Schlüssel
she shouts something at him	sie ruft ihm etwas zu
ear [ɪə]	Ohr
opposite ['ɒpəzɪt]	gegenüber (von)
alarm [ə'lɑːm]	Alarmanlage
71 **feeling** ['fiːlɪŋ] ➜	Gefühl ➜

→ The supermarket is *opposite* the museum.

→ He hates talking about his *feelings.* ➜   feel / feeling

Wordpower

72 **preposition** [prepə'zɪʃn]	Präposition, Verhältniswort

→ Words like 'under' or 'between' are *prepositions.*

Skills training

74 **hurricane** ['hʌrɪkən]	Orkan
theme park ['θiːmpɑːk]	Themenpark
12° Celsius (= 12 degrees Celsius) [dɪ'griːz, 'selsiəs]	12 Grad Celsius
space [speɪs] ➜	Weltraum ➜
astronaut ['æstrənɔːt]	Astronaut, Astronautin
Just a minute.	Einen Augenblick.
75 **Do you mind if I** sit here? [maɪnd]	Haben Sie etwas dagegen, wenn ich mich hier hinsetze?
Go ahead. [ə'hed]	Mach(t)/Machen Sie nur.
You're welcome.	Nichts zu danken; Bitte schön.
77 **reason** ['riːzn]	Grund
in my opinion [ə'pɪnjən]	meiner Meinung nach
believe [bɪ'liːv]	glauben

→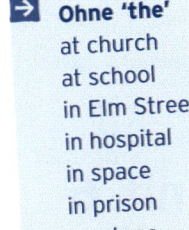

! 1 degree, 2 degrees

→ Imagine you could travel through *space.*

→ *Do you mind if I* open the window?

→ Can I open my presents now? – Yes, *go ahead.*

→ Thanks for your help.
– *You're welcome.*

→ *In my opinion,* that's a great idea.

→ You shouldn't *believe* everything that you hear.

➜ **Ohne 'the'**
at church
at school
in Elm Street
in hospital
in space
in prison
on stage

Look at language

78 ***grow** [grəʊ]	wachsen
economy [ɪ'kɒnəmi]	Wirtschaft
illegal [ɪ'liːgl]	ungesetzlich, illegal
papers ['peɪpəz]	(Ausweis-)Papiere
Mexico ['meksɪkəʊ]	Mexiko
employer [ɪm'plɔɪə]	Arbeitgeber, Arbeitgeberin
power ['paʊə]	Macht; Stärke
79 **adverb** ['ædvɜːb]	Adverb, Umstandswort

→ The tree *hasn't grown* in the last year.

→ It's *illegal* to smoke here.

→ This firm is one of the largest *employers* in the area.

*
Irregular verbs

Infinitive form	Simple past form	Present perfect form
grow [grəʊ]	I grew [gruː]	I've grown [grəʊn]
shake [ʃeɪk]	I shook [ʃʊk]	I've shaken ['ʃeɪkən]
spend [spend]	I spent [spent]	I've spent [spent]
wake up [weɪk'ʌp]	I woke up [wəʊk'ʌp]	I've woken up [wəʊkən'ʌp]

Hinweis: "Test yourself" findest du auf S.156.

Test yourself

1 Find the opposites and write them in your exercise book.

male – ... • behind – ... • happily – ... • fast – ... • sun – ... • quiet – ...

Tipp:
Schau dir die vorangegangenen Wortlisten gut an.

2 Who or what is it? Find and write in your exercise book a word for:

1 a big musical instrument   **3** somebody who travels in space

2 say something that isn't true   **4** somebody who gives people jobs

3 Find the missing words and write them in your exercise book.

1 She's great! Of course she'll win an ...   **4** I can't open the door. I don't have a ...

2 It's raining. You'll need an ...   **5** Nobody will steal my car. It has a car ...

3 He can't hear you. He's ...   **6** This king doesn't have much ...

Do you remember?

Write two lists in your exercise book: a) Music; b) Prepositions.

above • behind • between • concert • guitar • in front of • into •
musical instrument • musician • near • onto • opposite • piano • singer •
song • sound • stage • through • title • towards

Are your answers right? Check on page 198.

Unit 6

80	before [bɪ'fɔː]	vor
	it was called	es wurde genannt →
	trail [treɪl]	Pfad, Weg
	pioneer [paɪə'nɪə]	Pionier, Pionierin
81	wagon train ['wægəntreɪn]	Zug von Planwagen
	camp [kæmp]	lagern, zelten →
	Indian ['ɪndɪən]	Indianer, Indianerin; indianisch
	buffalo, buffaloes ['bʌfələʊ, 'bʌfələʊz]	Büffel →
	California [kælɪ'fɔːnɪə]	Kalifornien
82	scan [skæn]	überfliegen
	If I had the money, ...	Wenn ich das Geld hätte, ...
	enough [ɪ'nʌf]	genug
	e-pal ['iːpæl]	E-Mail-Freund/-Freundin
	county fair [kaʊntɪ'feə]	eine Art Landwirtschaftsschau
	coast [kəʊst]	Küste
	I'd teach you to ride [tiːtʃ]	ich würde dir das Reiten beibringen → →
	ride [raɪd]	reiten →
	excited [ɪk'saɪtɪd]	aufgeregt, begeistert
83	Historical Society [hɪ'stɒrɪklsə'saɪəti]	Geschichtsverein
	they were built [bɪlt]	sie wurden gebaut →
	establish [ɪ'stæblɪʃ]	einrichten; eröffnen
	name [neɪm]	nennen
	Farewell Bend [feə'welbend]	„Lebewohl-Biegung"
	change to	ändern in
	encyclopedia [ɪnsaɪklə'piːdɪə]	Lexikon, Enzyklopädie

→ it's called – it was called
they're sent – they were sent

→ camp
campfire
camping
tent

→ Last summer we *camped* at the river.

→ bear
beaver
buffalo
cougar
deer

→ I only *scanned* the newspaper today.

→ We don't have *enough* time to stop.

→ *on the coast* [an der Küste]

→ teach – I taught – I've/I had taught

→ ride – I rode – I've/I had ridden

→ teach
teacher

→ build – I built – I've/I had built

→ I had to *name* five wild animals in the quiz.

→ Her name was Mayer, but she *changed* it *to* May.

search engine [ˈsɜːtʃendʒɪn]	Suchmaschine	
nickname [ˈnɪkneɪm]	Spitzname	→ I'm Jack. My *nickname* in school is "Jackster".
skunk [skʌŋk]	Stinktier, Skunk	
jackalope [ˈdʒækələʊp]	*amerikanisches Fabeltier*	
disc golf [ˈdɪskɒlf]	Discgolf („Scheibengolf")	→

Story

84 *the flight was twelve hours* [flaɪt]	der Flug dauerte zwölf Stunden	
highway [ˈhaɪweɪ]	(AE) Fernstraße	
speed limit [ˈspiːdlɪmɪt]	Geschwindigkeitsbegrenzung	

kilometres per hour	Stundenkilometer	→ The speed limit is 50 *kilometres per hour*.
barn [bɑːn]	Scheune	
tractor [ˈtræktə]	Traktor ▐	
almost [ˈɔːlməʊst]	fast	→ Don't go! Dinner is *almost* ready.
typical [ˈtɪpɪkl]	typisch	❗ Aussprache: [ˈtɪpɪkl]
diner [ˈdaɪnə]	(AE) Imbissstube, Café	
soda [ˈsəʊdə]	(AE) Limonade	
refill [ˈriːfɪl]	Nachfüllung	→ Most diners offer *refills* of drinks.
85 *feel homesick* [ˈhəʊmsɪk]	Heimweh haben	
tubing [ˈtjuːbɪŋ]	*Benutzung eines Reifenschlauchs als Floß*	
tube [tjuːb]	Reifenschlauch	
all the time [ɔːlðəˈtaɪm]	die ganze Zeit	
s'mores [smɔːz]	*amerikanischer Lagerfeuersnack*	
grill [grɪl]	grillen	→ We *grilled* sausages on our campfire.
cracker [ˈkrækə]	Kräcker	
surprised [səˈpraɪzd]	überrascht	→ I wasn't *surprised* when they told me the news.

Sidebar:
→ barn
farm
farmer
field
tractor

Wordpower

86 *fizzy drink* [fɪziˈdrɪŋk]	Limonade	→ Would you like a *fizzy drink*?
passive [ˈpæsɪv]	Passiv	

Training

87 *reading log* [ˈriːdɪŋlɒg]	Lesetagebuch	
character [ˈkærəktə]	Figur, Person	→ The most important *character* in the book is Ron.
review [rɪˈvjuː]	Besprechung, Rezension	

Skills training

88 *book* [bʊk]	buchen, reservieren (lassen)	→

I've just *booked* the flights for our holiday.

double room [dʌblˈruːm]	Doppelzimmer	
form [fɔːm]	Formular	
fill in [fɪlˈɪn]	ausfüllen	→ You have to *fill in* a form on their website.
leave [liːv]	abreisen	
single room [sɪŋglˈruːm]	Einzelzimmer	
wildfire [ˈwaɪldfaɪə]	Großflächenbrand	
dry [draɪ]	trocken	❗ dry – drier – driest
89 *receptionist* [rɪˈsepʃənɪst]	Empfangschef, -dame ▐	

Sidebar:
→ **Hotel/Motel**
single/double room
receptionist
book a room
fill in a form
arrive – leave

Enjoy your stay. [ɪn'dʒɔɪ, steɪ]	Einen angenehmen Aufenthalt.	
90 *hero, heroes* ['hɪərəʊ, 'hɪərəʊz]	Held/Heldin, Helden/Heldinnen	→ Everybody called the brave girl a *hero*.
91 *describe* [dɪ'skraɪb]	beschreiben	

American English vocabulary ★ ★ ★ ★ ★ ★ ★ ★ ★ ★ ★

AE (American English)	BE (British English)	
diner ['daɪnə]	cafe	Imbissstube, Café
highway ['haɪweɪ]	trunk road ['trʌŋkrəʊd]	Fernstraße
soda ['səʊdə]	fizzy drink [fɪzi'drɪŋk]	Limonade

Extra Practice · Unit 1

97 *design* [dɪ'zaɪn]	entwerfen	→ all the pupils
all the time [ɔːlðə'taɪm]	die ganze Zeit →	all the time
98 *comparison* [kəm'pærɪsn]	Vergleich →	all weekend
joke [dʒəʊk]	Witz, Scherz	→ compare
World Trade Center [wɜːld'treɪdsentə]	Welthandelszentrum	comparison
skyscraper ['skaɪskreɪpə]	Wolkenkratzer, Hochhaus	
they flew [fluː]	sie flogen	→ in the background
hole [həʊl]	Loch	in the foreground
99 *in the background/foreground* ['bækgraʊnd, 'fɔːgraʊnd]	im Hintergrund/Vordergrund →	on the right on the left

Extra Practice · Unit 2

100 *describe* [dɪ'skraɪb]	beschreiben →	→ describe
surfing ['sɜːfɪŋ]	Surfen, Wellenreiten →	description
103 *Who can teach me?* [tiːtʃ]	Wer kann es mir beibringen?	→ surf
she has put an advert in the newspaper	sie hat eine Anzeige in die Zeitung gesetzt	surfboard surfer
anything ['eniθɪŋ]	irgendetwas →	surfing
Subject: ... ['sʌbdʒɪkt]	Betreff: ...	surfing gear
		→ something
		anything
		nothing

Extra Practice · Unit 3

104 *Lake Michigan* [leɪk'mɪʃɪgən]	Michigansee	
field [fiːld]	Sportplatz	
105 *sell* [sel]	sich verkaufen	→ book
library ['laɪbrəri]	Bücherei →	bookshop
106 *advice* [əd'vaɪs]	Rat	library
yearbook ['jɪəbʊk]	Jahrbuch	
107 *homecoming* ['həʊmkʌmɪŋ]	Ehemaligentreffen	

dance [dɑːns]	Tanzveranstaltung, Ball	
decorate ['dekəreɪt]	schmücken	
king [kɪŋ]	König ➜	
object ['ɒbdʒɪkt]	Gegenstand, Objekt	
shirt [ʃɜːt]	Hemd ➜	

➜ king
queen

➜ shirt
T-shirt
jacket

Extra Practice · Unit 4

108	*table* ['teɪbl]	Tabelle
	infinitive [ɪn'fɪnətɪv]	Infinitiv ➜
	building ['bɪldɪŋ]	Gebäude
109	*they thought of making Leavenworth a German town*	sie kamen darauf, aus Leavenworth eine deutsche Stadt zu machen
	Bavaria [bə'veəriə]	Bayern
	ski [skiː]	Ski fahren
110	*raven* ['reɪvn]	Rabe
	crow [krəʊ]	Krähe
111	*Subject: ...* ['sʌbdʒɪkt]	Betreff: ...
	Dear Sir/Madam, ... [sɜː, 'mædəm]	Sehr geehrte Damen und Herren, ...

➜ **-ive**
adjective
detective
expensive
imperative
infinitive
past/present
progressive

Extra Practice · Unit 5

112	*Independence Day* [ɪndɪ'pendənsdeɪ]	Unabhängigkeitstag
	hope [həʊp]	Hoffnung ➜
	celebration [selɪ'breɪʃn]	Feier ➜
	at 10th Street and Ocean Drive	an der Ecke 10. Straße und Ocean Drive
114	*rewrite* [riː'raɪt]	umschreiben

➜ **1** hope (verb)
2 hope (noun)

➜ celebration
festival
party

Extra Practice · Unit 6

116	*dune* [djuːn]	Düne ➜
	dune buggy ['djuːnbʌgi]	„Strandbuggy" *(offenes Freizeitauto)*
117	*in the 1860s* [eɪtiːn'sɪkstiz]	in den sechziger Jahren des 19. Jahrhunderts
	take [teɪk]	einnehmen
	land [lænd]	Land
	he was shown [ʃəʊn]	es wurde ihm gezeigt
	away [ə'weɪ]	weg, fort ➜
	war [wɔː]	Krieg
118	*if-clause* ['ɪfklɔːz]	if-Satz
	type [taɪp]	Typ
119	*penfriend* ['penfrend]	Brieffreund, Brieffreundin ➜

➜ ocean
sea
shore
beach
dune

➜ go away –
come back

➜ **Friends**
boyfriend
girlfriend
penfriend
e-pal

Alphabetische Liste der Wörter aus den Bänden 1–4 (Englisch – Deutsch)

mit Fundstellenangaben für den Lernwortschatz aus Band 4, z.B.
Next: 6 = Next stop: USA, S.6 oder U5: 70 = Unit 5, S.70

WF (wahlfrei): nicht zum Lernwortschatz gehörende Wörter
→ verweist auf die Grundform eines Wortes
(AE): überwiegend im amerikanischen Englisch benutzte Vokabeln; Schreibweise und Aussprache entsprechen generell dem britischen Englisch.

A

a [ə] ein, eine; **she's a bus driver** sie ist Busfahrerin; **24 hours a day** 24 Stunden am/pro Tag

about [ə'baʊt] **1** über; **The text is about ...** Der Text handelt von ...; **What about you?** Und du?/Was ist mit dir? **2** ungefähr

above [ə'bʌv] über U5: 70

academy [ə'kædəmi] Akademie WF

accident ['æksɪdənt] Unfall

accordion [ə'kɔːdɪən] Akkordeon WF

across [ə'krɒs] über; hinüber, herüber

act [ækt]: **Act the dialogue.** Spielt das Gespräch nach.

action film ['ækʃnfɪlm] Actionfilm

activity [æk'tɪvəti] Beschäftigung, Aktivität; **there was lots of activity** es war viel los, es gab viel Trubel WF

actor ['æktə] Schauspieler/in

address [ə'dres] Adresse

adjective ['ædʒɪktɪv] Adjektiv, Eigenschaftswort U4: 58

adult ['ædʌlt] Erwachsene, Erwachsener

adverb ['ædvɜːb] Adverb, Umstandswort U5: 79

advert ['ædvɜːt] Anzeige

advice [əd'vaɪs] Rat WF

afraid [ə'freɪd]: **I'm afraid ...** Leider ...

Africa ['æfrɪkə] Afrika

after ['ɑːftə] **1** nach; **after school** nach der Schule; **after a ball** hinter einem Ball her; **After that ...** Danach ... WF; **2** nachdem U4: 56

afternoon ['ɑːftə'nuːn] Nachmittag; **in the afternoon** am Nachmittag, nachmittags

again [ə'gen] noch einmal, (schon) wieder

against [ə'genst] gegen U2: 35

age [eɪdʒ] Alter

ago [ə'gəʊ]: **two years ago** vor zwei Jahren

agree [ə'griː]: **I agree (with you).** Ich stimme (dir) zu. Ich bin derselben Meinung (wie du).

ahead [ə'hed]: **Go ahead.** Mach(t)/Machen Sie nur. U5: 75

aid [eɪd]: **first aid** erste Hilfe U3: 39

airport ['eəpɔːt] Flughafen; **at Exeter Airport** am Flughafen Exeter

alarm [ə'lɑːm] Alarmanlage U5: 70

alarm clock [ə'lɑːmklɒk] Wecker WF

alcohol ['ælkəhɒl] Alkohol

alcoholic [ælkə'hɒlɪk] alkoholisch WF

all (the) [ɔːl] alle; **all in all** insgesamt U2: 35; **all the time** die ganze Zeit WF U6; **all weekend** das ganze Wochenende

almost ['ɔːlməʊst] fast WF U6

alone [ə'ləʊn] allein

along [ə'lɒŋ] entlang

alphabet ['ælfəbet] Alphabet

alphabetical [ælfə'betɪkl] alphabetisch

always ['ɔːlweɪz] immer

a.m. [eɪ'em] morgens, vormittags

am [æm] bin; **I'm (= I am) Sarah.** Ich heiße Sarah. **I'm from London.** Ich komme aus London. **How are you? – I'm fine, thanks.** Wie geht's? – Danke, gut. **Are you ...? – Yes, I am./ No, I'm not.** Bist du ...? – Ja./ Nein.

America [ə'merɪkə] Amerika U1: 14

American [ə'merɪkən] amerikanisch; Amerikaner/in Next: 8

amusement arcade [ə'mjuːzməntə'keɪd] Spielhalle

an [ən] ein, eine

and [ænd, ənd] und; **at 10th Street and Ocean Drive** an der Ecke 10. Straße und Ocean Drive WF

angry (with) ['æŋgri] böse, wütend (auf)

animal ['ænɪml] Tier; **animal rights** Tierrechte, Tierschutz- U4: 64

another [ə'nʌðə] **1** noch ein, eine, einer, eins; **2** ein anderer/anderes, eine andere

answer ['ɑːnsə] **1** (be)antworten; **answer the phone** ans Telefon gehen U2: 32; **2** Antwort

any ['eni] irgendein, -eine, -eines WF; irgendwelche U1: 18; **not ... any** kein, keine

anything ['eniθɪŋ] irgendetwas WF; **not ... anything** nichts

anywhere ['eniweə] überall WF; **not ... anywhere** nirgendwo, nirgendwohin, nirgendwoher

apartment [ə'pɑːtmənt] (AE) Wohnung Next: 9

apple ['æpl] Apfel

apply (for/to) [ə'plaɪ] sich bewerben (um/bei) U4: 63

appointment [ə'pɔɪntmənt] Termin, Verabredung U1: 18; **appointment card** (Patienten-) Terminkärtchen U1: 18

April ['eɪprəl] April

are [ɑː] bist; seid; sind; **aren't (= are not)** bist/seid/sind nicht; **How are you?** Wie geht's? **What are they in German?** Wie heißen sie auf Deutsch?

area ['eərɪə] Gegend

arm [ɑːm] Arm

around [ə'raʊnd]: **around them** um sie herum WF

arrangement [ə'reɪndʒmənt] Absprache; **make an arrangement** eine Absprache treffen

arrive [ə'raɪv] ankommen

art [ɑːt] Kunst

article ['ɑːtɪkl] Artikel

artist ['ɑːtɪst] Künstler/in WF

arts and crafts [ɑːtsənd'krɑːfts]: **arts and crafts club** Bastel-AG WF

as [æz, əz] **1** als U3: 38; **2** wie WF; **as many/... as** so viele/... wie U4: 54

Asia ['eɪʃə] Asien

Asian ['eɪʃn] asiatisch; Asiat/in

ask [ɑːsk] fragen; **ask a question** eine Frage stellen; **ask for** bitten um

assistant [ə'sɪstənt] Assistent, Assistentin U4: 63; **shop assistant** Verkäufer, Verkäuferin

astronaut ['æstrənɔːt] Astronaut, Astronautin U5: 74

at [æt, ət] bei; an; in; **at eight o'clock** um acht/zwanzig Uhr; **at Exeter Station** im Bahnhof Exeter; **at home** zu Hause, daheim; **at last** endlich WF; **at night** nachts, in der Nacht; **at the moment** zurzeit, im Moment; **at the weekend** am Wochenende; **she's at school** sie ist in der Schule; sie geht zur Schule

ate [et] (→ eat): **I ate** ich aß, ich habe gegessen U4: 56

athletics [æθ'letɪks] Leichtathletik

audio ['ɔːdiəʊ]: **audio device** akustisches Gerät WF

audition [ɔː'dɪʃn] Vorsprechen, Vorsingen U2: 28

August ['ɔːgəst] August; **August 20th** 20. August

aunt [ɑːnt] Tante

Austria ['ɒstriə] Österreich

auto feeder ['ɔːtəfiːdə] automatischer Papiereinzug WF

autograph ['ɔːtəgrɑːf] Autogramm

autumn ['ɔːtəm] Herbst

available [ə'veɪləbl] erhältlich WF

award [ə'wɔːd] Preis, Auszeichnung U5: 66

away [ə'weɪ] weg, fort WF

awesome ['ɔːsəm] (AE) irre, toll
Next: 8

B

baby ['beɪbi] Baby WF U6

babysitter ['beɪbɪsɪtə] Babysitter, Babysitterin WF

back [bæk] zurück; **back from school** aus der Schule zurück; **I'm back!** Ich bin wieder da! **at the back of the book** hinten im Buch

background ['bækgraʊnd] Hintergrund WF

backwards ['bækwədz] rückwärts WF

bacon ['beɪkən] Speck WF

bad [bæd] schlecht; schlimm; **Too bad!** Schade! U3: 42

badminton ['bædmɪntən] Badminton, Federball(spiel)

bag [bæg] (Schul-)Tasche

bagel ['beɪgl] Bagel (eine Art ringförmiges, festes Brötchen) WF

baggage handler ['bægɪdʒhændlə] Gepäckabfertiger/Gepäckabfertigerin

baker ['beɪkə] Bäcker, Bäckerin WF

ball [bɔːl] Ball

banana [bə'nɑːnə] Banane

band [bænd] Band, (Musik-)Gruppe

bank [bæŋk] Bank, Sparkasse

barn [bɑːn] Scheune WF U6

baseball ['beɪsbɔːl] Baseball U3: 41

basketball ['bɑːskɪtbɔːl] Basketball

bass guitar [beɪsgɪ'tɑː] Bassgitarre WF

bathroom ['bɑːθruːm] Badezimmer, Bad

battery ['bætri] Batterie WF

battery pack ['bætripæk] Akku WF

Bavaria [bə'veəriə] Bayern WF

be [biː, bi] (I/he was, you were; I've been) sein

beach [biːtʃ] Strand; **on the beach** am Strand U2: 29

bean [biːn] Bohne WF

bear [beə] Bär U4: 52

beard [bɪəd] Bart WF

beat [biːt] schlagen WF

beautiful ['bjuːtɪfl] schön, wunderschön

beaver ['biːvə] Biber U4: 55

became [bɪ'keɪm] (→ become): **I became** ich wurde, ich bin geworden

because [bɪ'kɒz] weil

become [bɪ'kʌm] (I became, I've become) werden; **I've become** ich bin geworden

bed [bed] Bett

bedroom ['bedruːm] Schlafzimmer

beef [biːf] Rindfleisch U1: 12

been [biːn, bɪn] (→ be): **I've been** ich bin gewesen; **I've been thinking that** ich habe das (immer wieder) gedacht WF

beep [biːp] piepen WF

beer [bɪə] Bier

before [bɪ'fɔː] **1** bevor; **2** vor WF U6

behind [bɪ'haɪnd] hinter

being ['biːɪŋ]: **dreams of being like ...** Träume, in denen ich wie ... bin WF

Belgium ['beldʒəm] Belgien

believe [bɪ'liːv] glauben U5: 77

belong to [bɪ'lɒŋtə] gehören WF

best [best] beste, bester, bestes; am besten U1: 11; **Best wishes, ...** Viele Grüße ...

better ['betə] besser

between [bɪ'twiːn] zwischen U2: 27

beverage ['bevərɪdʒ] Getränk WF

beware [bɪ'weə]: **Beware of ...** Nimm dich in Acht vor ... WF

big [bɪg] groß

bike [baɪk] Fahrrad, Rad

biology [baɪ'ɒlədʒi] Biologie WF

bird [bɜːd] Vogel

birthday ['bɜːθdeɪ] Geburtstag; **It's my birthday.** Ich habe Geburtstag.

biscuit ['bɪskɪt] Keks, Plätzchen WF

black [blæk] schwarz; **Black Forest** Schwarzwald WF; **black people** Schwarze U1: 14

blanket ['blæŋkɪt] Decke WF

block [blɒk] Häuserblock U1: 13

blog [blɒg] Blog (von Weblog; hier eine Art Online-Tagebuch)

blogger ['blɒgə] Blogger, Bloggerin (Autor/in eines Blogs)

blogging ['blɒgɪŋ] Bloggen (ein Blog führen und auf andere Blogs reagieren)

blonde [blɒnd] blond

blue [bluː] blau

board [bɔːd] **1** Tafel; **2** Board, Brett

boardwalk ['bɔːdwɔːk] (hölzerne) Strandpromenade U2: 25

boat [bəʊt] Boot; Schiff

book [bʊk] **1** Buch; Heft; **2** buchen, reservieren (lassen) WF U6

bookshop ['bʊkʃɒp] Buchladen, Buchhandlung

boot [buːt] Stiefel WF

border ['bɔːdə] Grenze

bored [bɔːd] gelangweilt; **I'm bored** ich langweile mich

boring ['bɔːrɪŋ] langweilig

born [bɔːn]: **I was born ...** ich wurde ... geboren

borrow ['bɒrəʊ]: **borrow a pen** sich einen Füller (aus)leihen

bought [bɔːt] (→ buy): **I bought** ich kaufte, ich habe gekauft; **I've bought** ich habe gekauft

box [bɒks] Kiste, Kasten

boy [bɔɪ] Junge

boyfriend ['bɔɪfrend] (fester) Freund U1: 16

brain [breɪn] Gehirn WF

brand [brænd] Marke U3: 41

brave [breɪv] mutig, tapfer

bread [bred] Brot

break [breɪk] Pause

breakfast ['brekfəst] Frühstück; **have breakfast** frühstücken

bridge [brɪdʒ] Brücke

bring [brɪŋ] (I brought, I've brought) bringen; **bring about** herbeiführen WF

DICTIONARY

Britain ['brɪtn] Großbritannien
British ['brɪtɪʃ] britisch; Brite/
Britin Next: 8
broccoli ['brɒkəli] Brokkoli WF
brochure ['brəʊʃə] Broschüre
brother ['brʌðə] Bruder; **brothers
and sisters** Geschwister
brought [brɔːt] (→ bring): **I brought**
ich brachte, ich habe gebracht
U4: 57; **I've brought** ich habe
gebracht U4: 153
brown [braʊn] braun; **brown bread**
Graubrot U1: 12
buddy ['bʌdi] „Kumpel" *(ältere/r
Schüler/in, der/die jüngeren hilft)*
buffalo, buffaloes ['bʌfələʊ,
'bʌfələʊz] Büffel WF U6
builder's helper ['bɪldəz'helpə]
Baugehilfe, Baugehilfin WF
building ['bɪldɪŋ] Gebäude WF
building site ['bɪldɪŋsaɪt] Baustelle
WF
built [bɪlt]: **she built** sie baute WF;
they were built sie wurden
gebaut WF U6
bully ['bʊli] Tyrann, „Mobber/in"
bullying ['bʊliɪŋ] Schikanieren,
Mobbing; **text bullying** SMS-
Terror
bus [bʌs] Bus
bus driver ['bʌsdraɪvə] Busfahrer,
Busfahrerin
business ['bɪznəs] Betrieb,
Geschäft(s-)
bus stop ['bʌstɒp] Bushaltestelle
busy ['bɪzi] beschäftigt; hektisch,
belebt U1: 11; **a busy road** eine
viel befahrene Straße
but [bʌt] aber
button ['bʌtn] Knopf; Taste
buy [baɪ] (I bought, I've bought)
kaufen
by [baɪ] **1** an, in der Nähe von,
neben; **2** von; durch; **by bike/
bus/car/...** mit dem Rad/Bus/
Auto/...; **by his arms** an den
Armen; **by October 15th** bis zum
15. Oktober U1: 21; **Learn it by
heart.** Lerne es auswendig. **play
by the rules** sich an die Spielregeln halten U3: 43
Bye. [baɪ] Tschüs. Wiedersehen.

C

cabin ['kæbɪn] Hütte WF
cable ['keɪbl] Kabel WF
cafe ['kæfeɪ] Café
cake [keɪk] Kuchen

California [kælɪ'fɔːniə] Kalifornien
WF U6
call [kɔːl] **1** anrufen; (herbei)rufen
U2: 32; **call back** zurückrufen
U2: 33; **call me at ...** ruf mich
unter ... an WF; **2** nennen,
bezeichnen U2: 30; **What do you
call ...?** Wie nennt/bezeichnet
man ...? U2: 30; **3 phone call**
Anruf U2: 32
calling ['kɔːlɪŋ]: **Thanks for calling.**
Danke für den Anruf.
came [keɪm] (→ come): **I came** ich
kam, ich bin gekommen
camera ['kæmərə] Fotoapparat,
Kamera U2: 36
camp [kæmp] lagern, zelten WF U6
campfire ['kæmpfaɪə] Lagerfeuer
U4: 54
campground ['kæmpgraʊnd] (AE)
Campingplatz, Zeltplatz U4: 54
camping ['kæmpɪŋ] Camping
can [kæn, kən] können, dürfen;
can't [kɑːnt] nicht können;
**Can you ...? – Yes, I can./No, I
can't.** Kannst du ...? – Ja./Nein.
canal [kə'næl] Kanal
canoe [kə'nuː] Kanu
canoeing [kə'nuːɪŋ] Kanufahren,
Paddeln
cap [kæp] Kappe
capital ['kæpɪtl] Hauptstadt
captain ['kæptɪn] Spielführer/in,
Mannschaftskapitän/in WF
car [kɑː] Auto
card [kɑːd] Karte
career [kə'rɪə] **1** Beruf, Berufs-
U3: 50; **2 career (in TV)** (Fern-
seh-)Karriere, berufliche Laufbahn (im Fernsehen) U2: 28
careful ['keəfl] vorsichtig
carnival ['kɑːnɪvl] Karneval
car park ['kɑːpɑːk] Parkplatz
carry ['kæri] tragen WF
cashier [kæ'ʃɪə] Kassierer,
Kassiererin U4: 63
castle ['kɑːsl] Schloss; Burg
cat [kæt] Katze
catch [kætʃ] fangen WF
category ['kætəgəri] Kategorie
WF
cauliflower ['kɒliflaʊə] Blumenkohl
WF
CD [siː'diː] CD
celebration [selɪ'breɪʃn] Feier WF
cellphone ['selfəʊn] (AE) Handy,
Mobiltelefon Next: 9
cent [sent] Cent U1: 12
centre ['sentə] Zentrum; Mitte
chair [tʃeə] Stuhl; Sessel

chairperson ['tʃeəpɜːsn] Vorsitzende, Vorsitzender
change [tʃeɪndʒ] **1** (sich) ändern,
(sich) verändern; **change to**
ändern in WF; **2** umsteigen
U1: 13; **change at 42nd Street to
line 7** an der 42. Straße in die
Linie 7 umsteigen U1: 13; **3** Veränderung WF
character ['kærəktə] Figur, Person
WF U6
charge [tʃɑːdʒ] aufladen WF
charged up [tʃɑːdʒd'ʌp]: **it's
charged up** es ist aufgeladen
charger ['tʃɑːdʒə] (Batterie-)Lade-
gerät
chat [tʃæt]: **have a chat** sich unterhalten
chat show ['tʃætʃəʊ] Talkshow
U2: 27
cheap [tʃiːp] billig, preiswert
check [tʃek] kontrollieren, überprüfen
cheer [tʃɪə] (zu)jubeln, hurra rufen
U3: 42
cheerleader ['tʃɪəliːdə] *Person, die
das Publikum bei einem Wett-
kampf zum Beifall anfeuert*
U3: 38
cheese [tʃiːz] Käse
cherry ['tʃeri] Kirsche WF
chess [tʃes] Schach WF
chicken ['tʃɪkɪn] Huhn;
(Brat-)Hähnchen
child, children [tʃaɪld, 'tʃɪldrən]
Kind, Kinder
chips [tʃɪps] Pommes frites
chocolate ['tʃɒklət] Schokolade
choir ['kwaɪə] Chor WF
Christmas ['krɪsməs] Weihnachten
church [tʃɜːtʃ] Kirche
cider ['saɪdə] Apfelwein
cinema ['sɪnəmə] Kino
city ['sɪti] Stadt, Großstadt
clarinet [klærə'net] Klarinette WF
class [klɑːs] Klasse; **extra classes**
Förderunterricht U3: 38
classical ['klæsɪkl] klassisch WF
classroom ['klɑːsruːm] Klassenzimmer
class teacher ['klɑː'tiːtʃə] Klassen-
lehrer, Klassenlehrerin
clean [kliːn] sauber
cleaner ['kliːnə] Putzhilfe, Raum-
pfleger/in U4: 63
clear [klɪə]: **clear tables** Tische
abräumen WF
cliff [klɪf] Klippe, Felsen
climb (a hill) [klaɪm] (auf einen
Hügel) klettern

climber ['klaɪmə] Kletterer, Kletterin

clock [klɒk] Uhr U3: 40

close [kləʊz] zumachen, schließen

closed [kləʊzd] geschlossen, zu

closet ['klɒzɪt] (AE) Wandschrank WF

clothes [kləʊðz] Kleidung, Kleider

cloud [klaʊd] Wolke

cloudy ['klaʊdi] bewölkt

club [klʌb] **1** Klub, Arbeitsgemeinschaft; Verein; **2** Disko

clue [kluː]: **I have no clue** ich habe keine Ahnung WF

coach [kəʊtʃ] Coach U3: 42

coast [kəʊst] Küste WF U6; **on the coast** an der Küste WF U6

coffee shop ['kɒfiʃɒp] Selbstbedienungscafé WF

cola ['kəʊlə] Cola

cold [kəʊld] kalt

collect [kə'lekt] sammeln

Colombia [kə'lɒmbiə] Kolumbien U5: 68

colour ['kʌlə] Farbe; **What colour is your room?** Welche Farbe hat dein Zimmer?

combine harvester [kɒmbaɪn'hɑːvɪstə] Mähdrescher WF

come [kʌm] (I came, I've come) kommen; mitkommen; **I've come** ich bin gekommen; **come in** hereinkommen; **come first in ...** Erste/Erster werden bei ...

comedy ['kɒmədi] Komödie, humorvoller Film/Roman U2: 27

comic ['kɒmɪk] Comic WF

communications [kəmjuːnɪ'keɪʃnz]: **information and communications technology** Informatik WF

compare [kəm'peə] vergleichen

comparison [kəm'pærɪsn] Vergleich WF

competition [kɒmpə'tɪʃn] Wettbewerb

complain [kəm'pleɪn] sich beschweren

complete [kəm'pliːt] vollständig

computer [kəm'pjuːtə] Computer, Rechner

concerned (about) [kən'sɜːnd] besorgt (wegen) WF

concert ['kɒnsət] Konzert U1: 18

confident ['kɒnfɪdənt] zuversichtlich, selbstsicher U3: 42

Congratulations! [kəngrætʃu'leɪʃnz] Herzlichen Glückwunsch!

connect [kə'nekt] anschließen, verbinden WF

context ['kɒntekst] Zusammenhang, Kontext U2: 31

conversation [kɒnvə'seɪʃn] Unterhaltung, Gespräch Next: 8

cook [kʊk] **1** kochen U4: 64; **2** Koch, Köchin

cool [kuːl] cool, toll

copy ['kɒpi] **1** abschreiben; kopieren U1: 21; **2** Kopie, Fotokopie WF

correct [kə'rekt] korrigieren, berichtigen

cost [kɒst] Preis WF

cotton ['kɒtn] Baumwolle WF

cougar ['kuːgə] (AE) Puma U4: 52

could [kʊd]: **I could(n't)** **1** ich konnte (nicht); **2** ich könnte (nicht) U2: 28

council ['kaʊnsl]: **school council** Schülermitverwaltung WF

country ['kʌntri] Land; **in the country** auf dem Land

county fair [kaʊnti'feə] eine Art Landwirtschaftsschau WF U6

courier ['kʊriə] Kurier/Kurierin, Bote/Botin

course [kɔːs]: **of course** natürlich, selbstverständlich

court [kɔːt] Spielfeld, Platz U3: 40

courtroom drama ['kɔːtruːmdrɑːmə] Gerichtsshow, -sendung WF

cousin ['kʌzn] Cousin, Cousine

cover ['kʌvə] **1** Abdeckung WF; **2** Umschlag WF

cover letter ['kʌvəletə] Anschreiben, Begleitbrief U4: 63

cow [kaʊ] Kuh

coward ['kaʊəd] Feigling WF

cowboy ['kaʊbɔɪ] Cowboy WF

cracker ['krækə] Kräcker WF U6

crash [kræʃ] abstürzen WF

crawl [krɔːl] kriechen; **crawl in** hineinkriechen

credit ['kredɪt] Guthaben

crime [kraɪm] Verbrechen U5: 66

crisps [krɪsps] Kartoffelchips

crow [krəʊ] Krähe WF

cry [kraɪ] weinen

cup [kʌp] Tasse; **a cup of tea** eine Tasse Tee

cupboard ['kʌbəd] Schrank

cycling ['saɪklɪŋ] Radfahren

Czech Republic [tʃekrɪ'pʌblɪk] Tschechische Republik

D

dad [dæd] Papa, Vati

dance [dɑːns] **1** tanzen; **2** Tanzveranstaltung, Ball WF

dancer ['dɑːnsə] Tänzer/in U5: 68

dancing ['dɑːnsɪŋ]: **go dancing** tanzen gehen

dangerous ['deɪndʒərəs] gefährlich

dare [deə] Mutprobe

date [deɪt] Datum

daughter ['dɔːtə] Tochter

day [deɪ] Tag

deaf [def] taub U5: 70

deal [diːl] (I dealt, I've dealt): **deal with bags** sich um Taschen kümmern

dear [dɪə]: **Dear ...** Liebe/Lieber ...; **Dear Sir/Madam, ...** Sehr geehrte Damen und Herren, ... WF

December [dɪ'sembə] Dezember

decorate ['dekəreɪt] schmücken WF

deer [dɪə] Hirsch, Hirsche U4: 52

definition [defɪ'nɪʃn] Definition U2: 30

degree [dɪ'griː] Grad U5: 74

deli ['deli] (AE) Feinkostgeschäft und -imbiss U1: 12

deliver [dɪ'lɪvə] austragen WF

Denmark ['denmɑːk] Dänemark

dentist ['dentɪst] Zahnarzt, Zahnärztin U1: 18

department store [dɪ'pɑːtməntstɔː] Kaufhaus

depressed [dɪ'prest] deprimiert WF

describe [dɪ'skraɪb] beschreiben WF U6

description [dɪ'skrɪpʃn] Beschreibung

design [dɪ'zaɪn] entwerfen WF

designated ['dezɪgneɪtɪd] gekennzeichnet WF

destination [destɪ'neɪʃn] (Reise-) Ziel WF

detail ['diːteɪl] Detail WF

detective [dɪ'tektɪv] Detektiv/in

devastated ['devəsteɪtɪd] erschüttert, am Boden zerstört

device [dɪ'vaɪs] Gerät WF

dialogue ['daɪəlɒg] Dialog, Gespräch

diary ['daɪəri] Tagebuch; **homework diary** Hausaufgabenheft; Schülerkalender

dictionary ['dɪkʃənri] Wörterbuch; Wörterverzeichnis

did [dɪd] (→ do): **I did** ich machte, ich habe gemacht

die [daɪ] sterben

difference ['dɪfrəns]: **make a difference** etwas bewegen, etwas verändern WF

different ['dɪfrənt] verschieden; anders; andere, anderer, anderes; **different from** anders als

difficult ['dɪfɪkəlt] schwierig, schwer U3: 50

diner ['daɪnə] (AE) Imbissstube, Café WF U6

dinner ['dɪnə] Abendessen U1: 12

director [də'rektə] Regisseur, Regisseurin U2: 28

dirty ['dɜːti] schmutzig

disc golf ['dɪskɒlf] Discgolf („Scheibengolf") WF U6

dislike [dɪs'laɪk] Abneigung

district ['dɪstrɪkt] Bezirk, Gebiet U1: 10

disturb [dɪ'stɜːb] stören WF

DJ ['diːdʒeɪ] DJ (= Discjockey)

do [duː] (he does; I did, I've done) **1** tun, machen; schaffen; **2 I don't (= do not)/He doesn't (= does not) live here.** Ich wohne/Er wohnt nicht hier. **Do you/Does he live here? – Yes, I do./No, I don't. / Yes, he does./No, he doesn't.** Wohnst du/Wohnt er hier? – Ja./Nein. **Don't eat.** Iss nicht.

document ['dɒkjumənt] Dokument, Schriftstück WF

documentary [dɒkju'mentri] Dokumentarfilm WF

does [dʌz] → do

dog [dɒg] Hund

doing ['duːɪŋ] **What are you doing?** Was machst du (da)? **How ya doin'?** (AE) Wie geht's? WF

dollar ($) ['dɒlə] Dollar (Währung) U1: 12

dolphin ['dɒlfɪn] Delfin

done [dʌn] (→ do) **I've done** ich habe gemacht

door [dɔː] Tür

double-decker bus [dʌbldekə'bʌs] Doppeldecker WF

double room [dʌbl'ruːm] Doppelzimmer WF U6

down [daʊn] hinunter/herunter, hinab/herab

download [daʊn'ləʊd] herunterladen U5: 68

drama ['drɑːmə] **courtroom drama** Gerichtsshow, Gerichtssendung WF; **family drama** Familienfilm WF

drank [dræŋk] (→ drink) **I drank** ich trank, ich habe getrunken

draw [drɔː] (I drew, I've drawn) zeichnen

dream [driːm] **1** träumen; **2** Traum

dressing ['dresɪŋ] Anziehen WF

drink [drɪŋk] **1** (I drank, I've drunk) trinken; **2** Getränk

drive [draɪv] (I drove, I've driven) fahren

driven ['drɪvn] (→ drive) **I've driven** ich bin gefahren U4: 153

driver ['draɪvə] (Auto-)Fahrer, Fahrerin

drove [drəʊv] (→ drive) **I drove** ich fuhr, ich bin gefahren U4: 56

drug [drʌg] Droge U2: 35

drug-free [drʌg'friː] drogenfrei WF

drums [drʌmz] Trommeln; Schlagzeug WF

dry trocken WF U6

Dubliner ['dʌblɪnə] Dubliner, Dublinerin

dumb [dʌm] dumm, blöd WF

dune [djuːn] Düne WF

dune buggy ['djuːnbʌgi] „Strandbuggy" (offenes Freizeitauto) WF

DVD [diːviː'diː] DVD

DVD player [diːviː'diːpleɪə] DVD-Player

E

each [iːtʃ] jede, jeder, jedes U3: 41

ear [ɪə] Ohr U5: 70

early ['ɜːli] früh

earn [ɜːn] verdienen WF

east [iːst] Osten; Ost-; östlich

easy ['iːzi] einfach, leicht

eat [iːt] (I ate, I've eaten) essen; fressen

eaten ['iːtn] (→ eat) **I've eaten** ich habe gegessen U4: 153

economy [ɪ'kɒnəmi] Wirtschaft U5: 78

education [edʒu'keɪʃn] Bildung, Ausbildung WF

egg [eg] Ei U1: 12

eighteensixties [eɪtiːn'sɪkstiz]: **in the 1860s** in den sechziger Jahren des 19. Jahrhunderts WF

electric [ɪ'lektrɪk] elektrisch

electricity [ɪlek'trɪsəti] Strom, Elektrizität

electronic [ɪlek'trɒnɪk] elektronisch

e-mail ['iːmeɪl] E-Mail

embarrassed [ɪm'bærəst] verlegen

emotional [ɪ'məʊʃənl] gefühlsbetont WF

employer [ɪm'plɔɪə] Arbeitgeber, Arbeitgeberin U5: 78

encyclopedia [ɪnsaɪklə'piːdiə] Lexikon, Enzyklopädie WF U6

end [end] Ende U1: 13; **in the end** letztendlich; schließlich

ending ['endɪŋ] Schluss; **happy ending** Happy End U3: 40

energy ['enədʒi] Energie; Kraft; **full of energy** energiegeladen WF

England ['ɪŋglənd] England

English ['ɪŋglɪʃ] englisch; Englisch; Engländer/Engländerin(nen); **English teacher** Englischlehrer/-lehrerin

enjoy [ɪn'dʒɔɪ] genießen WF; **Enjoy your stay.** Einen angenehmen Aufenthalt. WF U6; **everything for young men to enjoy** alles, was jungen Männern gefällt WF

enough [ɪ'nʌf] genug WF U6

entrance fee ['entrənsfiː] Eintrittspreis U4: 55

entry ['entri] Eintrag U2: 31

environment [ɪn'vaɪrənmənt] Umwelt; Umgebung

environmental studies [ɪnvaɪrən'mentl'stʌdiz] Umweltlehre WF

e-pal ['iːpæl] E-Mail-Freund/Freundin WF U6

equipment [ɪ'kwɪpmənt] Ausstattung, Ausrüstung U3: 40

errand ['erənd]: **run errands** Besorgungen machen WF

escape [ɪ'skeɪp] fliehen, entkommen WF

establish [ɪ'stæblɪʃ] einrichten; eröffnen WF U6

euro (€) ['jʊərəʊ] Euro

Europe ['jʊərəp] Europa

European [jʊərə'piːən] europäisch; Europäer, Europäerin U4: 60

evening ['iːvnɪŋ] Abend; **in the evening** am Abend, abends

event [ɪ'vent] Veranstaltung WF

ever ['evə] schon einmal, jemals; **the lowest price ever** der niedrigste Preis, den es je gab WF

evergreen ['evəgriːn] immergrün WF

every ['evri] jede, jeder, jedes

everybody ['evribɒdi] jeder, alle

everyone ['evriwʌn] jeder, alle WF

everything ['evriθɪŋ] alles

everywhere ['evriweə] überall, überallhin, überallher

exactly [ɪg'zæktli] genau WF

example [ɪg'zɑːmpl] Beispiel

exchange [ɪks'tʃeɪndʒ] Austausch-; Tausch- U3: 46

excited [ɪk'saɪtɪd] aufgeregt, begeistert WF U6

exciting [ɪk'saɪtɪŋ] aufregend, spannend

excuse [ɪkˈskjuːz]: **Excuse me, ...**
Entschuldigen Sie, ...

exercise [ˈeksəsaɪz] Übung

exercise book [ˈeksəsaɪzbʊk]
Schulheft

exhibition [eksɪˈbɪʃn] Ausstellung

expensive [ɪkˈspensɪv] teuer

experience [ɪkˈspɪəriəns] Erfahrung
U4: 63; **do work experience** ein
Berufspraktikum machen WF

expert [ˈekspɜːt] Fachmann/-frau,
Experte/Expertin U3: 41

explain [ɪkˈspleɪn] erklären;
explain something to her ihr
etwas erklären U1: 16

extinct [ɪkˈstɪŋkt] ausgestorben
WF

extra [ˈekstrə]: **extra classes**
Förderunterricht U3: 38

eye [aɪ] Auge

F

face [feɪs] Gesicht

fact [fækt] Tatsache Next: 7;
In fact, it was better. Es war
sogar besser.

factory [ˈfæktri] Fabrik

fair [feə]: **county fair** *eine Art
Landwirtschaftsschau* WF U6

fair play [feəˈpleɪ] Fair Play U3: 42

fall [fɔːl] (I fell, I've fallen) fallen

false [fɔːls] falsch, unwahr U1: 11

family [ˈfæməli] Familie; **family
name** Nachname, Familienname
U4: 63

famous [ˈfeɪməs] berühmt

fan [fæn] Fan, Anhänger/in

fantastic [fænˈtæstɪk] fantastisch
U5: 68

fantasy film [ˈfæntəsifɪlm] Fantasy-
film WF

far [fɑː] weit Next: 7

Farewell Bend [feəˈwelbend] „Lebewohl-Biegung" WF U6

farm [fɑːm] Bauernhof, Hof

farmer [ˈfɑːmə] Bauer, Bäuerin

fast [fɑːst] schnell

fast food [fɑːstˈfuːd] Fastfood
(schnell verzehrbare Gerichte)

father [ˈfɑːðə] Vater

favourite [ˈfeɪvərɪt] Lieblings-;
Favorit, Favoritin

February [ˈfebruəri] Februar

feed [fiːd] (I fed, I've fed) füttern,
zu essen geben

feel [fiːl] (I felt, I've felt) (sich) fühlen

feeling [ˈfiːlɪŋ] Gefühl U5: 71

feet [fiːt] Füße (→ foot)

fell [fel] (→ fall): **I fell** ich fiel, ich
bin gefallen

felt [felt] (→ feel): **I felt** ich fühlte
(mich), ich habe (mich) gefühlt;
I've felt ich habe (mich) gefühlt

female [ˈfiːmeɪl] weiblich U5: 69

festival [ˈfestɪvl] Festival; Fest
U4: 52

field [fiːld] Feld, Wiese; Sportplatz WF

fight [faɪt] (I fought, I've fought)
kämpfen; sich streiten U1: 14

file [faɪl] Karteikarte; Akte; Akten-
ordner WF

fill in [fɪlˈɪn] ausfüllen WF U6

film [fɪlm] Film

final [ˈfaɪnl] Finale WF

financial [faɪˈnænʃl] finanziell,
Finanz- U1: 10

find [faɪnd] (I found, I've found)
finden; **find out** herausfinden

fine [faɪn] gut, schön; **How are
you? – I'm fine, thanks.** Wie
geht's? – Danke, gut.

finish [ˈfɪnɪʃ] aufhören (mit);
beenden; **To finish, ...** Um zum
Ende zu kommen, ...

fire [ˈfaɪə] Feuer; Brand U4: 54

fireworks [ˈfaɪəwɜːks] Feuerwerk
U2: 36

first [fɜːst] **1** erste, erster, erstes;
first aid erste Hilfe U3: 39; **first
name** Vorname U4: 63; **2** zuerst

firstly [ˈfɜːstli] erstens

fish [fɪʃ] **1** Fisch, Fische; **2** fischen,
angeln U4: 57

fish and chip shop [fɪʃənˈtʃɪpʃɒp]
*Schnellimbiss für Fisch und
Pommes frites*

fishing [ˈfɪʃɪŋ] Fischen, Angeln

fit [fɪt] fit U3: 50

fix [fɪks] reparieren U3: 49

fizzy drink [fɪziˈdrɪŋk] Limonade
WF U6

flag [flæg] Fahne, Flagge

flat [flæt] Wohnung

flew [fluː]: **they flew** sie flogen WF

flight [flaɪt] Flug WF U6

flip phone [ˈflɪpfəʊn] Klapphandy

floor [flɔː] Fußboden, Boden

flyer [ˈflaɪə] Handzettel WF

follow [ˈfɒləʊ] folgen, verfolgen

food [fuːd] Essen; Lebensmittel

foot, feet [fʊt, fiːt] Fuß, Füße;
on foot zu Fuß

football [ˈfʊtbɔːl] Fußball;
American football American
Football *(ähnlich wie Rugby)*
U3: 41

for [fɔː, fə] **1** für; **2** zu; **3** denn WF;
for 14 years 14 Jahre lang; **for a
long time** lange U2: 28; **for
breakfast** zum Frühstück; **stay
for long** lange bleiben

foreground [ˈfɔːgraʊnd] Vordergrund WF

forest [ˈfɒrɪst] Wald, Waldgebiet
U4: 52

forget [fəˈget] (I forgot, I've
forgotten) vergessen

forgot [fəˈgɒt] (→ forget): **I forgot**
ich vergaß, ich habe vergessen
U4: 57

forgotten [fəˈgɒtn] (→ forget): **I've
forgotten** ich habe vergessen
U4: 153

form [fɔːm] **1** Form; **2** Formular
WF U6

forward [ˈfɔːwəd]: **I'm looking forward to hearing from you** ich
freue mich darauf, von Ihnen zu
hören U4: 56

forwards [ˈfɔːwədz] vorwärts WF

fought [fɔːt] (→ fight): **I fought** ich
kämpfte, ich habe gekämpft
U1: 144; **I've fought** ich habe
gekämpft U1: 144

foul [faʊl] Foul U3: 40

found [faʊnd] (→ find): **I found** ich
fand, ich habe gefunden; **I've
found** ich habe gefunden; **If
they found her ...** Wenn sie sie
fänden ... WF

fountain [ˈfaʊntən] Brunnen WF

France [frɑːns] Frankreich

freak [friːk] Freak *(jemand, der sich
sehr für etwas begeistert)*

free [friː] **1** frei; **2** kostenlos; **free
throw** Freiwurf U3: 40; **free
time** Freizeit

freedom [ˈfriːdəm] Freiheit U1: 14

freeway [ˈfriːweɪ] Autobahn *(in den
USA)* U2: 28

French [frentʃ] französisch; Französisch; Franzose(n), Franzö-
sin(nen)

Friday [ˈfraɪdeɪ, ˈfraɪdi] Freitag

friend [frend] Freund, Freundin

friendly [ˈfrendli] freundlich

frightened [ˈfraɪtnd]: **I'm
frightened** ich habe Angst

frightening [ˈfraɪtnɪŋ] beängstigend, Furcht erregend U5: 70

from [frɒm, frəm] aus; von; **I'm
from London.** Ich komme aus
London.

front [frʌnt]: **in front of** vor
U5: 68

fruit [fruːt] Obst, Früchte

DICTIONARY

full [fʊl] voll; vollständig WF

fun [fʌn] Spaß; **It's fun.** Es macht Spaß.

funfair ['fʌnfeə] Kirmes, Jahrmarkt

funny ['fʌni] lustig, komisch

furniture ['fɜːnɪtʃə] Möbel

future ['fjuːtʃə] Zukunft

G

Gaelic ['gælɪk] Gälisch *(keltische Sprache)*

game [geɪm] Spiel; **game show** Spielshow WF

gang [gæŋ] Gang, Bande, Clique

garage ['gærɑːʒ] Autowerkstatt WF

garden ['gɑːdn] Garten

gardener ['gɑːdnə] Gärtner/in

gas [gæs] (AE) Benzin WF

gate [geɪt] Tor

gave [geɪv] (→ give): **I gave** ich gab, ich habe gegeben

gear [gɪə] **1** Gang *(Fahrrad, Auto)*; **2** Ausrüstung U2: 29; **safety gear** Sicherheitsausrüstung; **3** Kleidung, Klamotten U2: 29

general ['dʒenrəl] allgemein U5: 68

geography [dʒi'ɒgrəfi] Erdkunde, Geografie

German ['dʒɜːmən] deutsch; Deutsch; Deutsche, Deutscher

Germany ['dʒɜːməni] Deutschland

get [get] (I got, I've got) **1** bekommen; **2** holen; **3** kommen, gelangen; **get lost** sich verirren U4: 59; **get on the bus** in den Bus einsteigen WF; **get out** rausgehen WF **I have to get out of this place.** Ich muss hier raus. **get up** aufstehen; **you can get yourself clean** du kannst dich waschen WF

ghost [gəʊst] Geist, Gespenst

Gimme five! [gɪmi'faɪv] (AE) *Aufforderung dazu, die (erhobenen) Hände aneinander zu klatschen* WF

girl [gɜːl] Mädchen

girlfriend ['gɜːlfrend] (feste) Freundin

give [gɪv] (I gave, I've given) geben; **Give the book to Tim.** Gib Tim das Buch. **give first aid** erste Hilfe leisten WF; **give to the poor** die Armen beschenken WF

give up [gɪv'ʌp] aufgeben; **give up TV** auf den Fernseher verzichten WF

given ['gɪvn] (→ give): **I've given** ich habe gegeben

giving ['gɪvɪŋ]: **Giving orders** Anweisungen geben, Befehle erteilen U3: 46

glass [glɑːs] Glas, Trinkglas

glove [glʌv] Handschuh WF

go [gəʊ] (I went, I've gone) gehen; fahren; fliegen; führen; **go in** hineingehen; **Go ahead.** Mach(t)/Machen Sie nur. U5: 75

goalkeeper ['gəʊlkiːpə] Torwart WF

going to ['gəʊɪŋtu, 'gəʊɪntə]: **I'm going to win** ich werde gewinnen, ich gewinne; **I'm going to be a ranger.** Ich werde Ranger.

golf [gɒlf] Golf

good [gʊd] gut; **good at** gut in; **a ball's no good** ein Ball nützt nichts WF; **Good evening/ morning/night.** Gute(n) Abend/ Morgen/Nacht. **Good luck!** Viel Glück! U3: 42

Goodbye. [gʊd'baɪ] Auf Wiedersehen.

goose [guːs] Gans WF

got [gɒt] (→ get): **I got 1** ich bekam, ich habe bekommen; **2** (AE) ich habe WF; **I've got** ich habe bekommen

gotta ['gɒtə]: **gotta find me a place** (ich) muss einen Ort finden WF

government ['gʌvənmənt] Regierung WF

grade [greɪd]: **grade 9** (AE) 9. Klasse U3: 38

grandad ['grændæd] Opa, Großvater

granddaughter ['grændɔːtə] Enkeltochter, Enkelin WF

grandma ['grænmɑː] Oma, Großmutter

grandparents ['grænpeərənts] Großeltern U4: 56

grass [grɑːs] Gras, Rasen U2: 28

grave [greɪv] Grab

great [greɪt] toll, großartig

great-grandmother ['greɪt'grænmʌðə] Urgroßmutter WF

Greektown ['griːktaʊn] „Griechenstadt" WF

green [griːn] grün

grew [gruː] (→ grow): **I grew** ich wuchs, ich bin gewachsen U5: 156

grey [greɪ] grau WF

grey whale ['greɪ'weɪl] Grauwal WF

grill [grɪl] grillen WF U6

grilled [grɪld] gegrillt WF

ground [graʊnd] Boden

grounded ['graʊndɪd]: **I'm grounded** ich habe Hausarrest/ Stubenarrest

group [gruːp] Gruppe

grow [grəʊ] (I grew, I've grown) wachsen U5: 78

grown [grəʊn] (→ grow): **I've grown** ich bin gewachsen U5: 156

guard [gɑːd]: **security guard** Wachfrau, Wachmann

guess [ges] raten; erraten

guest [gest] Gast WF

guide [gaɪd] **1** führen WF; **2** Führer/in *(für Sehenswürdigkeiten)*

guitar [gɪ'tɑː] Gitarre

guys [gaɪz]: **Hi you guys.** (AE) Hallo Leute. Next: 8

gym [dʒɪm] Turnhalle; Fitnessstudio

H

had [hæd, həd] (→ have): **I had** ich hatte, ich habe gehabt; **I've had** ich habe gehabt; **he had told** er hatte erzählt WF; **it had sent** es hatte geschickt U2: 28; **they had brought/sold/taken** sie hatten gebracht/verkauft/mitgenommen WF; **they had come** sie waren gekommen WF; **If I had the money, ...** Wenn ich das Geld hätte, ... WF U6

hair [heə] Haar, Haare

hairdresser ['heədresə] Friseur/in

half [hɑːf]: **half past nine** halb zehn; **three and a half** dreieinhalb

half-time [hɑːf'taɪm] Halbzeit U3: 42

Halloween [hæləʊ'iːn] Halloween

ham [hæm] Schinken

hamburger ['hæmbɜːgə] Hamburger

hamster ['hæmstə] Hamster

hand [hænd] Hand; **On the one hand, ... On the other hand, ...** Einerseits ... Andererseits ... U2: 35

hand out [hænd'aʊt] verteilen WF

hand signal ['hændsɪgnəl] Handzeichen

hang out [hæŋ'aʊt] herumhängen WF

happen ['hæpən] passieren, geschehen; **(it) so happened to be ...** zufälligerweise war es ... WF

happy ['hæpi] glücklich, froh; **I'm happy for her** ich freue mich für sie; **Happy birthday!** Herzlichen Glückwunsch zum Geburtstag! **happy ending** Happy End U3: 40

hard [hɑːd] hart; schwer

166

one hundred and sixty-six

harvest ['hɑːvɪst] ernten WF
has [hæz, həz] → have
hate [heɪt] hassen, nicht ausstehen können
hate-free [heɪt'friː] hassfrei WF
Havana [hə'vænə] Havanna U5: 66
have [hæv, həv] (he has; I had, I've had) **1** haben; **I'll have ...** Ich nehme ... *(Bestellung)* U1: 12; **have a chat** sich unterhalten; **have a cola** eine Cola trinken; **have a party** eine Party geben; **have a picnic** ein Picknick machen; **have an ice cream** ein Eis essen; **have breakfast** frühstücken; **Have a nice day!** (AE) (Einen) Schönen Tag noch! Next: 8; **2 I've (= I have)/he has finished** ich habe/er hat beendet; **I haven't (= have not)/he hasn't (= has not) finished** ich habe/er hat nicht beendet; **Have you ever ...? - Yes, I have./No, I haven't.** Bist/Hast du schon einmal ...? - Ja./Nein.
have to ['hævtu, 'hævtə] (I had to, I've had to) müssen
he [hiː] er; **he's (= he is)** er ist
head [hed] Kopf
heading ['hedɪŋ] Rubrik; Überschrift
healthy ['helθi] gesund
hear [hɪə] (I heard, I've heard) hören
heard [hɜːd] (→ hear): **I heard** ich hörte, ich habe gehört; **I've heard** ich habe gehört
hearing ['hɪərɪŋ] Gehör WF
heart [hɑːt]: **Learn it by heart.** Lerne es auswendig.
held [held] (→ hold): **I held** ich hielt, ich habe gehalten; **I've held** ich habe gehalten
Hello. [hə'ləʊ] Hallo. (Guten) Tag.
helmet ['helmɪt] Helm
help [help] **1** helfen; **Can I help you?** Kann ich Ihnen behilflich sein? U4: 61; **2** Hilfe
helper ['helpə] Helfer, Helferin
her [hɜː] **1** ihr, ihre; **2** ihr, sie
here [hɪə] hier; hierher; **Here you are.** Hier, bitte.
hero, heroes ['hɪərəʊ, 'hɪərəʊz] Held/Heldin, Helden/Heldinnen WF U6
Hi. [haɪ] Hallo.
high [haɪ] hoch
high jump ['haɪdʒʌmp] Hochsprung
highlight ['haɪlaɪt] Höhepunkt WF
high school ['haɪskuːl] Oberschule *(in den USA)* U3: 38

highway ['haɪweɪ] (AE) Fernstraße WF U6
hike [haɪk] wandern U4: 53
hiker ['haɪkə] Wanderer, Wanderin U4: 59
hill [hɪl] Hügel, (kleiner) Berg
him [hɪm] ihm, ihn
hip [hɪp] Hüfte U5: 68
hire ['haɪə] mieten; vermieten
his [hɪz] sein, seine
Hispanic [hɪ'spænɪk] Hispano-Amerikaner/in; hispanisch; spanischsprachig U5: 67
Historical Society [hɪ'stɒrɪklsə'saɪəti] Geschichtsverein WF U6
history ['hɪstri] Geschichte
hit [hɪt] **1** (I hit, I've hit) schlagen U3: 42; **I hit** ich schlug, ich habe geschlagen U3: 42; **I've hit** ich habe geschlagen U3: 150; **2** Hit U5: 77
hobby ['hɒbi] Hobby
hockey ['hɒki] Hockey
hold [həʊld] (I held, I've held) halten; (MP3-Player:) speichern
hole [həʊl] Loch WF
holiday, holidays ['hɒlədeɪ, -z] Ferien, Urlaub; **go on holiday** in den Urlaub fahren; **she's on holiday** sie macht Urlaub, sie ist im Urlaub
home [həʊm] Heim, Zuhause; **at home** zu Hause, daheim; **go home** nach Hause gehen; **children's home** Kinderheim WF
homecoming ['həʊmkʌmɪŋ] Ehemaligentreffen WF
home economics ['həʊmiːkə'nɒmɪks] Hauswirtschaftslehre WF
homeless ['həʊmləs] heimatlos; obdachlos U2: 25
home-made [həʊm'meɪd] selbst gemacht
homesick ['həʊmsɪk]: **feel homesick** Heimweh haben WF U6
homework ['həʊmwɜːk] Hausaufgaben, Schularbeiten; **I do my homework.** Ich mache (meine) Hausaufgaben.
homework diary [həʊmwɜːk'daɪəri] Hausaufgabenheft; Schülerkalender
hoop [huːp] (Basketball-)Korb U3: 40
hope [həʊp] **1** hoffen; **2** Hoffnung WF
horror ['hɒrə] Horror
horse [hɔːs] Pferd
horse riding ['hɔːsraɪdɪŋ] Reiten

hospital ['hɒspɪtl] Krankenhaus
hot [hɒt] heiß
hot dog ['hɒtdɒg] Hot Dog WF U6
hotel [həʊ'tel] Hotel
hour ['aʊə] Stunde
house [haʊs] **1** Haus; **at Tim's house** bei Tim (zu Hause); **Let's go to my house.** Gehen wir zu mir (nach Hause). **2** House *(Musikrichtung)* U1: 21
how [haʊ] wie; **how to find us** wie man uns findet; **How much is/are ...?** Was kostet/kosten ...? **How ya doin'?** (AE) Wie geht's? WF
hundred ['hʌndrəd] hundert
hungry ['hʌŋgri] hungrig; **I'm hungry.** Ich habe Hunger.
hunt [hʌnt] jagen U4: 57
hunter ['hʌntə] Jäger, Jägerin U4: 60
hurling ['hɜːlɪŋ] Hurling *(irische Sportart; ähnlich wie Hockey)*
hurricane ['hʌrɪkən] Orkan U5: 74
hurry ['hʌri]: **Hurry up!** Beeil dich!
hurt [hɜːt] (I hurt, I've hurt) verletzen, wehtun; **I hurt my hand** ich verletzte mir die Hand, ich habe mir die Hand verletzt

I

I [aɪ] ich; **I'd like ...** Ich möchte .../Ich hätte gern ...; **I'd like to go/...** Ich möchte gehen/...; **I'll (= I will) go** ich werde gehen; **I'll give you your invitations in the break.** Ich gebe euch eure Einladungen in der Pause. **I'll have ...** Ich nehme ... *(Bestellung)* U1: 12; **I'm (= I am)** ich bin
ice cream [aɪs'kriːm] (Speise-)Eis
idea [aɪ'dɪə] Idee, Einfall
idol ['aɪdl] Idol WF
if [ɪf] **1** wenn, falls; **2** ob U3: 49
if-clause ['ɪfklɔːz] if-Satz WF
ill [ɪl] krank
illegal [ɪ'liːgl] ungesetzlich, illegal U5: 78
illness ['ɪlnəs] Krankheit U4: 57
illuminations [ɪluːmɪ'neɪʃnz] Festbeleuchtung
imagine [ɪ'mædʒɪn] sich (etwas) vorstellen
immigrant ['ɪmɪgrənt] Immigrant/Immigrantin, Einwanderer/Einwandern U1: 11
imperative [ɪm'perətɪv] Befehlsform, Imperativ U3: 44
important [ɪm'pɔːtnt] wichtig

in [ɪn] in; **in 1971** (im Jahre) 1971; **in April** im April; **In fact, it was better.** Es war sogar besser. **in Fairfield Road** in der Fairfield Road; **in front of** [ɪnˈfrʌntəv] vor U5: 68; **in German** auf Deutsch; **in the car park** auf dem Parkplatz U3: 46; **in the country** auf dem Land; **in the morning/afternoon/evening** am Morgen/Nachmittag/Abend; **in the picture** auf dem Bild; **in the playground** auf dem Schulhof; **in the same place** am selben Ort; **in the street** auf der Straße; **in the world** auf der (ganzen) Welt; **in winter** im Winter; **come in** hereinkommen; **go in** hineingehen

Independence Day [ɪndɪˈpendənsdeɪ] Unabhängigkeitstag WF

Indian [ˈɪndɪən] Indianer, Indianerin; indianisch WF U6

indie (music) [ˈɪndi] „Indie-Musik" *(von großen Plattenfirmen unabhängige Musik)* WF

indoors [ɪnˈdɔːz] in der Halle, drinnen

infinitive [ɪnˈfɪnətɪv] Infinitiv WF

information [ɪnfəˈmeɪʃn] Informationen, Informations-; **information and communications technology** Informatik WF

in-line skating [ɪnlaɪnˈskeɪtɪŋ] Inlineskating WF

insert [ɪnˈsɜːt] einlegen WF

instead of [ɪnˈstedəv] statt

instructions [ɪnˈstrʌkʃnz] Gebrauchsanweisung

instrument [ˈɪnstrəmənt] Instrument

intercom [ˈɪntəkɒm] Sprechanlage

interest [ˈɪntrəst] Interesse

interested (in) [ˈɪntrəstɪd] interessiert (an)

interesting [ˈɪntrəstɪŋ] interessant

international [ɪntəˈnæʃnəl] international

Internet [ˈɪntənet] Internet; **on the Internet** im Internet

Internet kiosk [ˈɪntənetkiːɒsk] Internet-Kiosk *(öffentlich zugängliches Internet-Terminal)*

interpreting [ɪnˈtɜːprɪtɪŋ] Dolmetschen

interview [ˈɪntəvjuː] 1 Interview WF; 2 Vorstellungsgespräch WF

interviewer [ˈɪntəvjuːə] Gesprächsleiter/in eines Vorstellungsgesprächs WF

into [ˈɪntu, ˈɪntə] in (... hinein/herein); **into the street** auf die Straße (hinaus)

invitation [ɪnvɪˈteɪʃn] Einladung

invite (for) [ɪnˈvaɪt] einladen (zu)

Ireland [ˈaɪələnd] Irland

Irish [ˈaɪrɪʃ] irisch; Irisch; Ire(n), Irin(nen)

is [ɪz] ist; **isn't (= is not)** ist nicht; **What colour is your room?** Welche Farbe hat dein Zimmer?

island [ˈaɪlənd] Insel U4: 53

it [ɪt] 1 es (*nicht bei Personen:* er, sie); 2 ihm, es (*nicht bei Personen:* ihm, ihn; ihr, sie); **it's (= it is)** es ist; **it's 24–18 to North** es steht 24:18 für North U3: 42; **It's my birthday.** Ich habe Geburtstag. **It's Sarah.** Hier spricht Sarah.

Italy [ˈɪtəli] Italien U1: 10

its [ɪts] sein, seine; ihr, ihre

J

jackalope [ˈdʒækələʊp] *amerikanisches Fabeltier* WF U6

jacket [ˈdʒækət] Jacke

January [ˈdʒænjuəri] Januar

jealous (of) [ˈdʒeləs] neidisch (auf); eifersüchtig (auf)

jeans [dʒiːnz] Jeans

job [dʒɒb] 1 Aufgabe, Arbeit; 2 Arbeitsstelle; Beruf

jog [dʒɒg] joggen U2: 28

jogger [ˈdʒɒgə] Jogger, Joggerin

jogging [ˈdʒɒgɪŋ] Jogging

jogging trousers [ˈdʒɒgɪŋtraʊzəz] Jogginghose WF

join [dʒɔɪn]: **join a club** einem Klub beitreten, Mitglied in einem Klub werden; **join us for a party** an unserer Party teilnehmen WF

joke [dʒəʊk] Witz, Scherz WF

judo [ˈdʒuːdəʊ] Judo

juice [dʒuːs] Saft

July [dʒuˈlaɪ] Juli

jump [dʒʌmp] springen; **(the) high jump** Hochsprung

June [dʒuːn] Juni

junior [ˈdʒuːniə]: **junior ranger** Junior-Ranger U4: 54

jury [ˈdʒʊəri] Jury WF

just [dʒʌst] 1 gerade, soeben; 2 einfach WF; **Just a minute.** Einen Augenblick. U5: 74; **just before** kurz (be)vor

K

kayaking [ˈkaɪækɪŋ] Kajakfahren U4: 61

keen [kiːn]: **I'm not keen on it** ich habe nicht viel dafür übrig

keep [kiːp] (I kept, I've kept) halten, behalten U4: 54

kept [kept] (→ keep): **I kept** ich hielt, ich habe gehalten U4: 153; **I've kept** ich habe gehalten U4: 153

key [kiː] Schlüssel U5: 70

keyboard [ˈkiːbɔːd] Keyboard WF

kick [kɪk] kicken, treten U3: 40

kid [kɪd] Kind; Jugendliche/r

kill [kɪl] töten, umbringen U1: 14

kilometre [ˈkɪləmiːtə] Kilometer; **kilometres per hour** Stundenkilometer WF U6

kilt [kɪlt] Kilt *(Schottenrock)*

kind [kaɪnd]: **What kind of programmes?** Was für Sendungen? U2: 27

king [kɪŋ] König WF

kiosk [ˈkiːɒsk]: **Internet kiosk** Internet-Kiosk *(öffentlich zugängliches Internet-Terminal)*

kiss [kɪs] (sich) küssen U5: 70

kitchen [ˈkɪtʃɪn] Küche

knew [njuː] (→ know): **I knew** ich wusste, ich habe gewusst

know [nəʊ] (I knew, I've known) wissen; kennen; **he wanted to know her better** er wollte sie besser kennen lernen WF

L

label [ˈleɪbl] Schildchen, Etikett

lad [læd] Junge WF

laid [leɪd]: **he laid** er legte WF

lake [leɪk] (Binnen-)See Next: 7; **Lake Michigan** [leɪkˈmɪʃɪgən] Michigansee WF

lamb [læm] Lamm(fleisch) WF

lamp [læmp] Lampe WF

land [lænd] Land WF

landmark [ˈlændmɑːk] Wahrzeichen WF

language [ˈlæŋgwɪdʒ] Sprache

laptop [ˈlæptɒp] Laptop

last [lɑːst] letzte, letzter, letztes; **at last** endlich WF

late [leɪt] spät; zu spät, verspätet; **He's late (for school).** Er kommt zu spät (zur Schule).

laugh [lɑːf] lachen

law [lɔː] Gesetz WF

lawn [lɔːn] Rasen WF

lawyer [ˈlɔːjə] Rechtsanwalt, Rechtsanwältin WF

lead [liːd] (I led, I've led) führen U4: 59

lead singer [liːdˈsɪŋə] Leadsänger, Leadsängerin WF

lean [liːn] sich lehnen WF; **lean forwards/backwards** sich vorbeugen/zurücklehnen WF

learn [lɜːn] lernen; **learn about London** etwas über London erfahren; **Learn it by heart.** Lerne es auswendig.

leave [liːv] (I left, I've left) **1** verlassen, weggehen (von); abreisen WF U6; **2** (stehen/liegen) lassen, vergessen U3: 46

led [led] (→ lead): **I led** ich führte, ich habe geführt U4: 153; **I've led** ich habe geführt U4: 153

leek [liːk] Lauch/Porree(stange)

left [left] links; **on the left** auf der linken Seite; **on your left** links (von Ihnen)

left [left] (→ leave): **I left** ich verließ, ich habe verlassen; **I've left** ich habe verlassen U3: 150

lemonade [leməˈneɪd] (Zitronen-)Limonade

less [les] weniger U2: 27

lesson [ˈlesn] (Unterrichts-)Stunde

let [let]: **Let's finish.** Lasst uns aufhören./Hören wir auf.

letter [ˈletə] **1** Brief; **2** Buchstabe

letterboxing [ˈletəbɒksɪŋ] „Letterboxing" *(eine Art Schatzsuche)*

lettuce [ˈletɪs] (Kopf-)Salat U1: 12

library [ˈlaɪbrəri] Bücherei WF

lie [laɪ] lügen U5: 68

life [laɪf] Leben

lift [lɪft] anheben WF

light [laɪt] Licht, Lampe

light switch [ˈlaɪtswɪtʃ] Lichtschalter U5: 70

like [laɪk] **1** mögen, gern haben; **I like it.** Ich mag es./Es gefällt mir. **I (don't) like walking.** Ich laufe (nicht) gern. **I'd like ...** Ich möchte .../Ich hätte gern ...; **I'd like to go/...** Ich möchte gehen/...; **Who likes it best?** Wem gefällt es am besten? **2** wie; **like that/this** so U5: 68; **a job like that/this** so ein Job U2: 29; **What does she look like?** Wie sieht sie aus? **what the book is like** wie das Buch ist

likes and dislikes [ˈlaɪksənˈdɪslaɪks] Vorlieben und Abneigungen

line [laɪn] **1** Zeile; **2** Linie U1: 13; (AE) (Warte-)Schlange U2: 145; **wait in line** (AE) Schlange stehen U2: 28; **line of gear** Kollektion WF

link [lɪŋk] Link; Verbindung U5: 73

lip [lɪp] Lippe

list [lɪst] Liste

listen [ˈlɪsn] zuhören; **listen to** hören, sich anhören

litter [ˈlɪtə] Abfall

little [ˈlɪtl] klein U1: 10; **Little Italy** „Klein-Italien" U1: 10

live [lɪv] wohnen, leben

live [laɪv] live WF

living room [ˈlɪvɪŋruːm] Wohnzimmer

local [ˈləʊkl] örtlich, einheimisch WF

locker [ˈlɒkə] Schließfach, Spind U3: 38

lonely [ˈləʊnli] einsam

long [lɒŋ] lang; lange

longhouse [ˈlɒŋhaʊs] Langhaus WF

look [lʊk] **1** schauen, sehen; **look after** [lʊkˈɑːftə] sich kümmern um, aufpassen auf U4: 59; **look at** ansehen, sich ansehen; **look for** suchen; **I'm looking forward to hearing from you** ich freue mich darauf, von Ihnen zu hören U4: 56; **2** aussehen; **What does she look like?** Wie sieht sie aus?

lose [luːz] (I lost, I've lost) verlieren U1: 15

lost [lɒst] **1** (→ lose): **I lost** ich verlor, ich habe verloren U1: 15; **I've lost** ich habe verloren U1: 144; **2 get lost** sich verirren U4: 59

lots [lɒts]: **lots of** viele; viel

lottery [ˈlɒtəri]: **win a lottery** in einer Lotterie gewinnen WF

lotto [ˈlɒtəʊ] Lotto; **win the lotto** im Lotto gewinnen

loud [laʊd] laut U5: 70

love [lʌv] **1** lieben, sehr mögen; **I love reading.** Ich lese sehr gern. U1: 22; **2** Liebe; **(Lots of) Love, ...** (Viele) Liebe Grüße ...

luck [lʌk]: **Good luck!** Viel Glück! U3: 42

lucky [ˈlʌki]: **Lucky thing!** Der/Die/Du Glückliche/r! U2: 28

lunch [lʌntʃ] Mittagessen

lunch break [ˈlʌntʃbreɪk] Mittagspause

lunchtime [ˈlʌntʃtaɪm] Mittagszeit; Mittagspause

Luxembourg [ˈlʌksəmbɜːg] Luxemburg

M

machine [məˈʃiːn] Maschine, Gerät

madam [ˈmædəm]: **Dear Sir/Madam, ...** Sehr geehrte Damen und Herren, ... WF

made [meɪd] (→ make): **I made** ich machte, ich habe gemacht; **I've made** ich habe gemacht; **if they made me say goodbye** wenn man mich zwänge, mich zu verabschieden; **she made them feel happy** sie machte sie glücklich WF

magazine [mægəˈziːn] Zeitschrift

main point [ˈmeɪnˈpɔɪnt] Schwerpunkt U2: 35

make [meɪk] (I made, I've made) machen, herstellen; **make a difference** etwas bewegen, etwas verändern WF; **make an arrangement** eine Absprache treffen; **make groups** Gruppen bilden; **Make notes.** Mach dir Notizen. **nobody can make me eat this** keiner kann mich dazu zwingen, dies zu essen

make-up [ˈmeɪkʌp] Make-up U2: 30

make-up artist [ˈmeɪkʌpɑːtɪst] Visagist, Visagistin U2: 29

male [meɪl] männlich U5: 68

mall [mɔːl] (AE) Einkaufszentrum U1: 18

man, men [mæn, men] Mann, Männer

many [ˈmeni] viele; **many a man** so manchen Mann WF

map [mæp] Landkarte, Karte; Plan U1: 13

March [mɑːtʃ] März

market [ˈmɑːkɪt] Markt WF

married [ˈmærid] verheiratet

marshmallow [mɑːʃˈmæləʊ] Marshmallow („Mäusespeck") WF U6

master [ˈmɑːstə] Herr WF

match [mætʃ] **1** Spiel, Wettkampf; **2 Match the words with the pictures.** Ordne den Wörtern die Bilder zu.

maths [mæθs] Mathe(matik)

maximum [ˈmæksɪməm] Höchst- WF

May [meɪ] Mai

maybe [ˈmeɪbi] vielleicht

me [miː] **1** mir, mich; **2** ich

meal [miːl] Mahlzeit, (zubereitetes) Essen WF

mean [miːn] (I meant, I've meant) meinen; bedeuten

meaning ['miːnɪŋ] Bedeutung
U2: 31

meant [ment] (→ mean): **I meant**
ich meinte, ich habe gemeint;
I've meant ich habe gemeint

meat [miːt] Fleisch U1: 16

Mecca ['mekə] Mekka WF

media ['miːdiə]: **the media** die
Medien U2: 27

medical ['medɪkl] Medizin-; medizinisch U3: 38

meet [miːt] (I met, I've met)
1 (sich) treffen (mit); **2** kennen
lernen; **Nice to meet you.**
Schön, dich/Sie kennen zu lernen.

melon ['melən] Melone WF

men [men] Männer (→ man)

menu ['menjuː] Speisekarte U1: 12

message ['mesɪdʒ] Mitteilung,
Nachricht U1: 21; **Can I take a
message?** Kann ich (ihm/ihr)
etwas ausrichten? U2: 32; **phone
message** Telefonnotiz; telefonische Nachricht U2: 32

met [met] (→ meet): **I met** ich traf,
ich habe getroffen

metal ['metl] Metal (Musikrichtung)
U5: 68

metre ['miːtə] Meter

Mexico ['meksɪkəʊ] Mexiko U5: 78

mile [maɪl] Meile

milk [mɪlk] Milch

milking machine ['mɪlkɪŋməʃiːn]
Melkmaschine WF

million ['mɪljən] Million

mind [maɪnd]: **Do you mind if I sit
here?** Haben Sie etwas dagegen,
wenn ich mich hier hinsetze?
U5: 75

mind map ['maɪndmæp] Mindmap
(eine Art Gedankenkarte) U4: 59

minute ['mɪnɪt] Minute

mirror ['mɪrə] Spiegel U5: 70

miss [mɪs] **1** vermissen; **2** daneben
treffen; daneben gehen U3: 43

missing ['mɪsɪŋ]: **the missing
words** die fehlenden Wörter

mix up [mɪks'ʌp] durcheinander
bringen, mischen Next: 9

mobile (phone) ['məʊbaɪl] Handy

mobile home [məʊbaɪl'həʊm]
(Stand-)Wohnwagen

model ['mɒdl] (Foto-)Modell U2: 29

modern ['mɒdn] modern

mom [mɒm] (AE) Mama, Mutti
U1: 22

moment ['məʊmənt] Moment; **at
the moment** zurzeit, im Moment

Monday ['mʌndeɪ, 'mʌndi] Montag

money ['mʌni] Geld

monster ['mɒnstə] Monster

month [mʌnθ] Monat

moon [muːn] Mond U5: 70

moor [mɔː] (Hoch-)Moor

more [mɔː] mehr, weitere; **more
expensive** teurer

morning ['mɔːnɪŋ] Morgen; **in the
morning** am Morgen, morgens;
Monday morning Montagmorgen

moss [mɒs] Moos WF

most [məʊst] der/die/das meiste,
die meisten; **most expensive**
teuerste/teuerster/teuerstes,
am teuersten

motel [məʊ'tel] Motel WF U6

mother ['mʌðə] Mutter

motorbike ['məʊtəbaɪk] Motorrad

mountain ['maʊntən] Berg; **in the
mountains** im Gebirge

mountain bike ['maʊntənbaɪk]
Mountainbike

mountain biking ['maʊntənbaɪkɪŋ]
Mountainbikefahren

mountain board ['maʊntənbɔːd]
Mountainboard (eine Art Gelände-
Skateboard)

mountain boarding
['maʊntənbɔːdɪŋ] Mountainboardfahren

mourn [mɔːn]: **mourn for his life**
um sein Leben trauern WF

mouth [maʊθ] Mund U5: 70

move [muːv] **1** (sich) bewegen
U3: 42; **2** umziehen

movie ['muːvi] (AE) Film U1: 19

movie theater ['muːviθɪətə] (AE)
Kino WF

mow [məʊ] mähen WF

MP3 player [empiː'θriːpleɪə] MP3-
Player

Mr ['mɪstə]: **Mr Dunn** Herr Dunn

Mrs ['mɪsɪz]: **Mrs Jones** Frau
Jones

Ms [mɪz, məz]: **Ms Brown** Frau
Brown

much [mʌtʃ] viel

mum [mʌm] Mama, Mutti

museum [mjuː'ziːəm] Museum

mushroom ['mʌʃruːm] Champig-
non, Pilz WF

music ['mjuːzɪk] Musik

musical instrument
[mjuːzɪkl'ɪnstrəmənt] Musikinstrument

musician [mjuː'zɪʃn] Musiker, Musikerin U5: 67

Muslim ['mʊzlɪm] Muslim, Muslimin
U1: 14

must [mʌst] müssen

mustn't ['mʌsnt] nicht dürfen

my [maɪ] mein, meine

N

name [neɪm] **1** Name; **What's your
name?** Wie heißt du? **2** nennen
WF U6

narrow ['nærəʊ] schmal, eng

national park ['næʃnəl'pɑːk] Nationalpark

Native American ['neɪtɪvə'merɪkən]
amerik. Ureinwohner/in, Indianer/
Indianerin U4: 56

natural ['nætʃrəl] natürlich WF

navy (blue) ['neɪvi] marineblau WF

**NBA (National Basketball Associa-
tion)** [enbiː'eɪ] Nationaler Basket-
ball-Verband (in den USA) WF

near [nɪə] in der Nähe (von); nah

nearest ['nɪərɪst]: **the nearest airport** der nächste Flughafen

nearly ['nɪəli] fast WF

need [niːd] brauchen

neighbour ['neɪbə] Nachbar,
Nachbarin

neighbourhood ['neɪbəhʊd] Viertel,
Gegend U1: 11

nervous ['nɜːvəs] nervös, ängstlich

net [net] Netz WF

Netherlands ['neðələndz] Niederlande

network ['netwɜːk] Netz; Wortnetz,
Wörternetz

never ['nevə] (noch) nie, niemals

new [njuː] neu

news [njuːz] Nachricht(en);
Neuigkeit(en)

newspaper ['njuːzpeɪpə] Zeitung

next [nekst] nächste, nächster,
nächstes

next to ['nekstu, 'nekstə] neben

nice [naɪs] nett; schön

nickname ['nɪkneɪm] Spitzname
WF U6

night [naɪt] Nacht; **at night**
nachts, in der Nacht

no [nəʊ] **1** nein; **2** kein, keine;
There's no such thing. So
etwas gibt es nicht.

nobody ['nəʊbədi] niemand

noise [nɔɪz] Lärm; Geräusch
U4: 54

nominee [nɒmɪ'niː] Kandidat,
Kandidatin WF

nonsense ['nɒnsns] Unsinn, Blödsinn

north [nɔːθ] Norden; Nord-; nördlich; **in the north** im Norden

North Star [nɔːθˈstɑː] Nordstern WF

(the) north-west [nɔːθˈwest] (der) Nordwesten U4: 52

northern [ˈnɔːðən] Nord-, nördlich

Northern Ireland [ˈnɔːðənˈaɪələnd] Nordirland

not [nɒt] nicht

note [nəʊt] Notiz

nothing [ˈnʌθɪŋ] (gar) nichts

noticeboard [ˈnəʊtɪsbɔːd] Anschlagbrett, Schwarzes Brett

noun [naʊn] Nomen

November [nəʊˈvembə] November

now [naʊ] nun, jetzt

number [ˈnʌmbə] Nummer; Zahl; Ziffer; Anzahl WF U6

O

object [ˈɒbdʒɪkt] Gegenstand, Objekt WF

ocean [ˈəʊʃn] Ozean; Meer U4: 57

o'clock [əˈklɒk]: **at eight o'clock** um acht/zwanzig Uhr

October [ɒkˈtəʊbə] Oktober

of [ɒv, əv] von; **a picture of my dog** ein Bild meines Hundes; **a cup of tea** eine Tasse Tee; **think of** denken an

of course [əvˈkɔːs] natürlich, selbstverständlich

off [ɒf] von; **jump on and off** rein- und rausspringen WF

offer [ˈɒfə] **1** anbieten; **2** Angebot; **special offer** Sonderangebot

office [ˈɒfɪs] Büro WF; **tourist office** Touristeninformation, Fremdenverkehrsbüro

officer [ˈɒfɪsə]: **police officer** Polizist/Polizistin, Polizeibeamter/-beamtin

off-road [ˈɒfrəʊd] abseits der Straße, im Gelände

often [ˈɒfn] oft

oil [ɔɪl] Öl WF

OK [əʊˈkeɪ] okay, (schon) gut, in Ordnung; **Are you OK?** Ist alles in Ordnung bei dir? **That's OK.** Schon gut./Bitte.

old [əʊld] alt

Olympics [əˈlɪmpɪks]: **the Olympics** die Olympischen Spiele

on [ɒn] **1** auf; **2** an, eingeschaltet; **on August 5th** am 5. August; **on a reservation** in einer Reservation U4: 151; **on Dartmoor** in Dartmoor; **on foot** zu Fuß; **on holiday** in/im Urlaub;

on Saturdays samstags; **on school days** an Schultagen; **on special offer** im Sonderangebot; **on the beach** am Strand U2: 29; **on the board** an der Tafel; **on the bus** im Bus; **on the coast** an der Küste WF U6; **on the intercom** über die Sprechanlage; **on the Internet** im Internet; **On the one hand, ... On the other hand, ...** Einerseits ... Andererseits ... U2: 35; **on the phone** am Telefon; **on the road** unterwegs; **on the weekend** (AE) am Wochenende WF; **on TV** im Fernsehen; **get on the team** in die Mannschaft kommen; **jump on and off** rein- und rausspringen WF

one [wʌn] ein, eine, einer, eines; **one day** eines Tages

online [ɒnˈlaɪn] online U2: 34

only [ˈəʊnli] nur, bloß; erst

onto [ˈɒntʊ, ˈɒntə] auf (... hinauf/herauf)

open [ˈəʊpən] **1** öffnen, aufmachen; **2** sich öffnen, aufgehen; **3** offen, geöffnet

opening act [ˈəʊpənɪŋækt] Vorgruppe WF

opinion [əˈpɪnjən] Meinung U5: 77; **in my opinion** meiner Meinung nach U5: 77

opposite [ˈɒpəzɪt] **1** Gegenteil U1: 17; **2** gegenüber (von) U5: 70

or [ɔː] oder

orange [ˈɒrɪndʒ] Orange

order [ˈɔːdə] **1** Reihenfolge; **2** Anweisung, Befehl U3: 46; **out of order** außer Betrieb WF

organize [ˈɔːgənaɪz] ordnen; organisieren

orphan [ˈɔːfn] Waise WF

other [ˈʌðə] andere, weitere

our [ˈaʊə] unser, unsere

out [aʊt] hinaus/heraus, aus U1: 16; **find out** herausfinden

out of [ˈaʊtəv] aus (... hinaus/heraus); **out of order** außer Betrieb WF; **I have to get out of this place.** Ich muss hier raus.

outdoor [ˈaʊtdɔː]: **outdoor activity** Beschäftigung im Freien; **outdoor store** (AE) Geschäft mit Artikeln für Sport und Freizeit im Freien U4: 63

outdoors [aʊtˈdɔːz] im Freien, draußen

outlaw [ˈaʊtlɔː] Bandit, Banditin WF

over [ˈəʊvə] vorbei, zu Ende, aus; **Come on over!** Komm vorbei! WF; **over there** da drüben, dort drüben (hin) U3: 46

own [əʊn]: **your own room** dein eigenes Zimmer

P

Pacific [pəˈsɪfɪk] pazifisch WF

pack [pæk] packen, einpacken

page [peɪdʒ] Seite

paid [peɪd] (→ pay): **I paid** ich zahlte, ich habe gezahlt

pain [peɪn] Schmerzen; **Parents are a pain!** Eltern nerven!

palm tree [ˈpɑːmtriː] Palme WF

panic [ˈpænɪk] durchdrehen, in Panik geraten U3: 50

paper [ˈpeɪpə] Papier WF

papers [ˈpeɪpəz] (Ausweis-)Papiere U5: 78

paragraph [ˈpærəgrɑːf] Absatz

paramedic [pærəˈmedɪk] Rettungssanitäter, Rettungssanitärin U3: 50

parent, parents [ˈpeərənt, ˈpeərənts] Elternteil, Eltern

park [pɑːk] Park

part [pɑːt] Teil

partner [ˈpɑːtnə] Partner, Partnerin

part-time [pɑːtˈtaɪm] Teilzeit, Teilzeit- U4: 63

party [ˈpɑːti] Party

pass [pɑːs] vergehen WF

passage [ˈpæsɪdʒ] Gang, Korridor

passive [ˈpæsɪv] Passiv WF U6

past [pɑːst] Vergangenheit

past [pɑːst]: **past the house** am Haus vorbei; **five past ten** fünf nach zehn; **half past nine** halb zehn

past progressive [pɑːstprəˈgresɪv] Verlaufsform der Vergangenheit U2: 37

pasta [ˈpæstə] Nudeln WF

pavement [ˈpeɪvmənt] Bürgersteig, Gehsteig

pay [peɪ] **1** (I paid, I've paid) zahlen, bezahlen; **2** Bezahlung; Lohn WF

PE [piːˈiː] (= physical education) Sport(unterricht) WF

pear [peə] Birne WF

peer mediation [ˈpɪəmiːdiˈeɪʃn] Streitschlichtung WF

pen [pen] Füller

pence (p) [pens] Pence (britische Währung)

→ DICTIONARY

pencil ['pensl] Bleistift
pencil case ['penslkeɪs] Feder-mäppchen, Schreibetui
penfriend ['penfrend] Brieffreund, Brieffreundin WF
people ['piːpl] 1 Leute, Menschen; **black/white people** Schwarze/Weiße U1: 14; 2 Volk WF; **the Makah people** das Volk der Makah WF
pepper ['pepə] Paprikaschote WF
per [pɜː] pro U4: 63
per cent [pə'sent] Prozent U5: 67
percussion [pə'kʌʃn]: **percussion instrument** Schlaginstrument WF
permitted [pə'mɪtɪd] erlaubt WF
person ['pɜːsn] Person, Mensch U4: 55
pet [pet] Haustier, zahmes Tier
pet shop ['petʃɒp] Zoohandlung, Tierhandlung
petrol station ['petrəlsteɪʃn] Tank-stelle WF
phone [fəʊn] 1 anrufen, telefonie-ren; **phone back** zurückrufen U2: 33; 2 Telefon; **on the phone** am Telefon
phone call ['fəʊnkɔːl] Anruf U2: 32
phone message ['fəʊnmesɪdʒ] Tele-fonnotiz; telefonische Nachricht U2: 32
photo ['fəʊtəʊ] Foto; **take photos** Fotos machen, fotografieren U2: 29
photocopier ['fəʊtəʊkɒpɪə] Foto-kopierer, Kopiergerät WF
photographer [fə'tɒgrəfə] Fotograf, Fotografin U2: 29
photo shoot ['fəʊtəʊʃuːt] Foto-session, Fotoshooting U2: 28
phrase [freɪz] Ausdruck
piano [pi'ænəʊ] Klavier U5: 68
pick [pɪk] aussuchen, wählen
pick up [pɪk'ʌp] 1 aufheben, hoch-heben; 2 abholen
picnic ['pɪknɪk] Picknick
picture ['pɪktʃə] Bild, Foto
pier [pɪə] Pier, Anlegestelle
pig [pɪg] Schwein
pink [pɪŋk] rosa, pink
pioneer [paɪə'nɪə] Pionier/in WF U6
pirate ['paɪrət] Pirat, Piratin U2: 36
pita ['piːtə] Pita (Fladenbrot) WF
pizza ['piːtsə] Pizza
place [pleɪs] 1 Ort, Stelle, Platz; **a place to meet** ein Treffpunkt; 2 unterbringen WF
plan [plæn] 1 planen, vorhaben; 2 Plan

plane [pleɪn] Flugzeug
planner ['plænə] Planer, Planerin
play [pleɪ] spielen; **play by the rules** sich an die Spielregeln hal-ten U3: 43; **play sports** Sport treiben; **play the guitar** Gitarre spielen; **men playing games** Männer, die Spiele spielen U5: 66
player ['pleɪə] 1 Spieler, Spielerin; 2 Abspielgerät U3: 47
playground ['pleɪgraʊnd] Schulhof; **in the playground** auf dem Schul-hof
please [pliːz] bitte
plug in [plʌg'ɪn] anschließen WF
plum [plʌm] Pflaume WF
p.m. [piː'em] nachmittags, abends
pocket ['pɒkɪt] Tasche U1: 142
pocket money ['pɒkɪtmʌni] Taschengeld U1: 12
poem ['pəʊɪm] Gedicht
poet ['pəʊɪt] Dichter, Dichterin
point [pɔɪnt] Punkt
Poland ['pəʊlənd] Polen
police [pə'liːs] Polizei-
police officer [pə'liːsɒfɪsə] Poli-zist/in, Polizeibeamter/-beamtin
polite [pə'laɪt] höflich
pollution [pə'luːʃn] Umweltver-schmutzung WF
pony ['pəʊni] Pony
poor [pʊə] arm U1: 11; **Poor you!** Du Arme!/Du Armer! **the poor** die Armen WF
pop [pɒp] 1 Pop(musik) U5: 68; 2 (AE) Papa, Vati WF
popcorn ['pɒpkɔːn] Popcorn U1: 19
popular ['pɒpjələ] beliebt
population [pɒpju'leɪʃn] Bevölke-rung, Bevölkerungszahl Next: 7
pork [pɔːk] Schweinefleisch WF
porter ['pɔːtə] Gepäckträger/in WF
portfolio [pɔːt'fəʊliəʊ] Portfolio
postcard ['pəʊstkɑːd] Postkarte, Ansichtskarte
poster ['pəʊstə] Poster
post office ['pəʊstɒfɪs] Post(amt)
potato, potatoes [pə'teɪtəʊ, pə'teɪtəʊz] Kartoffel, Kartoffeln U1: 12
potato chips [pə'teɪtəʊtʃɪps] (AE) Kartoffelchips U1: 12
pound (£) [paʊnd] Pfund (britische Währung)
power ['paʊə] Macht; Stärke U5: 78
power button ['paʊəbʌtn] An-/Aus-schalter WF
power cord ['paʊəkɔːd] Netzkabel WF

practise ['præktɪs] üben; trainieren
prefer [prɪ'fɜː] vorziehen U2: 27
preposition [prepə'zɪʃn] Präposi-tion, Verhältniswort U5: 72
present [prɪ'zent] präsentieren
present ['preznt] 1 Geschenk; 2 **simple present** einfache Gegenwart
present progressive [prezntprə'gresɪv] Verlaufsform der Gegenwart
press [pres] drücken WF
price [praɪs] Preis
print out [prɪnt'aʊt] ausdrucken U3: 41
prison ['prɪzn] Gefängnis U1: 14; **go to prison** ins Gefängnis kommen U1: 14; **in prison** im Gefängnis U1: 14
prize [praɪz] Preis, Gewinn
problem ['prɒbləm] Problem
produce [prə'djuːs] herstellen, produzieren
programme ['prəʊgræm] (Radio-, Fernseh-)Sendung
progressive [prə'gresɪv]: **past progressive** Verlaufsform der Vergangenheit U2: 37; **present progressive** Verlaufsform der Gegenwart
prohibit [prə'hɪbɪt] verbieten U4: 57
prohibited [prə'hɪbɪtɪd] verboten U4: 54
project ['prɒdʒekt] Projekt, Projektarbeit
pronunciation [prənʌnsi'eɪʃn] Aussprache Next: 8
protector [prə'tektə] Protektor, Schützer
protest [prə'test] protestieren WF
punk [pʌŋk] Punk(musik) U5: 68
pupil ['pjuːpl] Schüler, Schülerin
push [pʊʃ] drücken
put [pʊt] (I put, I've put) stellen; legen; (an einen Ort) tun; **I put** ich tat, ich habe getan; **I've put** ich habe getan U4: 153; **put in the right order** in die richtige Reihenfolge bringen; **she has put an advert in the newspaper** sie hat eine Anzeige in die Zei-tung gesetzt WF
put in [pʊt'ɪn] 1 einfügen, hinzufü-gen; 2 eingeben WF
put up [pʊt'ʌp]: **put up a tent** ein Zelt aufstellen U4: 56; **Put up your hand.** Heb(t) die Hand. Next: 6

Q

quad (bike) [kwɒd, 'kwɒdbaɪk] Quad *(eine Art vierrädriges Gelände-Motorrad)*

quality ['kwɒləti]: **NBA quality sneakers** (AE) Sportschuhe in NBA-Qualität WF

quarter ['kwɔːtə]: **quarter to/past one** Viertel vor/nach eins

queen [kwiːn] Königin

question ['kwestʃən] Frage

questionnaire [kwestʃə'neə] Fragebogen

queue (up) [kjuː] Schlange stehen

quickly ['kwɪkli] schnell

quiet ['kwaɪət] ruhig

quietly ['kwaɪətli] leise WF

quiz [kwɪz] Quiz

quote [kwəʊt] Zitat U1: 14

R

R & B [ɑːrən'biː] R & B *(Musikrichtung)* U5: 68

racket ['rækɪt] Schläger WF

radiator ['reɪdieɪtə] Heizkörper

radio ['reɪdiəʊ] Radio

railings ['reɪlɪŋz] Geländer

railway line ['reɪlweɪlaɪn] Eisenbahnstrecke, Gleis

rain [reɪn] regnen

ran [ræn] (→ run): **I ran** ich rannte, ich bin gerannt

ranch [rɑːntʃ] Ranch WF U6

ranger ['reɪndʒə] Ranger *(Aufseher/in in Nationalparks)*

rap [ræp] Rap(musik)

rapper ['ræpə] Rapper/in, Rapsänger/in U1: 16

rat [ræt] Ratte

raven ['reɪvn] Rabe WF

RE [ɑː'riː] **(= religious education)** Religionslehre WF

read [riːd] (I read, I've read) lesen, vorlesen; **read something to her** ihr etwas vorlesen U1: 16

read [red] (→ read): **I read** ich las, ich habe gelesen; **I've read** ich habe gelesen

read out [riːd'aʊt] vorlesen, ablesen

reader ['riːdə] Leser, Leserin

reading log ['riːdɪŋlɒg] Lesetagebuch WF U6

reading week ['riːdɪŋwiːk] Lesewoche

ready ['redi] fertig, bereit

reality show [ri'ælətiʃəʊ] Reality-show *(Unterhaltungssendung, die wahre Begebenheiten zeigt oder nachstellt)* WF

really ['rɪəli] wirklich, eigentlich

reason ['riːzn] Grund U5: 77

receptionist [rɪ'sepʃənɪst] Empfangschef, -dame WF U6

recommend [rekə'mend] empfehlen U4: 61

recorder [rɪ'kɔːdə] Blockflöte WF

recording contract [rɪ'kɔːdɪŋkɒntrækt] Plattenvertrag WF

red [red] rot

referee [refə'riː] Schiedsrichter, Schiedsrichterin U3: 43

refill ['riːfɪl] Nachfüllung WF U6

reggae ['regeɪ] Reggae(musik) WF

relax [rɪ'læks] (sich) entspannen U2: 35

relaxed [rɪ'lækst] entspannt WF

release [rɪ'liːs] loslassen WF

remember [rɪ'membə] **1** sich erinnern (an); **2** daran denken U2: 28

rent [rent] mieten; ausleihen

repeat [rɪ'piːt] nachsprechen

report [rɪ'pɔːt] Bericht

reservation [rezə'veɪʃn] (Indianer-) Reservation, Reservat U4: 52; **on a reservation** in einer Reservation U4: 151

resort [rɪ'zɔːt] Urlaubsort WF

respectful [rɪ'spektfl] respektvoll WF

rest [rest] ruhen, sich ausruhen WF

restart [riː'stɑːt]: **restart the computer** einen Neustart machen WF

restaurant ['restrɒnt] Restaurant

result [rɪ'zʌlt] Ergebnis, Folge

résumé ['rezjumeɪ] (AE) Lebenslauf U4: 63

retirement home [rɪ'taɪəmənthəʊm] Seniorenheim WF

review [rɪ'vjuː] Besprechung, Rezension WF U6

reward [rɪ'wɔːd] Belohnung WF

rewrite [riː'raɪt] umschreiben WF

Rhine [raɪn] Rhein

rhyme (with) [raɪm] (sich) reimen (auf)

rhythm ['rɪðəm] Rhythmus U5: 69

rice [raɪs] Reis WF

rich [rɪtʃ]: **the rich** die Reichen WF

ridden ['rɪdn] (→ ride): **I've ridden** ich bin gefahren

ride [raɪd] **1** (I rode, I've ridden) reiten WF U6; **ride a bike/mountain board/quad** (mit einem) Rad/Mountainboard/Quad fahren; **2** Fahrt; **3** Fahrgeschäft, „Fahrattraktion" U2: 36

riding ['raɪdɪŋ]: **horse riding** Reiten WF; **quad/Trikke/... riding** Quadfahren/Trikkefahren/...

right [raɪt] **1** richtig; **You're right.** Du hast Recht. **2** Recht U1: 14; **animal rights** Tierrechte, Tierschutz- U4: 64; **3** rechts; **on the right** auf der rechten Seite; **on your right** rechts (von Ihnen)

ringtone ['rɪŋtəʊn] Klingelton

river ['rɪvə] Fluss; **the River Exe** der Exe

road [rəʊd] Straße; **in Fairfield Road** in der Fairfield Road; **on the road** unterwegs

road safety ['rəʊdseɪfti] Verkehrssicherheit

rob [rɒb] berauben WF; **rob a bank** eine Bank ausrauben WF

rock [rɒk] **1** Fels, großer Stein; **2** Rock(musik) WF

rock climber ['rɒkklaɪmə] Kletterer, Kletterin

rock climbing ['rɒkklaɪmɪŋ] Klettern

rodeo ['rəʊdiəʊ] Rodeo WF U6

role [rəʊl] Rolle U2: 28; **role card** Rollen(spiel)karte U2: 33

roll [rəʊl] Brötchen

roller coaster ['rəʊləkəʊstə] Achterbahn

romance [rəʊ'mæns] Liebesfilm, Liebesroman U2: 27

romantic [rəʊ'mæntɪk] romantisch

Rome [rəʊm] Rom

room [ruːm] Raum, Zimmer

root [ruːt] Wurzel U4: 56

round [raʊnd] um (... herum) WF

royal (blue) ['rɔɪəl] königsblau WF

RSVP [ɑːresviː'piː] u.A.w.g. (= um Antwort wird gebeten) U1: 21

rubber ['rʌbə] Radiergummi

rugby ['rʌgbi] Rugby

rule [ruːl] Regel, Vorschrift; **play by the rules** sich an die Spielregeln halten U3: 43

ruler ['ruːlə] Lineal

run [rʌn] (I ran, I've run) rennen, laufen; **run errands** Besorgungen machen WF

runner ['rʌnə] Läufer, Läuferin

running ['rʌnɪŋ] Laufen

S

sad [sæd] traurig

safe [seɪf] sicher, in Sicherheit

safety ['seɪfti]: **road safety** Verkehrssicherheit

safety gear ['seɪftigɪə] Sicherheitsausrüstung

said [sed] (→ say): **I said** ich sagte, ich habe gesagt; **I've said** ich habe gesagt

salad ['sæləd] Salat

sales clerk ['seɪlzklɑːk] (AE) Verkäufer, Verkäuferin U4: 63

salmon ['sæmən] Lachs U1: 142

same [seɪm]: **the same** der-/die-/dasselbe, der/die/das gleiche

sandwich ['sænwɪtʃ] Sandwich *(belegtes Brot)*

sang [sæŋ] (→ sing): **I sang** ich sang, ich habe gesungen

sat [sæt] (→ sit): **I sat** ich saß, ich habe gesessen

Saturday ['sætədeɪ, 'sætədi] Samstag, Sonnabend

sausage ['sɒsɪdʒ] Wurst, Würstchen

save [seɪv] **1** sparen; **2** retten U4: 64

saw [sɔː] (→ see): **I saw** ich sah, ich habe gesehen

saxophone ['sæksəfəʊn] Saxofon WF

say [seɪ] (I said, I've said) sagen; **say something to her** ihr etwas sagen U1: 16; **say goodbye to ...** sich von ... verabschieden; **Say hi to Dawn, please.** Grüße Dawn, bitte. **say sorry** sich entschuldigen

scan [skæn] überfliegen WF U6

scan in [skæn'ɪn] einscannen WF

scanner ['skænə] Scanner WF

scary ['skeəri] unheimlich WF

scene [siːn] Szene; Ansicht

school [skuːl] Schule; **she's at school** sie ist in der Schule; sie geht zur Schule

school band ['skuːlbænd] Schulorchester WF

school council ['skuːl'kaʊnsl] Schülermitverwaltung WF

school day ['skuːldeɪ] Schultag

science ['saɪəns] Naturwissenschaft

science fiction [saɪəns'fɪkʃn] Science-Fiction WF

score [skɔː] **1** (Punkte) erzielen, (Tor) schießen U3: 42; **2** Spielstand, Punktzahl U3: 40; **What's the score?** Wie steht's? U3: 148

Scotland ['skɒtlənd] Schottland

Scots [skɒts] Schottisch *(engl. Dialekt)*

Scottish ['skɒtɪʃ] schottisch; Schotte(n), Schottin(nen)

scream [skriːm] schreien

sea [siː] Meer

seal pup ['siːlpʌp] Seehundjunges WF

search engine ['sɜːtʃendʒɪn] Suchmaschine WF U6

seashell ['siːʃel] Muschel

seashore ['siːʃɔː] Küste, Strand

season ['siːzn] Jahreszeit

second ['sekənd]: **English as a Second Language** Englisch als Zweitsprache U3: 38

security check [sɪ'kjʊərətitʃek] Sicherheitskontrolle U3: 38

security guard [sɪ'kjʊərətigɑːd] Wachfrau, Wachmann

see [siː] (I saw, I've seen) sehen; **I see her mouth moving** ich sehe, wie sich ihr Mund bewegt WF; **See you.** Bis dann. **See you tomorrow/...** Bis morgen/...; **..., you see.** ..., verstehst du?

seen [siːn] (→ see): **I've seen** ich habe gesehen

self-control [selfkən'trəʊl] Selbstbeherrschung U3: 43

sell [sel] (I sold, I've sold) verkaufen; sich verkaufen WF

send [send] (I sent, I've sent) senden, schicken

sent [sent] (→ send): **I sent** ich sendete, ich habe gesendet; **I've sent** ich habe gesendet

sentence ['sentəns] Satz

September [sep'tembə] September

series ['sɪəriːz] Serie; Reihe U2: 27

serve [sɜːv] servieren WF

shake [ʃeɪk] (I shook, I've shaken) schütteln U5: 70; **she shakes her head** sie schüttelt den Kopf U5: 154

shaken ['ʃeɪkən] (→ shake): **I've shaken** ich habe geschüttelt U5: 156

share [ʃeə]: **share a room** sich ein Zimmer teilen

she [ʃiː] sie; **she's (= she is)** sie ist

sheep [ʃiːp] Schaf, Schafe

shelf, shelves [ʃelf, ʃelvz] Regal, Regale

sheriff ['ʃerɪf] Sheriff WF U6

ship [ʃɪp] Schiff

shirt [ʃɜːt] Hemd WF

shoe [ʃuː] Schuh

shook [ʃʊk] (→ shake): **I shook** ich schüttelte, ich habe geschüttelt U5: 70

shoot [ʃuːt] (I shot, I've shot) schießen; werfen U3: 40

shop [ʃɒp] Laden, Geschäft

shop assistant ['ʃɒpəsɪstənt] Verkäufer, Verkäuferin

shoplifter ['ʃɒplɪftə] Ladendieb/in

shopper ['ʃɒpə] Käufer, Käuferin

shopping ['ʃɒpɪŋ] Einkaufen U1: 11; **go shopping** einkaufen gehen

shopping centre ['ʃɒpɪŋsentə] Einkaufszentrum

shore [ʃɔː] Ufer, Strand WF

short [ʃɔːt] kurz; klein

shorts [ʃɔːts] Shorts, kurze Hosen U3: 40

shot [ʃɒt] Korbwurf U3: 40

shot [ʃɒt] (→ shoot): **I shot** ich schoss, ich habe geschossen U3: 150; **I've shot** ich habe geschossen U3: 150; **he was shot** er wurde erschossen WF

should [ʃʊd, ʃəd]: **you should** du solltest, du müsstest; **When should I ...?** Wann soll ich ...? U1: 19

shoulder ['ʃəʊldə] Schulter WF

shout [ʃaʊt] laut rufen, schreien; **she shouts something at him** sie ruft ihm etwas zu U5: 70

show [ʃəʊ] **1** (I showed, I've shown) zeigen; **2** Show

shown [ʃəʊn]: **he was shown** es wurde ihm gezeigt WF

Shut up! [ʃʌt'ʌp] Halt den Mund!

shuttle ['ʃʌtl] Shuttle U5: 74

shy [ʃaɪ] schüchtern

sick [sɪk]: **become sick** (AE) krank werden WF

side [saɪd] Seite

sidewalk ['saɪdwɔːk] (AE) Bürgersteig Next: 9

sigh [saɪ] seufzen U5: 70

sightseeing ['saɪtsiːɪŋ] Besichtigungen U1: 11

sign [saɪn] Schild; Zeichen

signal ['sɪgnəl] Zeichen, Signal

silly ['sɪli] dumm, albern

silver ['sɪlvə] silbern WF

simple past [sɪmpl'pɑːst] einfache Vergangenheit

simple present [sɪmpl'preznt] einfache Gegenwart

sing [sɪŋ] (I sang, I've sung) singen

Singapore ['sɪŋəpɔː] Singapur

singer ['sɪŋə] Sänger, Sängerin

single room ['sɪŋglruːm] Einzelzimmer WF U6

sir [sɜː]: **Dear Sir/Madam, ...** Sehr geehrte Damen und Herren, ... WF

sister ['sɪstə] Schwester; **brothers and sisters** Geschwister

sit [sɪt] (I sat, I've sat) sitzen; sich setzen

sitcom ['sɪtkɒm] „Situationskomödie", Comedy-Serie WF

skateboard ['skeɪtbɔːd] Skateboard U3: 47

skateboarder ['skeɪtbɔːdə] Skateboarder, Skateboarderin

skater ['skeɪtə] Skater, Skaterin

ski [skiː] Ski fahren WF

skiing ['skiːɪŋ] Skifahren WF

skin [skɪn] Haut WF

skunk [skʌŋk] Stinktier, Skunk WF U6

sky [skaɪ] Himmel WF

sky-high [skaɪ'haɪ] himmelhoch WF

skyscraper ['skaɪskreɪpə] Wolkenkratzer, Hochhaus WF

slave [sleɪv] Sklave, Sklavin WF

sleep [sliːp] (I slept, I've slept) schlafen

slept [slept]: **he/she slept** er/sie schlief, er/sie hat geschlafen WF

slip [slɪp] ausrutschen

slow [sləʊ] langsam U5: 69

small [smɔːl] klein

smile [smaɪl] lächeln

smog [smɒg] Smog U2: 25

smoke [sməʊk] rauchen U4: 54

smoked salmon [sməʊkt'sæmən] Räucherlachs U1: 12

s'mores [smɔːz] *amerikanischer Lagerfeuersnack mit Marshmallows* WF U6

sneaker ['sniːkə] (AE) Sportschuh U3: 41

sneaker wave ['sniːkəweɪv] überraschend hohe Uferwelle WF

snowboarder ['snəʊbɔːdə] Snowboarder, Snowboarderin

so [səʊ] so, also; daher

soap [səʊp] Seifenoper, Unterhaltungsserie WF

soccer ['sɒkə] Fußball U3: 41

social studies ['səʊʃl'stʌdiz] Gesellschaftslehre WF

soda ['səʊdə] (AE) Limonade WF U6

softball ['sɒftbɔːl] Softball *(ähnlich wie Baseball)* U3: 41

software ['sɒftweə] Software

sold [səʊld]: **they had sold** sie hatten verkauft WF

Somalia [sə'mɑːliə] Somalia

some [sʌm] **1** einige, ein paar; **2** etwas

somebody ['sʌmbədi] jemand

something ['sʌmθɪŋ] etwas; **something different** etwas anderes

sometimes ['sʌmtaɪmz] manchmal

song [sɒŋ] Lied

soon [suːn] bald

sorry ['sɒri]: **Sorry./I'm sorry.** Tut mir leid. **I'm sorry I ...** Tut mir leid, dass ich ...; **she felt sorry for him** er tat ihr leid WF

sound [saʊnd] **1** klingen, sich anhören; **2** Geräusch

soundtrack ['saʊndtræk] Filmmusik WF

soup [suːp] Suppe WF

south [saʊθ] Süden; Süd-; südlich

sow [səʊ] säen WF

space [speɪs] Weltraum U5: 74

Spain [speɪn] Spanien

Spanish ['spænɪʃ] spanisch; Spanisch; Spanier, Spanierin(nen) U5: 66

speak [spiːk] (I spoke, I've spoken) sprechen; **speak to** sprechen mit

speaker ['spiːkə] Redner, Rednerin WF; Sprecher, Sprecherin U5: 66

special ['speʃl] besondere, besonderer, besonderes

special offer [speʃl'ɒfə] Sonderangebot

speed [spiːd] Geschwindigkeit WF

speed limit ['spiːdlɪmɪt] Geschwindigkeitsbegrenzung WF U6

spell [spel] buchstabieren

spelling ['spelɪŋ] Rechtschreibung Next: 9

spend [spend] (I spent, I've spent) **1** ausgeben; **2** verbringen U5: 68

spent [spent] (→ spend): **I spent 1** ich gab aus, ich habe ausgegeben; **2** ich verbrachte, ich habe verbracht U5: 68; **I've spent** ich habe ausgegeben/verbracht U5: 156

spider ['spaɪdə] Spinne

splitting up [splɪtɪŋ'ʌp] Trennung WF

sponsored ['spɒnsəd] gesponsert

sport [spɔːt] Sport, Sportart; **play sports** Sport treiben

sports centre ['spɔːtssentə] Sportzentrum

sporty ['spɔːti] sportlich

spring [sprɪŋ] Frühling

squash [skwɒʃ] Squash

squid [skwɪd] Tintenfisch WF

stable ['steɪbl] Stall WF

stack [stæk]: **stack shelves** Regale auffüllen WF

stage [steɪdʒ] Bühne U5: 66; **on stage** auf der Bühne U5: 66

stall [stɔːl] (Verkaufs-)Stand U2: 24

stamp [stæmp] Stempel

stand [stænd] (I stood, I've stood) stehen; **I can't stand them** ich kann sie nicht ausstehen

star [stɑː] **1** Stern WF; **2** Star *(berühmte Persönlichkeit)*

start [stɑːt] **1** anfangen, beginnen; **I started to run** ich begann zu rennen; **start a programme** eine Sendung ins Leben rufen; **2** Start, Anfang

state [steɪt] (Bundes-)Staat, Land Next: 7

station ['steɪʃn] Bahnhof; **at Exeter Station** im Bahnhof Exeter

statue ['stætʃuː] Statue; **Statue of Liberty** ['stætʃuːəv'lɪbəti] Freiheitsstatue U1: 10

stay [steɪ] bleiben; übernachten

steal [stiːl] (I stole, I've stolen) stehlen U1: 14

step [step] Stufe

stew [stjuː] Eintopf WF

stole [stəʊl] (→ steal): **I stole** ich stahl, ich habe gestohlen U1: 144

stolen ['stəʊlən] (→ steal): **I've stolen** ich habe gestohlen U1: 144

stop [stɒp] **1** anhalten, stoppen; stehen bleiben; **2** Halt; Haltestelle Next: 6

store [stɔː] (AE) Laden, Geschäft Next: 9

story ['stɔːri] Geschichte

strawberry ['strɔːbəri] Erdbeere WF

street [striːt] Straße

stress [stres] betonen

strict [strɪkt] streng

strong [strɒŋ] stark WF

student ['stjuːdnt] (AE) Schüler, Schülerin U3: 38

studio ['stjuːdiəʊ] Studio U2: 28

stupid ['stjuːpɪd] dumm, blöd

subject ['sʌbdʒɪkt] **1** (Schul-)Fach; **2 Subject: ...** Betreff: ... WF

suburb ['sʌbɜːb] Vorort

subway ['sʌbweɪ] (AE) U-Bahn Next: 9

such [sʌtʃ]: **There's no such thing.** So etwas gibt es nicht.

suddenly ['sʌdnli] plötzlich

sugar ['ʃʊgə] Zucker WF

summary ['sʌməri] Zusammenfassung

summer ['sʌmə] Sommer
sun [sʌn] Sonne
Sunday ['sʌndeɪ, 'sʌndi] Sonntag
sung [sʌŋ] (→ sing): **I've sung** ich habe gesungen
sunglasses ['sʌnglɑːsɪz] Sonnenbrille WF
sunny ['sʌni] sonnig
super ['suːpə] super, toll
supermarket ['suːpəmɑːkɪt] Supermarkt
sure [ʃʊə] sicher
surf [sɜːf] surfen U2: 29
surfboard ['sɜːfbɔːd] Surfbrett U2: 28
surfer ['sɜːfə] Surfer, Surferin U2: 24
surfing ['sɜːfɪŋ] Surfen, Wellenreiten WF
surfing gear ['sɜːfɪŋgɪə] **1** Surfkleidung, -klamotten; **2** Surfausrüstung U2: 29
surprise [sə'praɪz] Überraschung
surprised [sə'praɪzd] überrascht WF U6
survey ['sɜːveɪ] Umfrage, Untersuchung
swam [swæm] (→ swim): **I swam** ich schwamm, ich bin geschwommen
sweet [swiːt] süß WF
swept [swept]: **she swept** sie fegte WF
swim [swɪm] (I swam, I've swum) schwimmen
swimmer ['swɪmə] Schwimmer, Schwimmerin
swimming ['swɪmɪŋ] Schwimmen; **go swimming** schwimmen gehen
swimming pool ['swɪmɪŋpuːl] Schwimmbad
Switzerland ['swɪtsələnd] Schweiz
symbol ['sɪmbl] Symbol

T

table ['teɪbl] **1** Tisch; **2** Tabelle WF
table tennis ['teɪbltenɪs] Tischtennis
take [teɪk] (I took, I've taken) nehmen; bringen; einnehmen WF; **Take a jacket.** Nimm/Bring eine Jacke mit. **take photos** Fotos machen, fotografieren U2: 29; **Can I take a message?** Kann ich (ihm/ihr) etwas ausrichten? U2: 32
take off [teɪk'ɒf]: **I take off my jacket** ich ziehe meine Jacke aus

taken ['teɪkən] (→ take): **I've taken** ich habe genommen
talent contest ['tæləntkɒntest] Talentwettbewerb WF
talk [tɔːk] **1 talk (to)** reden (mit), sprechen (mit), sich unterhalten (mit); **2** Vortrag
talk show ['tɔːkʃəʊ] (AE) Talkshow U5: 71
tall [tɔːl] groß (bei Personen)
taxi ['tæksi] Taxi
tea [tiː] Tee
teach [tiːtʃ] (I taught, I've taught) beibringen WF U6; **I'd teach you to ride** ich würde dir das Reiten beibringen WF U6; **Who can teach me?** Wer kann es mir beibringen? WF
teacher ['tiːtʃə] Lehrer, Lehrerin
team [tiːm] Team, Mannschaft
techno ['teknəʊ] Techno (Musikrichtung) U1: 21
technology [tek'nɒlədʒi] Technik, Technologie
teen, teenager ['tiːn, 'tiːneɪdʒə] Teenager
telephone line ['telɪfəʊnlaɪn] Telefonnetz WF
tell (about) [tel] (I told, I've told) erzählen (von); sagen
tennis ['tenɪs] Tennis
tent [tent] Zelt U4: 56
tepee ['tiːpiː] Tipi WF
terrible ['terəbl] schrecklich, furchtbar
test [test] Test, Klassenarbeit, Prüfung
text [tekst] **1** Text; **2** SMS
text bullying ['tekstbʊliːŋ] SMS-Terror
text message ['tekstmesɪdʒ] SMS (Textnachricht)
textile technology ['tekstaɪltek'nɒlədʒi] Textilgestaltung WF
than [ðæn, ðən]: **faster than** schneller als
thank [θæŋk]: **Thank you.** Danke (schön).
Thanks. [θæŋks] Danke.
that [ðæt] **1** das; der, die, das (da); **2** dass; **3** der, die, das (in Relativsätzen); **that evening** an diesem Abend; **That's OK.** Schon gut./Bitte. **That's why ...** Deshalb ..., Darum ...; **That's two pounds, please.** Das macht zwei Pfund, bitte.
the [ðə, ði] der, die, das; **The next day ...** Am nächsten Tag ...

theatre ['θɪətə] Theater U1: 11
their [ðeə] ihr, ihre
them [ðem] ihnen, sie
theme park ['θiːmpɑːk] Themenpark U5: 74
then [ðen] dann
there [ðeə] da, dort; dahin, dorthin; **there's (= there is)** da ist, es gibt/ist; **there are** da sind, es gibt/sind; **there was/were** da war(en), es gab/war(en)
these [ðiːz] die (hier); diese
they [ðeɪ] sie; **they're (= they are)** sie sind
thing [θɪŋ] Ding, Sache; **the right/best/... thing** das Richtige/Beste/...; **There's no such thing.** So etwas gibt es nicht.
think [θɪŋk] (I thought, I've thought) denken, nachdenken; finden; **think of** denken an; **What do you think of ...?** Was hältst du von ...? **they thought of making Leavenworth a German town** sie kamen darauf, aus Leavenworth eine deutsche Stadt zu machen WF
this [ðɪs] dies (hier), das (hier); diese, dieser, dieses; **this evening/...** heute Abend/...
those [ðəʊz] diese, jene, die (da)
thought [θɔːt] (→ think): **I thought** ich dachte, ich habe gedacht
thousand ['θaʊznd] tausend
threw [θruː] (→ throw): **I threw** ich warf, ich habe geworfen U3: 42
thriller ['θrɪlə] Thriller WF
through [θruː] durch, hindurch
throw [θrəʊ] **1** (I threw, I've thrown) werfen U3: 42; **2** Wurf U3: 40; **free throw** Freiwurf U3: 40
thrown [θrəʊn] (→ throw): **I've thrown** ich habe geworfen U3: 150
Thursday ['θɜːzdeɪ, 'θɜːzdi] Donnerstag
ticket ['tɪkɪt] Eintrittskarte; Fahrkarte, Flugschein
tied [taɪd]: **it was tied** es war unentschieden WF
till [tɪl] bis WF
time [taɪm] Zeit; Uhrzeit; **at that time** damals WF; **(for) a long time** lange U2: 28; **What time is it?** Wie spät ist es?
timetable ['taɪmteɪbl] Stundenplan
tip [tɪp] **1** Tipp; **2** Trinkgeld WF
tired ['taɪəd] müde
title ['taɪtl] Titel

to [tuː, tu, tə] **1** zu, nach; an; **fall to the ground** auf den Boden fallen; **go to bed** ins Bett gehen; **I've been to France.** Ich bin (schon einmal) in Frankreich gewesen. **it's 24–18 to North** es steht 24:18 für North U3: 42; **Jamie says goodbye to Tess.** Jamie sagt Tess auf Wiedersehen. **they help you to read** sie helfen dir zu lesen; **things to do** Sachen, die man machen kann; **to change things** um Dinge zu verändern U1: 14; **To finish, ...** Um zum Ende zu kommen, ...; **Welcome to London.** Willkommen in London. **2** bis; **It's five to ten.** Es ist fünf vor zehn.

tobacco [tə'bækəʊ] Tabak WF

today [tə'deɪ] heute

together [tə'geðə] zusammen

told [təʊld] (→ tell): **I told** ich erzählte, ich habe erzählt; **I've told** ich habe erzählt

tomato, tomatoes [tə'mɑːtəʊ, tə'mɑːtəʊz] Tomate, Tomaten U1: 12

tomorrow [tə'mɒrəʊ] morgen

tongue twister ['tʌŋtwɪstə] Zungenbrecher

too [tuː] **1** auch; **2** **too old** zu alt; **Too bad!** Schade! U3: 42

took [tʊk] (→ take): **I took** ich nahm, ich habe genommen

top [tɒp] Spitze, oberes Ende U1: 10; **at the top** ganz oben (auf), auf der Spitze U1: 10

topic ['tɒpɪk] Thema

touch [tʌtʃ] berühren, anfassen U3: 40

tough [tʌf] hart, zäh, stark

tour [tʊə] Tour; Rundgang, Führung U1: 11

tourist ['tʊərɪst] Tourist, Touristin

tourist office ['tʊərɪstɒfɪs] Touristeninformation, Fremdenverkehrsbüro

towards [tə'wɔːdz] auf ... zu, in Richtung

tower ['taʊə] Turm

town [taʊn] Stadt

town centre ['taʊnsentə] Stadtzentrum, Stadtmitte

toy [tɔɪ] Spielzeug

track [træk] **1** Weg, Pfad; **2** Bahn, Laufbahn

tractor ['træktə] Traktor WF U6

tradition [trə'dɪʃn] Tradition U4: 64

traffic ['træfɪk] Verkehr

traffic jam ['træfɪkdʒæm] (Verkehrs-)Stau WF

traffic light ['træfɪklaɪt] (Verkehrs-)Ampel

trail [treɪl] Pfad, Weg WF U6

train [treɪn] **1** trainieren; **2** Zug, Eisenbahn

trainer ['treɪnə] **1** Trainer; **2** Sportschuh

tram [træm] Straßenbahn

translate [træns'leɪt] übersetzen

trash [træʃ] (AE) Müll, Abfall WF

trash can ['træʃkæn] (AE) Mülltonne WF

travel ['trævl] **1** reisen, fahren; **2** Reise-, Reisen U1: 17

traveller ['trævələ] Reisende/r; Landfahrer/in

tray [treɪ] Tablett U3: 46

treasure hunt ['treʒəhʌnt] Schatzsuche

treat [triːt] Genuss, besonderes Vergnügen

tree [triː] Baum U4: 52

trick [trɪk] Streich WF

trip [trɪp] Ausflug, Reise

trouble ['trʌbl] Unruhe U4: 64; **I'm in big trouble** ich stecke in großen Schwierigkeiten

trousers ['traʊzəz]: **jogging trousers** Jogginghose WF

true [truː] wahr

truly ['truːli]: **Yours truly, ...** (AE) Mit freundlichen Grüßen ... U4: 63

trumpet ['trʌmpɪt] Trompete WF

try [traɪ] versuchen, (aus)probieren

T-shirt ['tiːʃɜːt] T-Shirt

tube [tjuːb] Reifenschlauch WF U6; **the tube** die (Londoner) U-Bahn

tubing ['tjuːbɪŋ] *Benutzung eines Reifenschlauchs als Floß* WF U6

Tuesday ['tjuːzdeɪ, 'tjuːzdi] Dienstag

tuna ['tjuːnə] Thunfisch WF

tunnel ['tʌnl] Tunnel

Turkey ['tɜːki] Türkei

turn (to the left) [tɜːn] sich (nach links) drehen U2: 29; **turn left/ right (into Market Street)** nach links/rechts (in die Market Street) abbiegen

turn off [tɜːn'ɒf] ausschalten

turn on [tɜːn'ɒn] einschalten

TV ['tiː'viː] Fernsehen; Fernsehgerät

twilight ['twaɪlaɪt] Dämmerung, Zwielicht WF

type [taɪp] Typ WF; **types of music** Musikrichtungen WF

typical ['tɪpɪkl] typisch WF U6

U

umbrella [ʌm'brelə] Schirm U5: 67

uncle ['ʌŋkl] Onkel U4: 57

uncool [ʌn'kuːl] nicht cool U2: 36

under ['ʌndə] unter

underground ['ʌndəgraʊnd] **1** unterirdisch; **2** U-Bahn Next: 9

underground station ['ʌndəgraʊndsteɪʃn] U-Bahnhof

underground train ['ʌndəgraʊndtreɪn] U-Bahn-Zug

underline [ʌndə'laɪn] unterstreichen

underlined [ʌndə'laɪnd] unterstrichen

understand [ʌndə'stænd] (I understood, I've understood) verstehen

understood [ʌndə'stʊd] (→ understand): **I understood** ich verstand, ich habe verstanden

undressing ['ʌndresɪŋ] Ausziehen WF

uniform ['juːnɪfɔːm] (Schul-)Uniform

unit ['juːnɪt] Lektion

up [ʌp]: **it's (= it was) up to me** es lag an mir WF; **What's up?** Was gibt's?

us [ʌs] uns

use [juːz] benutzen, verwenden

useful ['juːsfl] nützlich U2: 35

user ['juːzə]: **user's guide** Bedienungsanleitung WF

usually ['juːʒuəli] meistens, normalerweise, gewöhnlich

V

vacation [və'keɪʃn] (AE) Ferien, Urlaub WF

valuable ['væljuəbl] wertvoll WF

vegetable ['vedʒtəbl] (ein) Gemüse

vehicle ['viːəkl] Fahrzeug WF

venue ['venjuː] Veranstaltungsort WF

verb [vɜːb] Verb, Zeitwort

verse [vɜːs] Strophe

very ['veri] sehr

video ['vɪdiəʊ] Videofilm, Video

video game ['vɪdiəʊgeɪm] Videospiel U3: 47

viewer ['vjuːə] Fernsehzuschauer, -zuschauerin WF

Viking ['vaɪkɪŋ] Wikinger, Wikinger-

village ['vɪlɪdʒ] Dorf

violence ['vaɪələns] Gewalt, Gewalttätigkeit U1: 14

visit ['vɪzɪt] besuchen
visitor ['vɪzɪtə] Besucher/in, Gast
visitor centre ['vɪzɪtəsentə] Besucherzentrum U4: 55
voice [vɔɪs] Stimme U5: 69
volleyball ['vɒlibɔːl] Volleyball
vote [vəʊt]: vote for the winner über den Gewinner/die Gewinnerin abstimmen WF

W

wagon ['wægən] Planwagen WF U6; wagon train Zug von Planwagen WF U6
wait (for) [weɪt] warten (auf); I can't wait for it. Ich kann es kaum erwarten. Let's wait and see. Warten wir's ab. wait in line (AE) Schlange stehen U2: 28
waiter ['weɪtə] Kellner WF
waitress ['weɪtrəs] Kellnerin WF
wake up [weɪkʌp] (I woke up, I've woken up) aufwachen U5: 70
Wales [weɪlz] Wales
walk [wɔːk] gehen, laufen; walk dogs Hunde ausführen WF
walker ['wɔːkə] Spaziergänger/in, Wanderer, Wanderin
walking ['wɔːkɪŋ] Spazierengehen, Wandern
walking shoe ['wɔːkɪŋʃuː] Wanderschuh
wall [wɔːl] Wand; Mauer U4: 55
want [wɒnt] wollen; want to go gehen wollen
war [wɔː] Krieg WF
warm [wɔːm] warm
was [wɒz, wəz] war; wasn't (= was not) war nicht; they thought it was a good idea sie dachten, es wäre eine gute Idee; it was called es wurde genannt WF U6
Washington State [wɒʃɪŋtən'steɪt] der Bundesstaat Washington U4: 52
waste [weɪst] verschwenden; a waste of time Zeitverschwendung
watch [wɒtʃ] 1 beobachten, sich anschauen; zusehen; Watch me! Pass auf! watch TV fernsehen; 2 (Armband-)Uhr WF
water ['wɔːtə] Wasser
wave [weɪv] Welle U2: 29

way [weɪ] Weg; way of life Lebensweise WF
we [wiː] wir; we're (= we are) wir sind
wear [weə] (I wore, I've worn) tragen, anziehen
weather ['weðə] Wetter
webcode ['webkəʊd] Webcode
website ['websaɪt] Website
wedding ['wedɪŋ] Hochzeit U1: 21
wedding day ['wedɪŋdeɪ] Hochzeitstag
Wednesday ['wenzdeɪ,'wenzdi] Mittwoch
week [wiːk] Woche
weekend ['wiːk'end] Wochenende
welcome ['welkəm]: Welcome to London. Willkommen in London. we aren't welcome wir sind nicht willkommen; You're welcome. Nichts zu danken; Bitte schön. U5: 75
well [wel] 1 gut; Well done! Gut gemacht! U3: 42; 2 Well, ... Nun/Tja, ...
Welsh [welʃ] walisisch; Walisisch; Waliser, Waliserin(nen)
went [went] (→ go): I went ich ging, ich bin gegangen
were [wɜː] waren; warst; wart; weren't (= were not) waren/warst/wart nicht
west [west] Westen; West-; westlich
western ['westən] Western WF
wet [wet] nass, feucht
wetsuit ['wetsuːt] Surf-/Tauch-(schutz)anzug U2: 29
whale [weɪl] Wal
whale watching ['weɪlwɒtʃɪŋ] Walbeobachtung U4: 53; go whale watching auf Walbeobachtungstour gehen U4: 53
what [wɒt] 1 was; What a ...! Was für ein/eine ...! What about you? Und du?/Was ist mit dir? What are they in German? Wie heißen sie auf Deutsch? What time is it? Wie spät ist es? What's that? Was ist das? What's your name? Wie heißt du? What's up? Was gibt's? 2 welche, welcher, welches
whatever [wɒt'evə]: whatever the weather egal, wie das Wetter ist; you can do whatever you feel du kannst tun, wonach dir gerade ist WF

wheelchair ['wiːltʃeə] Rollstuhl; he's in a wheelchair er sitzt im Rollstuhl
when [wen] 1 wann; 2 wenn; 3 als
where [weə] wo; wohin; Where are you from? Woher kommst du?
whether ['weðə] ob
which [wɪtʃ] welche, welcher, welches
white [waɪt] weiß; white bread Weißbrot U1: 12; white people Weiße U1: 14
who [huː] 1 wer; 2 der, die, das (in Relativsätzen)
why [waɪ] warum, weshalb; That's why ... Deshalb ..., Darum ...
wide [waɪd] breit
wife [waɪf] Ehefrau WF
wild [waɪld] wild; wild lebend
wildfire ['waɪldfaɪə] Großflächenbrand WF U6
will [wɪl]: I'll (= I will) go ich werde gehen
win [wɪn] (I won, I've won) gewinnen
window ['wɪndəʊ] Fenster
winner ['wɪnə] Gewinner/Gewinnerin, Sieger/Siegerin
winter ['wɪntə] Winter
wishes ['wɪʃɪz]: Best wishes, ... Viele Grüße ...
witch [wɪtʃ] Hexe
with [wɪð] mit; bei
without [wɪ'ðaʊt] ohne
woke up [wəʊkʌp] (→ wake up): I woke up ich wachte auf, ich bin aufgewacht U5: 156
woken up [wəʊkən'ʌp] (→ wake up): I've woken up ich bin aufgewacht U5: 156
woman, women ['wʊmən, 'wɪmɪn] Frau, Frauen
won [wʌn] (→ win): I won ich gewann, ich habe gewonnen; I've won ich habe gewonnen
won't [wəʊnt]: I won't (= will not) go ich werde nicht gehen
wonder ['wʌndə] sich fragen WF
wood [wʊd] Wald
word [wɜːd] Wort; words (of a song) (Lied-)Text
wore [wɔː] (→ wear): I wore ich trug, ich habe getragen
work [wɜːk] 1 arbeiten; funktionieren; 2 Arbeit
work experience [wɜːkɪk'spɪəriəns] Berufserfahrung U4: 63; do work experience ein Berufspraktikum machen WF

worker ['wɜːkə] Arbeiter, Arbeiterin

world [wɜːld] Welt; **in the world** auf der (ganzen) Welt

World Trade Center [wɜːld'treɪdsentə] Welthandelszentrum WF

worried ['wʌrid]: **I'm worried (about)** ich mache mir Sorgen (um), ich bin beunruhigt (wegen)

worry (about) ['wʌri] sich Sorgen machen (um)

worse [wɜːs] schlechter; schlimmer

worst [wɜːst] schlechteste/r/s; schlimmste/r/s

would [wʊd]: **I'd (= I would)** ich würde U1: 22; **I'd like to go/...** Ich möchte gehen/...; **I wouldn't (= would not) like to go/...** Ich möchte nicht gehen/...; **Would you like ...?** Möchtest du/Möchten Sie ...?

Wow! [waʊ] Wow! Wahnsinn!

write [raɪt] (I wrote, I've written) schreiben

writer ['raɪtə] Schriftsteller/in

written ['rɪtn] (→ write): **I've written** ich habe geschrieben

wrong [rɒŋ] falsch; **What's wrong?** Ist etwas nicht in Ordnung?

wrote [rəʊt] (→ write): **I wrote** ich schrieb, ich habe geschrieben

Y

ya [jə]: **How ya doin'?** (AE) Wie geht's? WF

yeah [jeə] ja (besonders in wörtl. Rede)

year [jɪə] Jahr; Jahrgangsstufe; **a 13-year-old girl** ein 13-jähriges Mädchen; **What year are you in? – I'm in year 7.** In welcher Jahrgangsstufe bist du? – Ich bin in der 7. Stufe.

yearbook ['jɪəbʊk] Jahrbuch WF

yellow ['jeləʊ] gelb

yes [jes] ja

yesterday ['jestədeɪ, 'jestədi] gestern

yet [jet]: **not ... yet** noch nicht

YMCA [waɪemsiː'eɪ] CVJM WF

you [juː] **1** du; ihr; Sie; **2** dir, euch, Ihnen; dich, euch, Sie; **you're (= you are)** du bist; ihr seid; Sie sind; **I said you'd be in the shop tomorrow.** Ich habe gesagt, du wärst morgen im Laden.

young [jʌŋ] jung; **young kids** kleine Kinder U2: 36

your [jɔː] dein, deine; euer, eure; Ihr, Ihre

yours [jɔːz]: **Yours truly, ...** (AE) Mit freundlichen Grüßen ... U4: 63

yourself [jɔː'self] dir/dich (selbst); selbst U5: 69; **a picture of yourself** ein Bild von dir

youth club ['juːθklʌb] Jugendklub

Z

zone [zəʊn] Zone WF

Alphabetische Liste der Wörter aus den Bänden 1–4 (Deutsch–Englisch)

* = unregelmäßiges Verb; siehe auch *List of irregular verbs*, S.197/198

A

abbiegen: nach links/rechts (in die Hill Street) abbiegen turn left/right (into Hill Street)
Abend evening
Abendessen dinner
abends in the evening; *(mit Uhrzeit)* p.m.
aber but
Abfall litter
abholen pick up
ablesen *read out
Abneigung dislike
abreisen *leave
Absatz paragraph
abschreiben copy
abseits der Straße off-road
Abspielgerät player
Absprache arrangement; **eine Absprache treffen** *make an arrangement
Achterbahn roller coaster
Actionfilm action film
Adjektiv adjective
Adresse address
Adverb adverb
Afrika Africa
Ahnung: ich habe keine Ahnung I have no clue
Akademie academy
Akte file
Aktivität activity
Alarmanlage alarm
albern silly
Alkohol alcohol
alle all (the); *(jeder)* everybody
allein alone
alles everything
allgemein general
Alphabet alphabet
alphabetisch alphabetical
als **1** as; **2** *(Wann?)* when; **schneller als** faster than
also so
alt old
Alter age
am: am 5. August on August 5th; **am Morgen/...** in the morning/...; **Am nächsten Tag ...** The next day ...; **am selben Ort** in the same place; **am Strand** on the beach; **am Telefon** on the phone; **am Wochenende** (AE) on the weekend; **24 Stunden am Tag** 24 hours a day

American Football American football
Amerika America
Amerikaner/in American
amerikanisch American; **amerik. Ureinwohner/in** Native American
Ampel traffic light
an **1** *(bei)* at; **2** *(nach)* to; **3** *(in der Nähe von, neben)* by; **4** *(eingeschaltet)* on; **an den Armen** by his arms; **an der Küste** on the coast; **an der Tafel** on the board; **an Schultagen** on school days; **denken an** *think of
anbieten offer
andere other; **ein anderer/anderes, eine andere** another
andere/r/s, anders (als) different (from)
andererseits: Einerseits ... Andererseits ... On the one hand, ... On the other hand, ...
(sich) ändern change; **er änderte seinen Namen in ...** he changed his name to ...
Anfang start
anfangen start
anfassen touch
Angebot offer
angeln fish; **Angeln** fishing
angenehm: Einen angenehmen Aufenthalt. Enjoy your stay.
Angst: ich habe Angst I'm frightened
ängstlich nervous
Anhänger/in fan
anhalten stop
anhören: sich anhören sound; **sich die CD anhören** listen to the CD
ankommen arrive
Anlegestelle pier
Anruf phone call; **Danke für den Anruf.** Thanks for calling.
anrufen phone; call
anschauen: sich den Film anschauen watch the film
Anschlagbrett noticeboard
Anschreiben cover letter
ansehen: (sich) das Bild ansehen look at the picture
Ansicht scene
Ansichtskarte postcard

Antwort answer; **u.A.w.g.** (= um Antwort wird gebeten) RSVP
antworten answer
Anweisung order; **Anweisungen geben** Giving orders
Anzahl number
Anzeige advert
anziehen *(tragen)* *wear
Anzug: Surf-/Tauch(schutz)anzug wetsuit
Apfel apple
Apfelwein cider
April April
Arbeit work; job
arbeiten work
Arbeiter/in worker
Arbeitgeber/in employer
Arbeitsgemeinschaft *(Klub)* club
Arbeitsstelle job
Arm arm
arm poor; **Du Arme/r!** Poor you!
Artikel article
Asiat/in; asiatisch Asian
Asien Asia
Assistent/in assistant
Astronaut/in astronaut
auch too
auf on; *(auf ... hinauf/herauf)* onto; **auf das Haus zu** towards the house; **auf dem Bild** in the picture; **auf dem Land** in the country; **auf dem Parkplatz** in the car park; **auf dem Schulhof** in the playground; **auf den Boden fallen** *fall to the ground; **auf der (ganzen) Welt** in the world; **auf der Straße** in the street; **auf Deutsch** in German; **auf die Straße (hinaus)** into the street; **Auf Wiedersehen.** Goodbye.
Aufenthalt: Einen angenehmen Aufenthalt. Enjoy your stay.
Aufgabe job
aufgeben *give up
aufgehen *(sich öffnen)* open
aufgeladen: es ist aufgeladen it's charged up
aufgeregt excited
aufheben pick up
aufhören (mit) finish
aufmachen open
aufpassen auf look after; **Pass auf!** Watch me!
aufregend exciting
aufstehen *get up

aufstellen: ein Zelt aufstellen *put up a tent

aufwachen *wake up

Auge eye

Augenblick: Einen Augenblick. Just a minute.

August August; **20. August** August 20th

aus 1 from; *(hinaus/heraus)* out; *(aus … hinaus/heraus)* out of; **2** *(zu Ende)* over; **aus der Schule zurück** back from school

Ausbildung education

Ausdruck phrase

ausdrucken print out

Ausflug trip

ausfüllen fill in

ausgeben *spend

ausgestorben extinct

ausleihen *(mieten)* rent

ausprobieren try

ausrichten: Kann ich (ihm/ihr) etwas ausrichten? Can I take a message?

Ausrüstung equipment; gear

ausrutschen slip

ausschalten turn off

aussehen look; **Wie sieht sie aus?** What does she look like?

Aussprache pronunciation

Ausstattung equipment

ausstehen: ich kann sie nicht ausstehen I hate them; I can't stand them

Ausstellung exhibition

aussuchen pick

Austausch- exchange

Ausweispapiere papers

auswendig: Lerne es auswendig. Learn it by heart.

Auszeichnung award

ausziehen: ich ziehe meine Jacke aus I *take off my jacket

Auto car

Autobahn *(in den USA)* freeway

Autofahrer/in driver

Autogramm autograph

B

Baby baby

Bad, Badezimmer bathroom

Badminton badminton

Bahn *(Laufbahn)* track

Bahnhof station; **im Bahnhof Exeter** at Exeter Station

bald soon

Ball 1 ball; **2** *(Tanzveranstaltung)* dance

Banane banana

Band *(Musikgruppe)* band

Bande gang

Bank *(Sparkasse)* bank

Bär bear

Baseball baseball

Basketball basketball

Batterieladegerät charger

Bauer/Bäuerin farmer

Bauernhof farm

Baum tree

Bayern Bavaria

beängstigend frightening

beantworten answer

bedeuten *mean

Bedeutung meaning

beeilen: Beeil dich! Hurry up!

beenden finish

Befehl order; **Befehle erteilen** Giving orders

Befehlsform imperative

begeistert excited

beginnen start; **ich begann zu rennen** I started to run

Begleitbrief (AE) cover letter

behalten *keep

behilflich: Kann ich Ihnen behilflich sein? Can I help you?

bei 1 *(an)* at; **2** *(mit)* with; **bei Tim (zu Hause)** at Tim's house

beibringen *teach; **ich würde dir das Reiten beibringen** I'd teach you to ride; **Wer kann es mir beibringen?** Who can teach me?

Beispiel example

beitreten: einem Klub beitreten join a club

bekommen *get

belebt busy

Belgien Belgium

beliebt popular

benutzen use

beobachten watch

bereit ready

Berg mountain

Bericht report

berichtigen correct

Beruf job; **Beruf, Berufs-** career

Berufserfahrung work experience

berühmt famous

berühren touch

beschäftigt busy

Beschäftigung activity; *(im Freien)* outdoor activity

beschreiben describe

Beschreibung description

beschweren: sich beschweren complain

Besichtigungen sightseeing

besondere/r/s special

Besprechung *(Rezension)* review

besser better

beste/r/s best; **am besten** best

besuchen visit

Besucher/in visitor

Besucherzentrum visitor centre

betonen stress

Betreff: … Subject: …

Betrieb business

Bett bed

beunruhigt: ich bin beunruhigt (wegen) I'm worried (about)

Bevölkerung(szahl) population

bevor before

(sich) bewegen move

bewerben: sich bewerben (um/bei) apply (for/to)

bewölkt cloudy

bezahlen *pay

bezeichnen call

Bezirk district

Biber beaver

Bier beer

Bild picture

bilden: Gruppen bilden make groups

Bildung education

billig cheap

bin: ich bin I'm (= I am)

bis 1 to; **2** *(zeitlich)* till; **bis zum 15. Oktober** by October 15th; **Bis dann.** See you. **Bis morgen/…** See you tomorrow/…

bist: du bist you're (= you are); **Bist du schon einmal …? - Ja./Nein.** Have you ever …? - Yes, I have./No, I haven't.

bitte please; **Hier, bitte.** Here you are. **Bitte.** *(Schon gut.)* That's OK. **Bitte schön.** *(Nichts zu danken.)* You're welcome.

bitten um ask for

blau blue

bleiben stay

Bleistift pencil

blöd stupid

Blödsinn nonsense

Blog blog

Bloggen blogging

Blogger/in blogger

blond blonde

bloß only

Board *(Brett)* board

Boden floor; ground; **am Boden zerstört** devastated

Boot boat

böse (auf) angry (with)

Bote/Botin courier

Brand fire

brauchen need

braun brown

breit wide

Brett board; **Schwarzes Brett** noticeboard
Brief letter
Brieffreund/in penfriend
bringen *bring; *take; **in die richtige Reihenfolge bringen** *put in the right order
Brite/Britin British
britisch British
Broschüre brochure
Brot bread; **belegtes Brot** sandwich
Brötchen roll
Brücke bridge
Bruder brother
Buch book
buchen book
Bücherei library
Buchhandlung, Buchladen bookshop
Buchstabe letter
buchstabieren spell
Büffel buffalo, buffaloes
Bühne stage; **auf der Bühne** on stage
Bundesstaat state; **der Bundesstaat Washington** Washington State
Burg castle
Bürgersteig pavement; (AE) sidewalk
Bus bus
Busfahrer/in bus driver
Bushaltestelle bus stop

C

Café cafe; (AE) diner
Camping camping
Campingplatz (AE) campground
CD CD
Cent cent
Clique gang
Coach coach
Cola cola
Computer computer
cool cool; **nicht cool** uncool
Cousin/e cousin
Cowboy cowboy
CVJM YMCA

D

da: da(hin) there; **da ist** there's; **da sind** there are; **da war/waren** there was/were; **da drüben** over there; **Ich bin wieder da!** I'm back!

dagegen: Haben Sie etwas dagegen, wenn ich mich hier hinsetze? Do you mind if I sit here?
daheim at home
daher so
damals at that time
Dame: Sehr geehrte Damen und Herren, ... Dear Sir/Madam, ...
daneben treffen/gehen miss
Dänemark Denmark
Danke (schön). Thank you./Thanks.
danken: Nichts zu danken. You're welcome.
dann then
darauf: ich freue mich darauf, von Ihnen zu hören I'm looking forward to hearing from you
darum that's why
das the; (das da) that; (das hier) this; (in Relativsätzen) that; who; **Das ist ...** That's ...
dass that; **Tut mir leid, dass ich ...** I'm sorry I ...
dasselbe the same
Datum date
Definition definition
dein/e your
Delfin dolphin
denken (an) *think (of); **daran denken** remember
der the; (der da) that; (in Relativsätzen) that; who
derselbe the same
deshalb that's why
Detektiv/in detective
deutsch; Deutsch; Deutsche/r German
Deutschland Germany
Dezember December
Dialog dialogue
dich you; (dich selbst) yourself
Dichter/in poet
die the; (die da; Einzahl) that; (die da; Mehrzahl) those; (die hier; Mehrzahl) these; (in Relativsätzen) that; who; **Männer, die Spiele spielen** men playing games
Dienstag Tuesday
dies (hier) this
diese (Mehrzahl) these; (diese da) those
diese/r/s this; **an diesem Abend** that evening
dieselbe the same
Ding thing
dir you; (dir selbst) yourself; **ein Bild von dir** a picture of yourself

Discgolf disc golf
Discjockey (DJ) DJ
Disko club
Dollar dollar ($)
Dolmetschen interpreting
Donnerstag Thursday
Doppelzimmer double room
Dorf village
dort(hin) there
draußen (im Freien) outdoors
drehen: sich drehen turn; **sich nach links drehen** turn to the left
drinnen (in der Halle) indoors
Droge drug
drüben: da/dort drüben over there
drücken push
du you
Dubliner/in Dubliner
dumm silly; stupid
Düne dune
durch (hindurch) through
durchdrehen panic
durcheinander bringen (mischen) mix up
dürfen can; **nicht dürfen** mustn't
DVD DVD
DVD-Player DVD player

E

Ecke: an der Ecke 10. Straße und Ocean Drive at 10th Street and Ocean Drive
egal, wie das Wetter ist whatever the weather
Ehemaligentreffen homecoming
Ei egg
eifersüchtig (auf) jealous (of)
eigen: mein eigenes Zimmer my own room
Eigenschaftswort adjective
eigentlich really
ein/e a; an; (Zahl) one
eine/r/s one; **eines Tages** one day
einerseits: Einerseits ... Andererseits ... On the one hand, ... On the other hand, ...
einfach easy; **einfache Gegenwart** simple present; **einfache Vergangenheit** simple past
Einfall idea
einfügen *put in
eingeschaltet on
einige some
Einkaufen shopping
einkaufen gehen *go shopping

Einkaufszentrum shopping centre; (AE) mall
einladen (zu) invite (for)
Einladung invitation
einnehmen *take
einpacken pack
einrichten establish
einsam lonely
einschalten turn on
Eintrag entry
Eintrittskarte ticket
Eintrittspreis entrance fee
Einwanderer/Einwanderin immigrant
Einzelzimmer single room
Eis (Speiseeis) ice cream
Eisenbahn train
Eisenbahnstrecke railway line
elektrisch electric
Elektrizität electricity
elektronisch electronic
Eltern, Elternteil parents, parent
E-Mail e-mail
E-Mail-Freund/in e-pal
Empfangschef/-dame receptionist
empfehlen recommend
Ende end; **oberes Ende** top; **Um zum Ende zu kommen, ...** To finish, ...; **zu Ende** over
Energie energy
eng narrow
Engländer/in(nen): er ist Engländer he's English
England England
englisch; Englisch English
entlang along; **die Straße entlang** along the street
entschuldigen: sich entschuldigen *say sorry; **Entschuldigen Sie, ...** Excuse me, ...
(sich) entspannen relax
entwerfen design
Enzyklopädie encyclopedia
er he; (nicht bei Personen) it
Erdkunde geography
erfahren: etwas über London erfahren learn about London
Erfahrung experience
Ergebnis result
erinnern: sich erinnern (an) remember
erklären explain; **ihr etwas erklären** explain something to her
eröffnen establish
erraten guess
erschüttert devastated
erst only
erste/r/s first; **erste Hilfe** first aid

erstens firstly
Erwachsene/r adult
erwarten: Ich kann es kaum erwarten. I can't wait for it.
erzählen (von) *tell (about)
erzielen (Punkte) score
es it; **es ist/gibt** there's; **es sind/gibt** there are; **es war(en)/gab** there was/were
essen *eat; **ein Eis essen** *have an ice cream; **zu essen geben** *feed
Essen food; (zubereitet) meal
Etikett label
etwas something; **etwas anderes** something different; **etwas Schokolade** some chocolate
euch you
euer/eure your
Euro euro (€)
Europa Europe
Europäer/in; europäisch European
Experte/Expertin expert

F

Fabrik factory
Fach (Schulfach) subject
Fachmann/-frau expert
Fahne flag
„Fahrattraktion" (im Vergnügungspark) ride
fahren *go; (ein Auto/einen Bus) *drive; (reisen) travel; **Mountainboard/Quad/Rad fahren** *ride a mountain board/quad/bike
Fahren: Quadfahren/Trikkefahren/... quad/Trikke/... riding
Fahrer/in driver
Fahrgeschäft ride
Fahrkarte ticket
Fahrrad bike
Fahrrad fahren *ride a bike
Fahrt ride
Fair Play fair play
fallen *fall; **auf den Boden fallen** *fall to the ground
falls if
falsch wrong; false
Familie family
Familienname family name
Fan fan
fantastisch fantastic
Farbe colour
fast almost; nearly
Fastfood fast food
Favorit/in favourite

Februar February
Federball(spiel) badminton
Federmäppchen pencil case
fehlend: die fehlenden Wörter the missing words
Feier celebration
Feinkostgeschäft und -imbiss (AE) deli
Feld field
Fels rock
Felsen (Klippe) cliff
Fenster window
Ferien holiday/s
fernsehen watch TV
Fernsehen, Fernsehgerät TV
Fernsehkarriere career in TV
Fernstraße (AE) highway
fertig ready
Fest; Festival festival
Festbeleuchtung illuminations
feucht wet
Feuer fire
Feuerwerk fireworks
Figur (Person) character
Film film; (AE) movie
Finanz-, finanziell financial
finden *find; *think
Fisch, Fische fish
fischen fish; **Fischen** fishing
fit fit
Fitnessstudio gym
Flagge flag
Fleisch meat
fliegen *go
flogen: sie flogen they flew
Flug flight
Flughafen airport; **am Flughafen Exeter** at Exeter Airport
Flugschein (plane) ticket
Flugzeug plane
Fluss river
Folge result
folgen follow
Förderunterricht extra classes
Form form
Formular form
fort away
Foto photo; picture; **Fotos machen** *take photos
Fotoapparat camera
Fotograf/in photographer
fotografieren *take photos
Fotosession, Fotoshooting photo shoot
Foul foul
Frage question; **eine Frage stellen** ask a question
Fragebogen questionnaire
fragen ask
Frankreich France

Franzose(n)/Französin(nen); französisch; Französisch French

Frau, Frauen woman, women; *(Anrede allgemein)* Ms; *(Anrede für verheiratete Frauen)* Mrs

Freak freak

frei free; **im Freien** outdoors; **Beschäftigung im Freien** outdoor activity

Freiheit freedom

Freiheitsstatue Statue of Liberty

Freitag Friday

Freiwurf free throw

Freizeit free time

Fremdenverkehrsbüro tourist office

fressen *eat

freuen: ich freue mich darauf, von Ihnen zu hören I'm looking forward to hearing from you; **ich freue mich für sie** I'm happy for her

Freund/in friend; *(feste/r Freundin/Freund)* boyfriend/girlfriend

freundlich friendly; **Mit freundlichen Grüßen ...** (AE) Yours truly, ...

Friseur/in hairdresser

froh happy

Früchte fruit

früh early

Frühling spring

Frühstück breakfast

frühstücken *have breakfast

(sich) fühlen *feel

führen *go; *lead

Führer/in *(für Sehenswürdigkeiten)* guide

Führung *(Rundgang)* tour

Füller pen

funktionieren work

für for; **es steht 24:18 für North** it's 24–18 to North

furchtbar terrible

furchterregend frightening

Fuß, Füße foot, feet

Fußball football; soccer

Fußboden floor

füttern *feed

G

Gälisch Gaelic

Gang **1** *(Bande)* gang; **2** *(Fahrrad/Auto/...)* gear; **3** *(Korridor)* passage

ganz: das ganze Wochenende all weekend; **die ganze Zeit** all the time

gar nichts nothing

Garten garden

Gärtner/in gardener

Gast visitor

Gebäude building

gebaut: sie wurden gebaut they were built

geben *give; **Gib Tim das Buch.** Give the book to Tim. **eine Party geben** *have a party; **Was gibt's?** What's up?

Gebiet district

Gebirge: im Gebirge in the mountains

geboren: ich wurde ... geboren I was born ...

Gebrauchsanweisung instructions

Geburtstag birthday

gedacht: ich habe das (immer wieder) gedacht I've been thinking that

Gedicht poem

gefährlich dangerous

gefallen: Es gefällt mir. I like it. **Wem gefällt es am besten?** Who likes it best? **alles, was jungen Männern gefällt** everything for young men to enjoy

Gefängnis prison; **im/ins Gefängnis** in prison; **ins Gefängnis kommen** *go to prison

Gefühl feeling

gefühlsbetont emotional

gegen against

Gegend area; *(Viertel)* neighbourhood

Gegenstand object

Gegenteil opposite

gegenüber (von) opposite

Gegenwart: einfache Gegenwart simple present

gehen *go; walk; **ans Telefon gehen** answer the phone; **sie geht zur Schule** she's at school; **Wie geht's?** How are you?/(AE) How ya doin'?

Gehör hearing

Gehsteig pavement

Geist ghost

gekommen: sie waren gekommen they had come

Gelände: im Gelände off-road

Geländer railings

gelangen *get

gelangweilt bored

gelb yellow

Geld money

Gemüse vegetable/s

genug enough

Genuss treat

geöffnet open

Geografie geography

Gepäckabfertiger/in baggage handler

gerade just

Gerät machine

Geräusch noise; sound

gern: gern haben like; **Ich laufe (nicht) gern.** I (don't) like walking. **Ich lese sehr gern.** I love reading.

Geschäft business; *(Laden)* shop; (AE) store

geschehen happen

Geschenk present

Geschichte **1** *(Erzählung)* story; **2** *(Schulfach)* history

Geschichtsverein Historical Society

geschickt: es hatte geschickt it had sent

geschlossen closed

Geschwindigkeitsbegrenzung speed limit

Geschwister brothers and sisters

gesetzt: sie hat eine Anzeige in die Zeitung gesetzt she has put an advert in the newspaper

Gesicht face

Gespenst ghost

gesponsert sponsored

Gespräch conversation; dialogue

gestern yesterday

gesund healthy

Getränk drink

Gewalt(tätigkeit) violence

Gewinn prize

gewinnen *win; **im Lotto gewinnen** *win the lotto

Gewinner/in winner

gewöhnlich usually

gezeigt: es wurde ihm gezeigt he was shown

Gitarre guitar; **Gitarre spielen** play the guitar

Glas glass

glauben believe

gleich: der/die/das gleiche the same

Gleis railway line

Glück: Viel Glück! Good luck!

glücklich happy

Glückliche/r: Der/Die Glückliche! Du Glückliche/r! Lucky thing!

Glückwunsch: Herzlichen Glückwunsch! Congratulations! *(zum Geburtstag)* Happy birthday!

Golf golf

Grab grave

Grad degree

Gras grass

Graubrot brown bread
Grauwal grey whale
Grenze border
grillen grill
groß big; *(bei Personen)* tall
großartig great
Großbritannien Britain
Großeltern grandparents
Großflächenbrand wildfire
Großmutter *(Oma)* grandma
Großstadt city
Großvater *(Opa)* grandad
grün green
Grund reason
Gruppe group
Grüße: Mit freundlichen Grüßen ...
(AE) Yours truly, ...; **Viele
Grüße ...** Best wishes, ...; **(Viele)
Liebe Grüße ...** (Lots of) Love, ...
grüßen: Grüße Dawn, bitte. Say hi
to Dawn, please.
gut good; fine; *(schon gut)* OK;
gut in good at; **gut kennen/...**
know/... well; **Gut gemacht!**
Well done! **Gute(n) Abend/
Morgen/Nacht.** Good evening/
morning/night. **Guten Tag.**
Hello. **Wie geht's? – Danke, gut.**
How are you? – I'm fine, thanks.
Guthaben credit

H

Haar, Haare hair
haben *have; **ich habe** (AE) I got;
Ich habe Geburtstag. It's my
birthday. **Welche Farbe hat
dein Zimmer?** What colour is
your room?
Hähnchen *(Brathähnchen)* chicken
halb: halb zwei/... half past one/...;
dreieinhalb three and a half
Halbzeit half-time
Halle: in der Halle indoors
Hallo. Hello./Hi.
Halloween Halloween
Halt stop
halten *hold; *keep; **sich an die
Spielregeln halten** play by the
rules; **Halt den Mund!** Shut up!
Was hältst du von ...? What do
you think of ...?
Haltestelle stop
Hamburger hamburger
Hamster hamster
Hand hand
handeln: Der Text handelt von ...
The text is about ...
Handy mobile (phone); (AE) cell-
phone

Handzeichen hand signal
Happy End happy ending
hart hard; tough
Hase rabbit
hassen hate
**hast: Hast du schon einmal ...?
– Ja./Nein.** Have you ever ...?
– Yes, I have./No, I haven't.
hätte: Ich hätte gern ... I'd like ...;
Wenn ich das Geld hätte, ... If I
had the money, ...
Hauptstadt capital
Haus house; **nach Hause gehen**
*go home; **zu Hause** at home;
bei Tim zu Hause at Tim's
house; **Gehen wir zu mir nach
Hause.** Let's go to my house.
**Hausarrest: ich habe Haus-
arrest** I'm grounded
Hausaufgaben homework
Hausaufgabenheft homework
diary
Häuserblock block
Haustier pet
Haut skin
Havanna Havana
heben: Heb(t) die Hand. Put up
your hand.
Heft book
Heim home
heimatlos homeless
Heimweh haben *feel homesick
heiß hot
heißen: Ich heiße Sarah. I'm
Sarah. **Wie heißt du?** What's
your name? **Wie heißen sie auf
Deutsch?** What are they in
German?
Heizkörper radiator
hektisch busy
Held/in, Held(inn)en hero, heroes
helfen help
Helfer/in helper
Helm helmet
Hemd shirt
herausfinden *find out
herbeiführen *bring about
herbeirufen call
Herbst autumn
hereinkommen *come in
Herr *(Anrede)* Mr; **Sehr geehrte
Damen und Herren, ...** Dear Sir/
Madam, ...
herstellen *make; produce
herüber across
herumhängen *hang out
herunterladen download
**herzlich: Herzlichen Glück-
wunsch!** Congratulations! *(zum
Geburtstag)* Happy birthday!

heute today; **heute
Morgen/...** this morning/...
Hexe witch
hier(her) here; **Hier, bitte.** Here
you are. **Hier spricht Sarah.**
It's Sarah.
Hilfe help; **erste Hilfe** first aid
himmelhoch sky-high
hinab/herab down
hinaus/heraus out
hinein in; **hineingehen** *go in;
hineinkriechen crawl in
hinten: hinten im Buch at the
back of the book
hinter behind; **hinter einem Ball
her** after a ball
Hintergrund background
hinüber across
hinunter/herunter down
hinzufügen *put in
Hirsch, Hirsche deer
**hispanisch; Hispano-Amerika-
ner/in** Hispanic
Hit hit
Hobby hobby
hoch high
Hochhaus skyscraper
hochheben pick up
Hochsprung (the) high jump
Hochzeit wedding
Hochzeitstag wedding day
Hockey hockey
Hof *(Bauernhof)* farm
hoffen hope
Hoffnung hope
höflich polite
holen *get
hören *hear; *(sich anhören)* listen
to
Horror horror
Hose: kurze Hosen shorts
Hot Dog hot dog
Hotel hotel
House house
Hüfte hip
Hügel hill
Huhn chicken
Hund dog
hundert hundred
Hunger: Ich habe Hunger. I'm
hungry.
hungrig hungry
Hurling hurling
hurra rufen cheer

I

ich I; **Dies bin ich.** This is me.
Idee idea
if-Satz if-clause

ihm, ihn him; *(nicht bei Personen)* it
ihnen them
Ihnen you
ihr 1 *(Wer?)* you; **2** *(Wem?)* her; *(nicht bei Personen)* it
ihr/e 1 *(Einzahl)* her; *(nicht bei Personen)* its; **2** *(Mehrzahl)* their
Ihr/e your
illegal illegal
im: im April in April; **im Bahnhof Exeter** at Exeter Station; **im Bus** on the bus; **im Fernsehen** on TV; **im Internet** on the Internet; **im Jahre 1971** in 1971; **im Norden** in the north; **im Sonderangebot** on special offer; **im Urlaub** on holiday; **im Winter** in winter
Imbissstube *(Café)* (AE) diner
immer always
immergrün evergreen
Immigrant/in immigrant
Imperativ imperative

in in; at; *(in … hinein/herein)* into; **in Dartmoor** on Dartmoor; **in den Urlaub fahren** *go on holiday; **in der Fairfield Road** in Fairfield Road; **in der Nacht** at night; **in der Schule** at school; **in die Mannschaft kommen** *get on the team; **in einer Reservation** on a reservation; **In welcher Jahrgangsstufe bist du? – Ich bin in der 7. Stufe.** What year are you in? – I'm in year 7. **ins Bett gehen** *go to bed; **eine Sendung ins Leben rufen** start a programme; **Willkommen in London.** Welcome to London. **Ich bin (schon einmal) in Frankreich gewesen.** I've been to France.
Indianer/in Indian; *(amerik. Ureinwohner/in)* Native American
indianisch Indian
Infinitiv infinitive
Informationen, Informations- information
Insel island
insgesamt all in all
interessant interesting
Interesse interest
interessiert (an) interested (in)
international international
Internet Internet; **im Internet** on the Internet
Internet-Kiosk Internet kiosk
Ire(n)/Irin(nen); irisch; Irisch Irish

irgendetwas anything
irgendwelche any
Irland Ireland
irre (AE) awesome
ist is
Italien Italy

J

ja yes; *(besonders in wörtl. Rede)* yeah
Jacke jacket
jagen hunt
Jäger/in hunter
Jahr year; **ein 13-jähriges Mädchen** a 13-year-old girl
Jahrbuch yearbook
Jahreszeit season
Jahrgangsstufe year; **In welcher Jahrgangsstufe bist du?** What year are you in?
Jahrmarkt funfair
Januar January
Jeans jeans
jede/r/s each; every
jeder *(alle)* everybody
jemals ever
jemand somebody
jene *(Mehrzahl)* those
jetzt now
joggen jog
Jogger/in jogger
Jogging jogging
jubeln cheer
Judo judo
Jugendklub youth club
Jugendliche/r kid
Juli July
jung young
Junge boy
Juni June
Junior-Ranger junior ranger

K

Kajakfahren kayaking
Kalifornien California
kalt cold
Kamera camera
kämpfen *fight
Kanal canal
Kanu canoe; **Kanufahren** canoeing
Kappe cap
Karneval carnival
Karriere career
Karte card; *(Landkarte)* map
Karteikarte file

Kartoffel, Kartoffeln potato, potatoes
Kartoffelchips crisps; (AE) potato chips
Käse cheese
Kassierer/in cashier
Kasten box
Katze cat
kaufen *buy
Käufer/in shopper
Kaufhaus department store
kein/e no; not … any
kennen *know; **kennen lernen** *meet; **Schön, dich/Sie kennen zu lernen.** Nice to meet you.
kicken kick
Kilometer kilometre
Kilt *(Schottenrock)* kilt
Kind, Kinder child, children; kid, kids
Kinderheim children's home
Kino cinema
Kirche church
Kirmes funfair
Kiste box
Klamotten gear
Klapphandy flip phone
Klasse class; **9. Klasse** (AE) grade 9
Klassenarbeit test
Klassenlehrer/in class teacher
Klassenzimmer classroom
Klavier piano
Kleider, Kleidung clothes; *(Klamotten)* gear
klein little; short; small; **kleine Kinder** young kids; **„Klein-Italien"** Little Italy
Kletterer/Kletterin (rock) climber
klettern climb; **auf einen Hügel klettern** climb a hill; **Klettern** (rock) climbing
Klingelton ringtone
klingen sound
Klippe cliff
Klub club
Knopf button
Koch/Köchin cook
kochen cook
Kolumbien Colombia
komisch funny
kommen *come; *(gelangen)* *get; **Ich komme aus London.** I'm from London. **Er kommt zu spät.** He's late. **ins Gefängnis kommen** *go to prison; **sie kamen darauf, aus Leavenworth eine deutsche Stadt zu machen** they thought of making Leavenworth a German town

Komödie comedy
König king
Königin queen
können can
konnte: ich konnte (nicht) I could(n't)
könnte: ich könnte (nicht) I could(n't)
Kontext context
kontrollieren check
Konzert concert
Kopf head
kopieren copy
Korb *(Basketball)* hoop
Korbwurf shot
Korridor passage
korrigieren correct
kosten: Was kostet/kosten ...? How much is/are ...?
kostenlos free
Kräcker cracker
Kraft energy
Krähe crow
krank ill; **krank werden** (AE) *become sick
Krankenhaus hospital
Krankheit illness
kriechen crawl
Krieg war
Küche kitchen
Kuchen cake
Kuh cow
kümmern: sich kümmern um look after; **sich um Taschen kümmern** *deal with bags
Kumpel buddy
Kunst art
Kurier/in courier
kurz short; **kurz (be)vor** just before
(sich) küssen kiss
Küste coast; *(Strand)* seashore; **an der Küste** on the coast

L

lächeln smile
lachen laugh
Lachs salmon
Ladegerät charger
Laden shop; (AE) store
Ladendieb/in shoplifter
lag: es lag an mir it's (= it was) up to me
Lagerfeuer campfire
lagern camp
Lampe lamp; light
Land 1 land; **2** *(ländliche Gegend)* country; **auf dem Land** in the country; **3** *(Staat)* state

Landfahrer/in traveller
Landkarte map
Landwirtschaftsschau county fair
lang: 14 Jahre lang for 14 years
lang/e long
lange (for) a long time; **lange bleiben** stay for long
Langhaus longhouse
langsam slow
langweilen: ich langweile mich I'm bored
langweilig boring
Laptop laptop
Lärm noise
lassen: stehen/liegen lassen *leave; **Lasst uns aufhören.** Let's finish.
Lauch(stange) leek
Laufbahn 1 *(Bahn)* track; **2** *(berufliche Laufbahn (im Fernsehen))* career (in TV)
laufen *run; walk; **Laufen** running
Läufer/in runner
laut loud
leben live
Leben life
Lebenslauf (AE) résumé
Lebensmittel food
Lebensweise way of life
„Lebewohl-Biegung" Farewell Bend
legen *put
Lehrer/in teacher
leicht easy
Leichtathletik athletics
leid: Tut mir leid. I'm sorry./Sorry.
Leider ... I'm afraid ...
leihen: sich einen Füller (aus)leihen borrow a pen
leisten: erste Hilfe leisten *give first aid
Lektion unit
lernen learn; **Lerne es auswendig.** Learn it by heart.
lesen *read
Leser/in reader
Lesetagebuch reading log
Lesewoche reading week
„Letterboxing" letterboxing
letzte/r/s last
letztendlich in the end
Leute people; **Hallo Leute.** (AE) Hi you guys.
Lexikon encyclopedia
Licht light
Lichtschalter light switch
lieb: Liebe/r ... Dear ...; **(Viele) Liebe Grüße ...** (Lots of) Love, ...
Liebe love

lieben love
Liebesfilm, Liebesroman romance
Lieblings- favourite
Lied song
Limonade fizzy drink; (AE) soda; *(Zitronen-)* lemonade
Lineal ruler
Linie line
Link link
links left; **auf der linken Seite** on the left; **links (von Ihnen)** on your left
Lippe lip
Liste list
Loch hole
los: es war viel los there was lots of activity
loslassen release
Lotterie: in einer Lotterie gewinnen *win a lottery
Lotto lotto
lügen lie
lustig funny
Luxemburg Luxembourg

M

machen *do; *make; **ein Picknick machen** *have a picnic; **Das macht zwei Pfund, bitte.** That's two pounds, please. **Es macht Spaß.** It's fun. **Ich mache Hausaufgaben.** I *do my homework. **Mach dir Notizen.** *Make notes. **Mach(t) / Machen Sie nur.** Go ahead. **sie macht Urlaub** she's on holiday **Was machst du (da)?** What are you doing?
Macht power
Mädchen girl
Mahlzeit meal
Mai May
Make-up make-up
Mama mum; (AE) mom
manchmal sometimes
Mann, Männer man, men
männlich male
Mannschaft team
Marke brand
Marshmallow marshmallow
März March
Maschine machine
Mathe(matik) maths
Mauer wall
Medien: die Medien the media
Medizin-; medizinisch medical
Meer sea; ocean
mehr more
Meile mile

mein/e my
meinen *mean
Meinung opinion; **meiner Meinung nach** in my opinion; **Ich bin derselben Meinung (wie du).** I agree (with you).
meiste/n: der/die/das meiste, die meisten most
meistens usually
Mekka Mecca
Mensch person; **Menschen** people
Metal metal
Meter metre
Mexiko Mexico
mich me
Michigansee Lake Michigan
mieten rent; *(Fahrrad/Kanu/...)* hire
Milch milk
Million million
Mindmap mind map
Minute minute
mir me
mischen mix up
mit with; **mit dem Rad/Bus/Auto/...** by bike/bus/car/...
mitbringen *take
Mitglied in einem Klub werden join a club
mitnehmen *take
Mittagessen lunch
Mittagspause lunch break; lunchtime
Mittagszeit lunchtime
Mitteilung message
Mittwoch Wednesday
„Mobber/in" bully
Mobbing bullying
Möbel furniture
Mobiltelefon mobile (phone); (AE) cellphone
Modell model
modern modern
mögen like; **sehr mögen** love; **Ich möchte (gehen/...)** I'd like (to go/...); **Ich möchte nicht gehen/...** I wouldn't like to go/...; **Möchtest du/Möchten Sie ...?** Would you like ...?
Moment moment; **im Moment** at the moment
Monat month
Mond moon
Monster monster
Montag Monday
Moor *(Hochmoor)* moor
morgen tomorrow
Morgen morning; **Montagmorgen** Monday morning

morgens in the morning; *(mit Uhrzeit)* a.m.
Motel motel
Motorrad motorbike
Mountainbike mountain bike
Mountainbikefahren mountain biking
Mountainboard mountain board
Mountainboardfahren mountain boarding
MP3-Player MP3 player
müde tired
Mund mouth; **Halt den Mund!** Shut up!
Muschel seashell
Museum museum
Musik music
Musiker/in musician
Musikinstrument musical instrument
Muslim/in Muslim
müssen *have to; must; **du müsstest** you should; **(ich) muss einen Ort finden** gotta find me a place
mutig brave
Mutprobe dare
Mutter mother
Mutti mum; (AE) mom

N

nach 1 *(Wann?)* after; **nach der Schule** after school; **fünf nach zehn** five past ten; **Viertel nach elf** quarter past eleven; **2** *(zu)* to; **nach Hause gehen** *go home
Nachbar/in neighbour
nachdem after
nachdenken *think
Nachfüllung refill
Nachmittag afternoon
nachmittags in the afternoon; *(mit Uhrzeit)* p.m.
Nachname family name
Nachricht(en) news; *(Mitteilung)* message
nachsprechen repeat
nächste/r/s: der nächste Flughafen the nearest airport; **nächste Woche** next week
Nacht night
nachts at night
Nähe: in der Nähe von by; near
Name name
nass wet
Nationalpark national park
natürlich of course

Naturwissenschaft science
neben by; next to
nehmen *take; **Ich nehme ...** *(Bestellung)* I'll have ...
neidisch (auf) jealous (of)
nein no
nennen call; name
nerven: Eltern nerven! Parents are a pain!
nervös nervous
nett nice
Netz network
neu new
Neuigkeit(en) news
nicht not; **Iss nicht.** Don't eat.
nichts nothing; not ... anything
nie never
Niederlande Netherlands
niemals never
niemand nobody
nirgendwo(-hin/-her) not ... anywhere
noch: noch ein/e/er/s another; **noch einmal** again; **noch nicht** not ... yet; **noch nie** never
Nomen noun
Nord- north; northern
(im) Norden (in the) north
Nordirland Northern Ireland
nördlich north; northern
Nordwesten: der Nordwesten the north-west
normalerweise usually
Notiz note
November November
Nummer number
nun now; **Nun, ...** Well, ...
nur only
nützen: ein Ball nützt nichts a ball's no good
nützlich useful

O

ob if; whether
obdachlos homeless
oben: ganz oben (auf) at the top
Oberschule *(in den USA)* high school
Objekt object
Obst fruit
oder or
offen open
(sich) öffnen open
oft often
ohne without
Ohr ear
okay OK
Oktober October

Öl oil
olympisch: die Olympischen Spiele the Olympics
Oma grandma
Onkel uncle
online online
Opa grandad
Orange orange
ordnen organize
Ordnung: in Ordnung OK; Ist alles in Ordnung bei dir? Are you OK? Ist etwas nicht in Ordnung? What's wrong?
organisieren organize
Orkan hurricane
Ort place
Osten; Ost- east
Österreich Austria
östlich east
Ozean ocean

P

paar: ein paar some
packen pack
Paddeln canoeing
Panik: in Panik geraten panic
Papa dad
Papiere papers
Park park
Parkplatz car park
Partner/in partner
Party party
passieren happen
Passiv passive
Pause break
Pence pence (p)
Person person; (Figur) character
Pfad track; trail
Pferd horse
Pfund (brit. Währung) pound (£)
Picknick picnic
Pier pier
pink pink
Pionier/in pioneer
Pirat/in pirate
Pizza pizza
Plan plan; (Karte) map
planen plan
Planer/in planner
Planwagen wagon
Platz place; (Spielfeld) court
plötzlich suddenly
Polen Poland
Polizei- police
Polizist/in police officer
Pommes frites chips
Pony pony
Popcorn popcorn

Pop(musik) pop
Porree(stange) leek
Portfolio portfolio
Post(amt) post office
Poster poster
Postkarte postcard
Präposition preposition
präsentieren present
Preis 1 (Kaufpreis) price; 2 (Gewinn) prize; 3 (Auszeichnung) award
preiswert cheap
pro per; 24 Stunden pro Tag 24 hours a day
probieren try
Problem problem
produzieren produce
Projekt(arbeit) project
Protektor protector
protestieren protest
Prozent per cent
Prüfung test
Puma (AE) cougar
Punk(musik) punk
Punkt point
Punktzahl score

Q

Quad quad (bike)
Quiz quiz

R

Rabe raven
Rad (Fahrrad) bike; Rad fahren *ride a bike
Radfahren cycling
Radiergummi rubber
Radio radio
Ranch ranch
Ranger ranger
Rap(musik) rap
Rapper/in, Rapsänger/in rapper
Rasen grass
Rat advice
raten guess
Ratte rat
rauchen smoke
Räucherlachs smoked salmon
Raum room
Raumpfleger/in cleaner
raus: Ich muss hier raus. I have to get out of this place.
Rechner computer
Recht right; Du hast Recht. You're right.

rechts right; auf der rechten Seite on the right; rechts (von Ihnen) on your right
Rechtsanwalt, -anwältin lawyer
Rechtschreibung spelling
reden (mit) talk (to)
Redner/in speaker
Regal, Regale shelf, shelves
Regel rule
Regisseur/in director
regnen rain
Reifenschlauch tube
Reihe (Serie) series
Reihenfolge order
(sich) reimen (auf) rhyme (with)
Reise trip; Reise- travel
reisen travel; Reisen travel
Reisende/r traveller
reiten *ride; Reiten horse riding
rennen *run
reparieren fix
Reservat(ion) reservation
reservieren (lassen) book
Restaurant restaurant
retten save
Rettungssanitäter/in paramedic
Rezension review
Rhein Rhine
Rhythmus rhythm
richtig right; das Richtige/Beste/... the right/best/... thing
Richtung: in Richtung Haus towards the house
Rindfleisch beef
Rodeo rodeo
Rolle role
Rollen(spiel)karte role card
Rollstuhl wheelchair; er sitzt im Rollstuhl he's in a wheelchair
Rom Rome
romantisch romantic
rosa pink
rot red
Rubrik heading
rufen call; (laut rufen) shout
Rugby rugby
ruhig quiet
Rundgang tour

S

Sache thing; Sachen, die man machen kann things to do
Saft juice
sagen *say; *tell; ihr etwas sagen say something to her; Jamie sagt Tess auf Wiedersehen. Jamie says goodbye to Tess.

Salat salad; *(Kopfsalat)* lettuce
sammeln collect
Samstag Saturday
samstags on Saturdays
Sandwich sandwich
Sänger/in singer
Satz sentence
sauber clean
Schade! Too bad!
Schaf, Schafe sheep
Schatzsuche treasure hunt
schauen look
Schauspieler/in actor
Scherz joke
Scheune barn
schicken *send
Schiedsrichter/in referee
schießen *shoot; *(Tor)* score
Schiff boat; ship
Schikanieren bullying
Schild sign
Schildchen label
Schinken ham
Schirm umbrella
schlafen *sleep
Schlafzimmer bedroom
schlagen *hit
Schlange *(Warteschlange)*
    (AE) line; **Schlange stehen**
    queue (up); (AE) wait in line
schlecht bad
schlechter worse
schlechteste/r/s worst
schließen close
Schließfach locker
schließlich in the end
schlimm bad
schlimmer worse
schlimmste/r/s worst
Schloss castle
Schluss ending
Schlüssel key
schmal narrow
Schmerzen pain
schmücken decorate
schmutzig dirty
schnell fast; quickly
Schnellimbiss *(für Fisch/Pommes
    frites)* fish and chip shop
Schokolade chocolate
schon: schon einmal ever; **Schon
    gut. (Bitte.)** That's OK. **schon
    wieder** again
schön beautiful; fine; nice;
    (Einen) Schönen Tag noch!
    (AE) Have a nice day!
Schotte(n)/Schottin(nen)
    Scottish
Schottisch *(engl. Dialekt)* Scots
Schottland Scotland

Schrank cupboard
schrecklich terrible
schreiben *write
Schreibetui pencil case
schreien scream; shout
Schriftsteller/in writer
schüchtern shy
Schuh shoe
Schularbeiten homework
Schule school
Schüler/in pupil; (AE) student
Schülerkalender homework diary
Schulheft exercise book
Schulhof playground; **auf dem
    Schulhof** in the playground
Schultag school day
Schultasche bag
schütteln *shake; **sie schüttelt
    den Kopf** she shakes her head
Schützer protector
schwarz black
Schwarze black people
Schwein pig
Schweiz Switzerland
schwer hard; *(schwierig)* difficult
Schwerpunkt main point
Schwester sister
schwierig difficult
**Schwierigkeiten: ich stecke in
    großen Schwierigkeiten** I'm in
    big trouble
Schwimmbad swimming pool
schwimmen *swim; **Schwimmen**
    swimming
schwimmen gehen *go swimming
Schwimmer/in swimmer
**sechziger: in den sechziger Jah-
    ren des 19. Jahrhunderts** in the
    1860s
See *(Binnensee)* lake
sehen look; *see
sehr very; **Sehr geehrte Damen
    und Herren, ...** Dear Sir/
    Madam, ...
seid: ihr seid you're (= you are)
sein *be
sein/e his; *(nicht bei Personen)* its
Seite side; *(Buch, Heft)* page
selbst gemacht home-made
Selbstbeherrschung self-control
selbstsicher confident
selbstverständlich of course
senden *send
Sendung *(Radio, TV)* programme
September September
Serie series
Sessel chair
setzen: sich setzen *sit
seufzen sigh
Sheriff sheriff

Shorts shorts
Show show
Shuttle shuttle
sicher sure; *(in Sicherheit)* safe
Sicherheit: in Sicherheit safe
Sicherheitsausrüstung safety
    gear
Sicherheitskontrolle security
    check
sie **1** *(Wer?)* she; *(nicht bei Per-
    sonen)* it; *(Mehrzahl)* they;
    2 *(Wen?)* her; *(nicht bei Per-
    sonen)* it; *(Mehrzahl)* them
Sie you
Sieger/in winner
Signal signal
sind are
Singapur Singapore
singen *sing
sitzen *sit; **er sitzt im Rollstuhl**
    he's in a wheelchair
Skateboard skateboard
Skateboarder/in skateboarder
Skater/in skater
Ski fahren ski
Skifahren skiing
Sklave, Sklavin slave
Skunk skunk
Smog smog
SMS text (message)
SMS-Terror text bullying
Snowboarder/in snowboarder
so **1** so; **2** like that/this; **so ein
    Job** a job like that/this; **So
    etwas gibt es nicht.** There's no
    such thing. **so viele/... wie** as
    many/... as
soeben just
Softball softball
Software software
sogar: Es war sogar besser. In
    fact, it was better.
sollen: Wann soll ich ...? When
    should I ...? **du solltest** you
    should
Somalia Somalia
Sommer summer
Sonderangebot special offer
Sonnabend Saturday
Sonne sun
sonnig sunny
Sonntag Sunday
Sorgen: sich Sorgen machen (um)
    worry (about); **ich mache mir
    Sorgen (um)** I'm worried
    (about)
spannend exciting
Spanien Spain
**Spanier/in(nen); spanisch;
    Spanisch** Spanish

spanischsprachig Hispanic

sparen save

Spaß fun; **Es macht Spaß.** It's fun.

spät, zu spät late; **Er kommt zu spät.** He's late. **Wie spät ist es?** What time is it?

später later

Spazierengehen walking

Spaziergänger/in walker

speichern *(MP3-Player)* *hold

Speiseeis ice cream

Speisekarte menu

Spiegel mirror

Spiel game; *(Wettkampf)* match

spielen play; **Gitarre spielen** play the guitar; **Spielt das Gespräch nach.** Act the dialogue.

Spieler/in player

Spielfeld court

Spielhalle amusement arcade

Spielregel: sich an die Spielregeln halten play by the rules

Spielstand score

Spielzeug toy

Spind locker

Spinne spider

Spitze top; **auf der Spitze** at the top

Spitzname nickname

Sport, Sportart sport; **Sport treiben** play sports

sportlich sporty

Sportplatz field

Sportschuh trainer; (AE) sneaker

Sportzentrum sports centre

Sprache language

Sprechanlage intercom

sprechen (mit) *speak to; talk (to); **Hier spricht Sarah.** It's Sarah.

Sprecher/in speaker

springen jump

Squash squash

Staat state

Stadt town; *(Großstadt)* city

Stadtmitte, -zentrum town centre

Stand *(Verkaufsstand)* stall

Star star

stark tough

Stärke power

Start start

statt instead of

Statue statue

stehen *stand; **es steht 24:18 für North** it's 24–18 to North; **Wie steht's?** What's the score?

stehen bleiben stop

stehlen *steal

Stein *(Fels)* rock

Stelle place

stellen *put

Stempel stamp

sterben die

Stimme voice

Stinktier skunk

stoppen stop

Strand beach; *(Küste)* seashore; **am Strand** on the beach

„Strandbuggy" dune buggy

Strandpromenade boardwalk

Straße road; street

Straßenbahn tram

streiten: sich streiten *fight

streng strict

Strom electricity

Strophe verse

Stubenarrest: ich habe Stubenarrest I'm grounded

Studio studio

Stufe step; *(Jahrgangsstufe)* year; **Ich bin in der 7. Stufe.** I'm in year 7.

Stuhl chair

Stunde hour; *(Unterrichtsstunde)* lesson

Stundenkilometer kilometres per hour

Stundenplan timetable

suchen look for

Suchmaschine search engine

Süden; Süd-; südlich south

super super

Supermarkt supermarket

Surf(schutz)anzug wetsuit

Surfausrüstung surfing gear

Surfbrett surfboard

surfen surf; **Surfen** surfing

Surfer/in surfer

Surfkleidung, -klamotten surfing gear

Symbol symbol

Szene scene

T

Tabelle table

Tablett tray

Tafel board

Tag day

Tagebuch diary

Talkshow chat show; (AE) talk show

Tante aunt

tanzen dance; **tanzen gehen** *go dancing

Tänzer/in dancer

Tanzveranstaltung dance

tapfer brave

Tasche bag; *(Kleidung)* pocket

Taschengeld pocket money

Tasse cup; **eine Tasse Tee** a cup of tea

Taste button

Tatsache fact

taub deaf

Tauch(schutz)anzug wetsuit

Tausch- exchange

tausend thousand

Taxi taxi

Team team

Technik technology

Techno techno

Technologie technology

Tee tea

Teenager teenager, teen

Teil part

teilen: sich ein Zimmer teilen share a room

Teilzeit, Teilzeit- part-time

Telefon phone; **am Telefon** on the phone; **ans Telefon gehen** answer the phone

telefonieren phone

Telefonnotiz phone message

Tennis tennis

Termin *(Verabredung)* appointment

Terminkärtchen appointment card

Terror: SMS-Terror text bullying

Test test

teuer expensive

Text text; *(Liedtext)* words (of a song)

Theater theatre

Thema topic

Themenpark theme park

Tier animal; *(zahmes Tier, Haustier)* pet

Tierhandlung pet shop

Tierrechte, Tierschutz- animal rights

Tipi tepee

Tipp tip

Tisch table

Tischtennis table tennis

Titel title

Tja, ... Well, ...

Tochter daughter

toll cool; great; super; (AE) awesome

Tomate, Tomaten tomato, tomatoes

Tor gate

töten kill

Tour tour

Tourist/in tourist

Touristeninformation tourist office
Tradition tradition
tragen *(anziehen)* *wear
Trainer trainer
trainieren train; practise
Traktor tractor
Traum dream
träumen dream
traurig sad
treffen, sich treffen (mit) *meet; **eine Absprache treffen** *make an arrangement
Treffpunkt: ein Treffpunkt a place to meet
treten kick
trinken *drink; **eine Cola trinken** *have a cola
trocken dry
Trubel: es gab viel Trubel there was lots of activity
Tschechische Republik Czech Republic
Tschüs. Bye.
T-Shirt T-shirt
tun *do; *(an einen Platz tun)* *put
Tunnel tunnel
Tür door
Türkei Turkey
Turm tower
Turnhalle gym
Tut mir leid. I'm sorry./Sorry.
Tüte bag
Typ type
typisch typical
Tyrann bully

U

U-Bahn underground; (AE) subway; **die (Londoner) U-Bahn** the tube
U-Bahnhof underground station
U-Bahn-Zug underground train
üben practise
über 1 above; **2** *(über die Straße)* across (the road); **3** about; **über die Sprechanlage** on the intercom
überall(-hin, -her) everywhere
überfliegen scan
übernachten stay
überprüfen check
überrascht surprised
Überraschung surprise
Überschrift heading
übersetzen translate

übrig: ich habe nicht viel dafür übrig I'm not keen on it
Übung exercise
Uhr clock; **um acht/zwanzig Uhr** at eight o'clock
Uhrzeit time
um: um acht/zwanzig Uhr at eight o'clock; **um Dinge zu verändern** to change things
umbringen kill
Umfrage survey
Umgebung environment
umschreiben *rewrite
Umstandswort adverb
umsteigen change
Umwelt environment
umziehen move
Unabhängigkeitstag Independence Day
und and; **Und du?** What about you?
unentschieden: es war unentschieden it was tied
Unfall accident
ungefähr about
ungesetzlich illegal
Uniform uniform
Unruhe trouble
uns us
unser/e our
Unsinn nonsense
unter under
unterhalten: sich unterhalten (mit) *have a chat (with); talk (to)
Unterhaltung conversation
unterirdisch underground
Unterrichtsstunde lesson
unterstreichen underline
unterstrichen underlined
Untersuchung *(Umfrage)* survey
unterwegs on the road
unwahr false
Urlaub holiday/s; **in den Urlaub fahren** *go on holiday; **sie macht Urlaub, sie ist im Urlaub** she's on holiday

V

Vater father
Vati dad
Verabredung appointment
verabschieden: sich von ... verabschieden *say goodbye to ...
Veränderung change
Verb verb

verbieten prohibit
Verbindung link
verboten prohibited
verbrachte: ich verbrachte I spent
Verbrechen crime
verbringen *spend
verdienen earn
Verein club
verfolgen follow
Vergangenheit past
vergessen *forget; *(stehen/liegen lassen)* *leave
Vergleich comparison
vergleichen compare
Vergnügen: besonderes Vergnügen treat
Verhältniswort preposition
verheiratet married
verirren: sich verirren *get lost
(sich) verkaufen *sell
Verkäufer/in shop assistant; (AE) sales clerk
Verkehr traffic
Verkehrssicherheit road safety
verlassen *leave
Verlaufsform der Gegenwart/ Vergangenheit present/past progressive
verlegen embarrassed
verletzen *hurt; **ich habe mir die Hand verletzt** I hurt my hand
verlieren *lose
vermieten hire
vermissen miss
verschieden different
verschwenden waste
verspätet late
verstehen *understand; **..., verstehst du?** ..., you see.
versuchen try
verwenden use
Video(film) video
Videospiel video game
viel lots of; much; **eine viel befahrene Straße** a busy road; **Viel Glück!** Good luck!
viele lots of; many; **Viele Grüße ...** Best wishes, ...
vielleicht maybe
Viertel neighbourhood
Viertel vor/nach eins quarter to/ past one
Visagist/in make-up artist
Vogel bird
Volk people; **das Volk der Makah** the Makah people
Volleyball volleyball

vollständig complete

von 1 of; 2 from; 3 (vom/von ... herab/herunter) off; 4 (durch) by

vor 1 (Wo?) in front of; 2 (Wann?) before; vor zwei Jahren two years ago; fünf vor zehn five to ten

vorbei (zu Ende) over; am Haus vorbei past the house

Vordergrund foreground

vorhaben plan

vorlesen *read (out); ihr etwas vorlesen read something to her

Vorlieben und Abneigungen likes and dislikes

Vormittag morning

vormittags (mit Uhrzeit) a.m.

Vorname first name

Vorort suburb

Vorschrift rule

vorsichtig careful

Vorsingen audition

Vorsitzende/r chairperson

Vorsprechen audition

vorstellen: sich (etwas) vorstellen imagine

Vortrag talk

vorziehen prefer

W

Wachfrau/-mann security guard

wachsen *grow

wählen pick

Wahnsinn! Wow!

wahr true

Wal whale

Walbeobachtung whale watching; auf Walbeobachtungstour gehen *go whale watching

Wald wood; (Waldgebiet) forest

Wales Wales

Waliser/in(nen); walisisch; Walisisch Welsh

Wand wall

Wanderer, Wanderin walker; hiker

wandern hike

Wandern walking

Wanderschuh walking shoe

Wandschrank (AE) closet

wann when

war was

wäre: sie dachten, es wäre eine gute Idee they thought it was a good idea

waren, warst, wart were

warm warm

wärst: Ich habe gesagt, du wärst morgen im Laden. I said you'd be in the shop tomorrow.

warten (auf) wait (for); Warten wir's ab. Let's wait and see.

Warteschlange (AE) line

warum why

was what; Was für ein/e ...! What a ...! Was für Sendungen? What kind of programmes? Was gibt's? What's up? Was ist das? What's that? Was ist mit dir? What about you?

waschen: du kannst dich waschen you can get yourself clean

Wasser water

Webcode webcode

Website website

weg away

Weg way; (Pfad) track; trail

weggehen (von) *leave

wehtun *hurt

weiblich female

Weihnachten Christmas

weil because

weinen cry

weiß white

Weißbrot white bread

Weiße white people

weit far

weitere 1 (mehr) more; 2 (andere) other

welche/r/s what; which; Welche Farbe hat dein Zimmer? What colour is your room?

Welle wave

Wellenreiten surfing

Welt world; auf der (ganzen) Welt in the world

Weltraum space

weniger less

wenn if; when

wer who

werden *become; ich werde gehen I'll (= I will) go; ich werde nicht gehen I won't (= will not) go; ich werde gewinnen, ich gewinne I'm going to win; Ich werde Ranger. I'm going to be a ranger. Erste/r werden bei ... *come first in ...

werfen *throw; *shoot

weshalb why

Westen; West- west

westlich west

Wettbewerb competition

Wetter weather

Wettkampf match

wichtig important

wie 1 how; Wie geht's? How are you? Wie heißen sie auf Deutsch? What are they in German? Wie heißt du? What's your name? Wie nennt/ bezeichnet man ...? What do you call ...? Wie spät ist es? What time is it? wie man uns findet how to find us; ich sehe, wie sich ihr Mund bewegt I see her mouth moving; 2 (so wie) like; wie das Buch ist what the book is like; Wie sieht sie aus? What does she look like? Träume, in denen ich wie ... bin dreams of being like ...

wieder again; Ich bin wieder da! I'm back!

Wiedersehen. Bye.

Wiese field

Wikinger Viking

wild wild

willkommen: wir sind nicht willkommen we aren't welcome; Willkommen in London. Welcome to London.

Winter winter

wir we

wirklich really

Wirtschaft economy

wissen *know

Witz joke

wo where

Woche week

Wochenende weekend

woher: Woher kommst du? Where are you from?

wohin where

wohnen live

Wohnung flat; (AE) apartment

Wohnwagen (Standwohnwagen) mobile home

Wohnzimmer living room

Wolke cloud

Wolkenkratzer skyscraper

wollen want; gehen wollen want to go

wonach: du kannst tun, wonach dir gerade ist you can do whatever you feel

Wort word

Wörterbuch, -verzeichnis dictionary

Wortnetz, Wörternetz network

Wow! Wow!
wunderschön beautiful
wurde: es wurde genannt it was called
würde: ich würde I'd (= I would)
Wurf throw
Wurst, Würstchen sausage
Wurzel root
wütend (auf) angry (with)

Z

zäh tough
Zahl number
zahlen *pay
zahmes Tier pet
Zahnarzt/-ärztin dentist
Zeichen sign; signal
zeichnen *draw
zeigen *show
Zeile line
Zeit time
Zeitschrift magazine
Zeitung newspaper
Zeitverschwendung a waste of time
Zeitwort verb
Zelt tent
zelten camp
Zeltplatz (AE) campground
Zentrum centre
Ziffer number
Zimmer room
Zitat quote
Zoohandlung pet shop
zu 1 to; **sie helfen dir zu lesen** they help you to read; **zu Fuß** on foot; **zu Hause** at home; **2** for; **3 zu alt** too old; **zu spät** late; **4** (geschlossen) closed
zuerst first
zufälligerweise war es ... (it) so happened to be ...
Zug train; **Zug von Planwagen** wagon train
Zuhause home
zuhören listen
zujubeln cheer
Zukunft future
zum: zum Frühstück/Mittagessen for breakfast/lunch
zumachen close
Zungenbrecher tongue twister
zuordnen match
zur: sie geht zur Schule she's at school; **Er kommt zu spät zur Schule.** He's late for school.

zurück back
zurückrufen call/phone back
zurufen: sie ruft ihm etwas zu she shouts something at him
zurzeit at the moment
zusammen together
Zusammenfassung summary
Zusammenhang context
zusehen watch
zustimmen: Ich stimme (dir) zu. I agree (with you).
zuversichtlich confident
Zweitsprache: Englisch als Zweitsprache English as a Second Language
zwingen: keiner kann mich dazu zwingen, dies zu essen nobody can make me eat this; **wenn man mich zwänge** if they made me
zwischen between

Girls/Women

Adrienne [eɪdri'en]
Alexa [ə'leksə]
Alice ['ælɪs]
Amanda [ə'mændə]
Angela ['ændʒələ]
Ashley ['æʃli]
Brianna [bri'ænə]
Britany ['brɪtəni]
Britney ['brɪtni]
Caitlin ['keɪtlɪn]
Calina [kə'li:nə]
Candice ['kændɪs]
Destiny ['destɪni]
Halma ['hælmə]
Janet ['dʒænɪt]
Jazmin ['dʒæzmɪn]
Katherine ['kæθrɪn]
Kaylee ['keɪli]
Kimberley ['kɪmbəli]
Lana ['lɑːnə]
Laura ['lɔːrə]
Leanne [li'æn]
Mariela [meəri'elə]
Natalie/Nattalie ['nætəli]
Pauline ['pɔːliːn]
Rita ['riːtə]
Sancha ['sæntʃə]
Sophie ['səʊfi]
Stephanie ['stefəni]
Sue Li [suː'liː]

Boys/Men

Bob [bɒb]
Damon ['deɪmən]
Diego [di'eɪgəʊ]
Dylan ['dɪlən]
Frank [fræŋk]
Hassan ['hɑːsən]
Joel [dʒəʊəl]
Joseph ['dʒəʊzɪf]
Josh [dʒɒʃ]
Kenichi [kə'nɪtʃi]
Kyle [kaɪl]
Lanh [læn]
Lee [liː]
Luke [luːk]
Mack [mæk]
Miguel [mɪ'gel]
Pete [piːt]
Ramon [rə'mɒn]
Richard ['rɪtʃəd]
Robert ['rɒbət]
Steph [stiːv]
Taylor ['teɪlə]
Thomas ['tɒməs]
Toby ['təʊbi]
Tyrell [taɪ'rel]

People

Abi Russell ['eɪbi'rʌsəl]
Akon ['eɪkɑːn]
Alicia Keys [ə'liːʃə'kiːz]
Ben Gordon [ben'gɔːdən]
Beyoncé [biːɒn'seɪ]
Calvin Klein ['kælvɪn'klaɪn]
Carlos Oliva ['kɑːlɒsə'lɪvə]
Carmelo Anthony [kɑː'meləʊ'æntəni]
Courtney Long ['kɔːtni'lɒŋ]
Eddie Murphy ['edi'mɜːfi]
Elizabeth Urban [ɪ'lɪzəbəθ'ɜːbən]
Gerard Way ['dʒerɑːd'weɪ]
Geronimo [dʒə'rɒnɪməʊ]
Goyathlay [gɔɪ'æŋklɑː]
Gwen Stefani ['gwenste'fɑːni]
Harriet Tubman ['hæriet'tʌbmən]
Jennifer Lopez ['dʒenɪfə'ləʊpez]
Jesse James ['dʒesi'dʒeɪmz]
Justin Timberlake ['dʒʌstɪn'tɪmbəleɪk]
Kelly Clarkson ['keli'klɑːksən]
Lady Sovereign ['leɪdi'sɒvrɪn]
Lil' Kim [lɪl'kɪm]
Little Steven ['lɪtl'stiːvn]
Madonna [mə'dɒnə]
Malcolm X ['mælkəm'eks]
Marc Anthony [mɑːk'æntəni]
Notorious B.I.G. [nəʊ'tɔːriəs'bɪg]
Robin Hood ['rɒbɪn'hʊd]
Robin Thicke ['rɒbɪn'θɪk]
Scarlett Johansson ['skɑːlətdʒəʊ'hænsən]
Sean Penn [ʃɔːn'pen]
Shakira [ʃə'kiːrə]
Wyclef Jean ['waɪkləf'dʒiːn]

Families

Bailey ['beɪli]
Brodess ['brəʊdes]
Cortez [kɔː'tez]
Dunn [dʌn]
Garcia [gɑː'siːə]
Greene [griːn]
Harris ['hærɪs]
Howard [haʊəd]
Hughes [hjuːz]
Jones [dʒəʊnz]
Kennedy ['kenədi]
Moore [mɔː]
Nguyen [nuː'jen]
Ramirez [rə'mɪərez]
Stone [stəʊn]
Wilson ['wɪlsən]

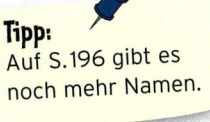

Tipp:
Auf S.196 gibt es noch mehr Namen.

NAMES

Places

Anacortes [ænə'kɔːtes]
Arizona [ærɪ'zəʊnə]
Bandon ['bændən]
Berlin [bɜː'lɪn]
Calle Ocho [kʌjeɪ'ɒtʃəʊ]
Central Park [sentrəl'paːk]
Chambers Street ['tʃeɪmbəzstriːt]
Chicago [ʃɪ'kɑːgəʊ]
Chinatown ['tʃaɪnətaʊn]
Cleveland ['kliːvlənd]
Commercial Avenue [kə'mɜːʃəl'ævənjuː]
Costa Rica [kɒstə'riːkə]
Crater Lake [kreɪtə'leɪk]
Deschutes County [də'ʃuːts'kaʊnti]
Disneyland ['dɪznɪlænd]
Dulles Airport ['dʌləs'eəpɔːt]
Ellis Island [elɪs'aɪlənd]
Empire State Building [empaɪə'steɪtbɪldɪŋ]
Epcot ['epkət]
Everglades ['evəgleɪdz]
Fidalgo Island [fɪ'dælgəʊ'aɪlənd]
Florida ['flɒrɪdə]
Fort Laramie [fɔː't'lærəmi]
Fort Lauderdale [fɔːt'lɔːdədeɪl]
Friday Harbor ['fraɪdi'hɑːbə]
Glendale ['glendeɪl]
Grand Canyon [grænd'kænjən]
Grand Central [grænd'sentrəl]
Greenville ['griːnvɪl]
Ground Zero [graʊnd'zɪərəʊ]
Harlem ['hɑːləm]
Hobuck Beach ['həʊbʌk'biːtʃ]
Hollywood Boulevard ['hɒliwʊd'buːləvɑːd]
Hurricane Ridge ['hʌrɪkəɪn'rɪdʒ]
Independence [ɪndɪ'pendəns]
Leavenworth ['levənwəθ]
Lincoln Center ['lɪŋkən'sentə]
Los Angeles [lɒs'ændʒɪliːz]
Madison Square Garden ['mædɪsən'skweə'gɑːdn]
Manhattan [mæn'hætən]
Maryland ['meərilænd]
Miami [maɪ'æmi]
Millennium Park [mɪ'leniəmpɑːk]
Missouri [mɪ'zʊəri]
Neah Bay ['niːə'beɪ]
Nebraska [nə'bræskə]
New Jersey [njuː'dʒɜːzi]
New York City [njuːjɔːk'sɪti]
Anacortes [ænə'kɔːtes]
Ohio [ɔʊ'haɪəʊ]
Olympic National Park [ə'lɪmpɪk'næʃnəl'pɑːk]
Omaha ['əʊməhɑː]
Oregon ['ɒrɪgən]
Panther Parkway ['pænθə'pɑːkweɪ]
Pennsylvania [pensɪl'veɪnɪə]
Philadelphia [fɪlə'delfɪə]
Port Angeles [pɔːt'ændʒɪliːz]
Portland ['pɔːtlənd]
Port Townsend [pɔːt'taʊnzend]

Puerto Rico [pwɜːtəʊ'riːkəʊ]
Richmond ['rɪtʃmənd]
Roche Harbor ['rəʊtʃ'hɑːbə]
Santa Monica ['sæntə'mɒnɪkə]
Sears Tower ['sɪəztaʊə]
Seattle [si'ætl]
Snake River ['sneɪk'rɪvə]
South Carolina ['saʊθkærə'laɪnə]
Tennessee [tenə'siː]
Times Square ['taɪmz'skweə]
Tropical Park ['trɒpɪkəl'pɑːk]
United Center [jʊ'naɪtɪdsentə]
Venice ['venɪs]
Vietnam [vjet'næm]
Washington Square [wɒʃɪŋtən'skweə]
West Palm Beach [westpɑːm'biːtʃ]
Yellowstone ['jeləʊstəʊn]
Yosemite [jəʊ'semɪti]

Other names

Amy's Place ['eɪmiz'pleɪs]
Chicago Bulls [ʃɪ'kɑːgəʊ'bʊlz]
Daddio's Pizza ['dædiəʊz'piːtsə]
Greenpeace ['griːnpiːs]
Makah [mə'kɑː]
My Chemical Romance [maɪ'kemɪkəlrəʊ'mæns]
Odeon Cinema ['əʊdiən'sɪnəmə]
Peter Pan ['piːtə'pæn]
Radio Cascades ['reɪdɪəʊkæs'keɪdz]
San Juan Safaris [sæn'hwɑːnsə'fɑːriz]
Segway ['segweɪ]
Spinreel Dunes ['spɪnriːl'djuːnz]
Sullivan High ['sʌlɪvən'haɪ]
Sunset Motel ['sʌnsetməʊ'tel]
The Chorus [ðə'kɔːrəs]
The Pirates of the Caribbean [ðə'paɪrətsɒvðəkærɪ'biːən]
The Pixies [ðə'pɪksiz]
The Splash Mountain [ðə'splæʃ'maʊntən]
The Starbury One [ðə'stɑːbəri'wʌn]
Warner Brothers ['wɔːnəbrʌðəz]
Wikipedia [wɪkɪ'piːdiə]
Within Temptation [wɪ'ðɪntemp'teɪʃn]

Tipp:
Auf S.195 gibt es
noch mehr Namen.

IRREGULAR VERBS

Infinitive form (Grundform)	Simple past form (Einfache Vergangenheit)	Present perfect form (Vollendete Gegenwart)	
be	I was, you were, she was	I've been	sein
have	I had	I've had	haben
do	I did	I've done [dʌn]	tun, machen
become	I became	I've become	werden
bring	I brought	I've brought	bringen
buy	I bought	I've bought	kaufen
come	I came	I've come	kommen
deal	I dealt [delt]	I've dealt [delt]	sich kümmern
draw	I drew	I've drawn	zeichnen
drink	I drank	I've drunk	trinken
drive	I drove	I've driven ['drɪvn]	fahren
eat	I ate [et]	I've eaten	essen
fall	I fell	I've fallen	fallen
feed	I fed	I've fed	füttern
feel	I felt	I've felt	(sich) fühlen
fight	I fought	I've fought	kämpfen; sich streiten
find	I found	I've found	finden
forget	I forgot	I've forgotten	vergessen
get	I got	I've got	bekommen; holen
give	I gave	I've given	geben
go	I went	I've gone [gɒn]	gehen; fahren
grow	I grew	I've grown	wachsen
hear	I heard [hɜːd]	I've heard [hɜːd]	hören
hit	I hit	I've hit	schlagen
hold	I held	I've held	halten
hurt	I hurt	I've hurt	verletzen
keep	I kept	I've kept	halten, behalten
know	I knew	I've known	wissen; kennen
lead	I led	I've led	führen
leave	I left	I've left	verlassen; (liegen) lassen
lose	I lost	I've lost	verlieren
make	I made	I've made	machen
mean	I meant [ment]	I've meant [ment]	meinen; bedeuten
meet	I met	I've met	treffen; kennen lernen
pay	I paid	I've paid	zahlen, bezahlen
put	I put	I've put	stellen, legen, tun
read	I read [red]	I've read [red]	lesen, vorlesen
ride	I rode	I've ridden	(Rad/Quad) fahren
run	I ran	I've run	rennen
say	I said [sed]	I've said [sed]	sagen
see	I saw	I've seen	sehen
sell	I sold	I've sold	verkaufen
send	I sent	I've sent	senden
shake	I shook	I've shaken	schütteln
shoot	I shot	I've shot	schießen; werfen
show	I showed	I've shown	zeigen

Lösungen (S.144–156)

IRREGULAR VERBS

Infinitive form (Grundform)	Simple past form (Einfache Vergangenheit)	Present perfect form (Vollendete Gegenwart)	
sing	I sang	I've sung	singen
sit	I sat	I've sat	sitzen; sich setzen
sleep	I slept	I've slept	schlafen
speak	I spoke	I've spoken	sprechen
spend	I spent	I've spent	ausgeben; verbringen
stand	I stood	I've stood	stehen
steal	I stole	I've stolen	stehlen
swim	I swam	I've swum	schwimmen
take	I took	I've taken	nehmen; bringen
tell	I told	I've told	erzählen; sagen
think	I thought	I've thought	(nach)denken; finden
throw	I threw	I've thrown	werfen
understand	I understood	I've understood	verstehen
wake up	I woke up	I've woken up	aufwachen
wear	I wore	I've worn	tragen, anziehen
win	I won	I've won	gewinnen
write	I wrote	I've written	schreiben

Bildquellen

Alamy, Abingdon (S.8 Kenichi / Vova Pomorttzeff, Kaylee / Dynamic Graphics Group / IT Stock Free; S.9.2 / Barry Mason, 3 / Mark Hamilton, u-re / Sylvia Cordaiy Photo Library Ltd; S.10.1 / AA World Travel Library, 3 / Black Star, 5 / Sylvia Cordaiy Photo Library Ltd; S.11 mittig / Alex Segre, o-re / Ambient Images; S.17 Greenville / James Schwabel, Britney / Stockdisc Classic, re / Mark Baigent; S.24 u-re / EuroStyle Graphics, u-li / Glow Images, u-re / LHB Photo; S.25 F / Peter Jordan, G / LHB, H / dreamtours; S.44 Bild 4 / Rodolfo Arpia; S.45 oben / Dennis MacDonald; S.46 li / Steve Skjold ; S.47 u-re / Judith Collins; S.48 D / Charles Ridgeway; S.53 u-re / Jeff Greenberg; S.56 Mi / imagebroker; S.59 / Jeff Greenberg; S.62 li / Steve Skjold; S.66C / Jeff Greenberg; S.67F / Stock Connection Blue; S.68 li / Steve Skjold; S.70 unten / geogphotos; S.71 li / Ken Weingart, re / Ingram Publishing (Superstock Limited); S.73 / David Levenson; S.78 oben / David R Frazier Photolibrary Inc, Mitte / Jim West; S.81 u-re / Index Stock; S.82 li / Digital Vision, re / Buzzshotz; S.83 o-li / Andre Jenny, S.84 / Stan Rohrer; S.85 oben / William S.Kuta; S.92 o-re / America, u-re / Dennis McDonald, Mitte / Jupiter Images / Comstock Images; S.101 re / Vlad; S.102.2 / Visions of America LLC, Bild 4 / James Nesterwitz; S.104a / TNT Magazine, b / David Ball, e / Chuck Eckert; S.110 o-re / Brian Atkinson; S.113a / David J. Green – Lifestyle, c / Formcourt, d / Thinkstock; S.118 / Patrick Blake; S.119 / Digital Vision; S.122 / North Wind Picture Archives); **Associated Press**, New York (S.103); **Avenue Images**, Hamburg (S.32 unten / Image Source; S.44 Bilder 1 & 2 / Image 100, Bild 6 / Radius Images; S.46 re / Blend Images; S.50 / ImageSource; S.52 o-li / Index Stock; S.55 beaver / Alaska Express; S.56 oben / Bananastock; S.66A / Stockbyte; S.67E / Index Stock; S.83 u-li / Index Stock; S.88 / Index Stock; S.104 C & D / Index Stock; S.112 / BrandX; S.113b / Digital Vision, f / Radius Images); **Annette Bondzio-Abbit**, Bielefeld (S.74 oben); **Steve Berentsen**, Anacortes (S.53 o-li; S.60.1); **Bridgeman Art Library**, Berlin (S.57 / William Page; S.80 Peter Newark American Pictures); **Anna Catania**, Berlin (S.36); **Corbis**, Düsseldorf (S.14 / Bettman; S.15 / Bettmann; S.44 Bild 3 / moodboard; S.53 o-re / Kevin Schafer; S.66B / Tim Mosenfelder & D / Buddy Mays; S.67G / Nathan Benn; S.76 re / Reuters; S.104F / Angelo Hornak; S.108 / Michael S.Lewis; S.122 unten / Richard Cummins; S.123 li / Louie Psihoyos ;S.124 / Bettmann; S.125 oben / Bettmann, u-li); **Corel Library** (S.47 skull; S.126 pasta, soup, stew); **George Delgado**, New York (S.41 oben; S.42 – 43; S.106); **Denver Public Library**, USA (S.81 o-li & re / Colorado Historical Society & Denver Art Museum); **Frank Donoghue**, Nenagh (S.53 u-li; S.54 u-re; S.56 unten; S.60.2 & 3; S.88a& b; S.101 star; S.111 o-li); **EUP-Images**, Brussels (S.120 & 121 / Gorm K. Gaare); **F1Online**, Frankfurt (S.92 mi-re / Wildgruber); **Gundula Friese**, Berlin (S.12 o-re / S.19); **Getty Images**, München (S.41 unten; S.67H; S.68re / WireImage; S.69 / Scott Gries; S.70 oben / SW Productions; S.72 / Tom Sadler; S.76 li; S.105; S.115 unten / Donald Kravitz; S.117 unten / Hulton Archive; S.123 re); **Helicopter Flight Services Inc.**, New York (S.17 unten); **IFABilderteam**, München (S.11 Bild 9); **Ingram Publishing**, Cheshire (S.12 tomato & lettuce); **Interfoto**, München (S.98 o-re / Archiv Friedrich); **invitationconsultants.com** (S.20 o.li); **Jupiter Images**, Ottobrunn / München (S.53 o-mi / Tom Brakefield); **Kennedy Space Center**, Florida (S.74 unten); **The Kobal Collection**, London (S.100 / Polygram); **LA Youth** (S.34 o-li); **Los Angeles Magazine**, Los Angeles (S.26 unten); **Lower Manhattan Development Corporation**, New York (S.98 Freedom Tower); **Makah Museum**, Neah Bay (S.61 unten); **Mauritius Images**, Mittenwald (S.10 o-mi / Pixtal); **Christine Maxwell**, Berlin (S.47.3 T-shirt; S.48 Bilder 2,3,4 & B; S.49 unten); **Robert Nadolny**, Berlin (S.52 – 53 Hintergrund); **National Parks Service Photo**, Washington DC (S.52 bear; S.54 fire, bear); **New York City Transit**, New York (S.13); **Guy Noffsinger**, Los Angeles (S.28; S.29; S.32 o-re); **Vaughan Oliver**, London (S.34 u-li); **Oregon Parks & Recreation Department**, Salem (S.54 o-re; S.59 o-li); **Photofusion**, London (S.48C / Brian Mitchell); **Photographers Direct**, UK (S.25l /Buddy Mays; S.52 u-re / Francis Caldwell; S.109 / Merrilyn McDonald; S.111 o-re / Steve MacAulay); **Photolibrary**, London (S.92 u-li / ImageS.com); **Picture Alliance**, Frankfurt / Main (S.78 u-li & re / dpa; S.97.1 / dpa / dpaweb, 2 / Schroewig / Cyberimage, 3 / dpa, 4 / Schroewig / Cyberimage, 5 / dpa-Report); **Redferns**, London (S.115 oben / gna); **Reuters**, Berlin (S.64 / Anthony Bolante); **Rex Features**, London (S.16 / David Fisher); **San Juan Safaris**, Friday Harbor, WA (S.61 o & mi); **Salt & Light Ministries, Inc.**, N. Bend, (S.116); **Santa Monica Pier Restoration Corporation**, Santa Monica, (S.26 oben); **Segway** (S.31); **Shutterstock**, New York (S.8 Emily / Cathleen Clapper, Luke / Galina Barskaya, Shanna / Lorelyn Medina; S.9.1 / Jan Vancura, 5 / 6169758076, 4 / William Perugini; S.10 licence plate, u-li / Luca Flor; S.11.6 / Donald R. Swartz; S.12 u-li / Sharon D, bagel / Olga Lyubkina; S.17 li / Albo; S.18 bags / prism_68, tooth / Timashov Sergiy; S.22 li / Lorelyn Medina, re / Dana E. Fry; S. 24 o-li / Susan McKenzie; S.25 E / Ingus Kruklitis; S.34 o-re / Edyta Pawlowska, witch / Simone van den Berg, mi-li / barrirret, u-re / ene; S.44 Bild 5 / kristian sekulic, Bild 6 / Larry St. Pierre; S.47 Bild 1 / maxstockphoto, Bild 2 / Stocksnapper, Bild 4 / JoLin, Bild 5 / Jessica Bilen, u-li / Scott Waldren; S.48 A / Jenny Solomon; S.49 oben / J. Helgason; S.52 deer / Mike Rogal, cougar / Tony Campbell; S.53 Mi-li / Hiep Nguyen; S.55 deer / Andrew Taylor, unten / Jamie cross; S.58.1 / red06, 2 / Fernando Jose Vasconcelos Soares, 3 / Slobodan Djajic, 4 / Kirsty Pargeter, 5 / Elisabeth Perotin, 6 / Grzegorz Japol; S.62 li / About-Life; S.63 oben / Rafa Irusta, unten / Chris Turner; S.77 li / Peter Albrektsen, re / Lisa F. Young; S.80 oben / Najin; S.83 o-re / Eric Patterson, u-re / Robynrg; S.85 unten / Tyler Olsen; S.87 / Anita Patterson Peppers; S.92 o-li / Jinglebeez Photo Gallery, mittig-li / Natalia Bratlavsky; S.94 oben / Jan Carbol, u-li / Miguel Angel Salinas Salinas, u-re / Andryianava Alena; S.95 oben / Heath Doman, unten / Szymon Apanowicz; S.96 / Scott A. Maxwell; S.98 Mi-li / Natalia Bratlavsky, re / Marcin Wasilewski; S.99 / Emin Kuliyev; S.102.1 / Roger Dale Pleis, 3 / Stephen Finn, 5 / Dana Bartekoska; S.106A / Graca Victoria, B / Morgan Lane Photography, C / Joszef Szasz-Fabian, D / Anubhav Suri, E / lev dolgachov, F / vnlit; S.111 unten / Martine Oger; S.113 E / Grischa Georgiew; S.114 / Yuri Arcurs; S.117 oben / Ronald Sherwood, Mitte / Jamie Cross; S.126 pork / Colour, lamb / Robyn Mackenzie, squid / Pawel Strykowski, bacon / VanHart, tuna / Karin Lau, plums / Isidore Milic, strawberries / bhathaway, pears / Olga Shelego, cherries / JoLin, melon / Stefano Tiraboschi, cauliflower / Jow Gough, beans / Sally Scott, pepper / Marc Dietrich, mushrooms / arnaud weisser, broccoli / LockStockBob, rice / Elena moiseeva, biscuits / Gabi Garcia; S.127 western / Jim Parkin, scifi / Antonis Papantoniou, newspapers / 4736202690, magazines / Tan Wei Ming, detective / Peter Hansen, scales / Le Loft 1911; S.128 shorts / Johanna Goodyear, glove / Byron W. Moore, helmet / Panagiotis Mouzakis, boots / oddech, referee / george green, cheerleader / Jaimie Duplass, goalkeeper / Vova Pomortzeff, athletics / Petur Asgeirsson, kick / Shawn Pecor, throw / Rena Schild, court / Albo, racket / Denis Pepin, net / Elena Eliseeva, pool / Billy Lobo H; S.129 PE / Jerry Sharp, art / Amanda Flagg, textiles / Susanne Karlsson, environment / Cathy Keifer, orchestra / WizData Inc., chess / PhotoCreate, arts and crafts / Jyothi Joshi, judo / Tito Wong; S.130 oben / Andresr, u-li / Nikolay Okhitin, u-re / Joe Gough; S.131 accordion / Alexei Novikov, bass guitar / Jaimie Duplass, clarinet / Kiselev Andrey Valerevich, drums / iofoto, electric guitar / Robynrg, keyboard / Peter Albrektsen, piano / Brian Chase, recorder / Thomas M Perkins, saxophone / Kiselev Andrey Valerevich, trumpet / photobank.ch, goose / Zaichenko Olga, milking machine / Nitipong Ballapavanich, tractor / Olga Zaporozhskaya, combine harvester / Gilmanshin, barn / David Scheuber, stable / Jakez, sow / Chepko Danil Vitalevich, feed / Rtimages; S.141 / Stephen Aaron Rees; S.142 / David Dea; S.145 / Tatiana Sayig; S.151 / James Steidl; S.155 / Lynne Barrows; S.156 / Najin; S.157 sign / Julien, frisbee-golf / Jason Maehl); **Stills Online**, Hamburg (S.128 jogging trousers); **Stockdisc** (S.106 u-re pencil case); **Sullivan High School**, Chicago (S.38, S.39, S.45 unten; S.106 Mitte; S.107); **Ullstein Bild**, Berlin (S.98 WTC / Reuters); **US Postal Service** (S.125 u-re); **Silvia Wiedemann**, Berlin (S.60, 124 map)

Umschlag: George Delgado, New York

Lied- und Textquellen

S.31: *Das Oxford Schulwörterbuch* © Oxford University Press, 2007; S.34: *L.A. Youth*, Los Angeles; S.40: *YMCA*, T: Belolo, Henri © Scorpio Music. Für D/A/CH: Roba Music Verlag GmbH; S.70/71: *A life without music* © 2007 Elizabeth Urban.

New Highlight
Band 4

Im Auftrage des Verlages herausgegeben von
Frank Donoghue, Nenagh, Irland

Erarbeitet von
Frank Donoghue, Nenagh, Irland • Rebecca Robb Benne, Otterup, Dänemark

Verlagsredaktion
Susanne Döpper (Projektleitung) • Silvia Wiedemann (verantwortliche Redakteurin)
Christine Maxwell (Bildredaktion)

Anhang
Redaktionsbüro Birgit Herrmann, Freudenstadt

Beratende Mitwirkung
Hans Bebermeier, Bielefeld • Hartmut Bondzio, Bielefeld • Annette Bondzio-Abbit, Bielefeld •
Gisela Feldmann, Haltern • Prof. Dr. Liesel Hermes, Karlsruhe • Ingrid-Barbara Hoffmann, Böblingen •
Dagmar Höffner, Ingelheim • Barbara Hohkamp, Stuttgart • Petra Klein, Runkel • Martina Kriebel, Brigachtal •
Inge Kronisch, Flensburg • Christa Lüdemann, Hannover • Konstanze Stöckermann-Borst, Leimen •
Ellen Wiegard-Kaiser, Bielefeld • Herbert Willms, Herford • Gunhild Wolf, Unna

Illustration/Grafik
Adrian Barclay, Bristol • John Batten, London • Dr. Volkhard Binder, Berlin • Carlos Borrell, Berlin •
Klaus Ensikat, Berlin

Umschlaggestaltung
Leonardi.Wollein, Berlin

Layoutkonzept
Christoph Schall

Layout und technische Umsetzung
Klein & Halm Grafikdesign, Berlin

www.cornelsen.de

Alle Drucke dieser Auflage sind inhaltlich unverändert und können im Unterricht
nebeneinander verwendet werden.

Druck: Mohn Media Mohndruck, Gütersloh

1. Auflage, 8. Druck 2020
ISBN 978-3-464-34462-0
broschiert

1. Auflage, 7. Druck 2019
ISBN 978-3-464-34346-3
gebunden

PEFC zertifiziert
Dieses Produkt stammt aus nachhaltig
bewirtschafteten Wäldern und kontrollierten
Quellen.

PEFC
PEFC/04-31-1033

www.pefc.de